Monty Python, Shakespeare and
English Renaissance Drama

Monty Python, Shakespeare and English Renaissance Drama

Darl Larsen

Foreword by William Proctor Williams

McFarland & Company, Inc., Publishers

Jefferson, North Carolina, and London

Library of Congress Cataloguing-in-Publication Data

Larsen, Darl, 1963–
     Monty Python, Shakespeare and English Renaissance drama /
     Darl Larsen ; foreword by William Proctor Williams.
           p.   cm.
     Includes bibliographical references and index.

     ISBN 0-7864-1504-5 (softcover : 50# alkaline paper)

     1. Shakespeare, William 1564–1616 — Criticism and interpretation.
     2. Shakespeare, William, 1564–1616 — Knowledge — History.
     3. Historical drama, English — History and criticism.   4. English
     drama (Comedy) — History and criticism.   5. English wit and
     humor — History and criticism.   6. Shakespeare, William,
     1564–1616 — Humor.   7. Performing arts — Great Britain — History.
     8. Monty Python (Comedy troupe)   9. Renaissance — England.
     10. Comedy.   I. Title.
     PR2976.L23   2003
     822.3'3 — dc21   2002154653

British Library cataloguing data are available

On the cover: Images from Art Today ©2003 and PhotoSpin ©2003

Manufactured in the United States of America

*McFarland & Company, Inc., Publishers
     Box 611, Jefferson, North Carolina 28640
        www.mcfarlandpub.com*

For Nycole, Keir, Emrys,
Brynmor, Eamonn, Dathyl, Ransom,
and Culainn

Acknowledgments

I would be remiss if I did not give thanks for the inestimable assitance I received as this book progressed.

I owe a debt of gratitude to Dr. William Proctor Williams, formerly of Northern Illinois University, whose classroom discussions helped shape this challenging topic, and who read and responded to every word. The subject matter raised more than a few academic eyebrows, but Dr. Williams pushed us on anyway. His passion for the subjects— Shakespeare, Jonson and just English Renaissance drama and Monty Python in general — made the process fun.

I thank my parents, Dr. Norbert William and Patricia Tenney Larsen, who were a constant support and tireless cheering section. Their help was financial, emotional, spiritual, and always gladly offered. It will always be gratefully remembered.

A special thanks must go to my wife, Nycole, and my wonderful children Keir, Emrys, Brynmor, Eamonn, Dathyl, Ransom, and Culainn. They all moved where and when I needed to move, and back again, and just plain endured me. Nycole was and is certain there are no challenges we cannot overcome, and this work is dedicated to the whole family.

Also included in my thoughts are Jan Arwood, Dr. Robert Self, the NIU English Department faculty and staff, Maria Krull, Dr. Robert Nelson, my brother Mark, sisters Stacey, Liesl, Amalie, Katie and their families, Lynn and Maude Tenney, and Daniel and Monica Malcolm. They all helped in meaningful ways.

Table of Contents

Foreword

On my shelves I have a book which proclaims on its front cover *The Complete Works of Shakespeare and Monty Python*, vol. I, Monty Python, published in 1981. According to WorldCat (OCLC), twelve libraries in the world hold this volume, among them the New York Public Library, Yale University, the Bodleian Library, and the British Library. It is not held, apparently, by the Folger Shakespeare Library nor by the Shakespeare Collection at the University of Birmingham. It is not to be found in the *World Shakespeare Bibliography Online*, whose coverage is now 1971 to 2002. This is odd, for my copy has a charge slip from the Ferndean School Library pasted onto the front endpaper indicating that between 17 November and 12 February of some year the book was checked out by W. H. Auden, J. P. Sartre, E. Waugh, S. Davis, Jr., D. G. Rosetti, and others. However, the last person to check this book out is one M. Thatcher on "12th Feb." (there is no indication that she ever returned it), and we know that one Margaret Hilda Thatcher told, not very well, the "Dead Parrot" joke in 1990 and by the end of that year she had had to resign as Prime Minister of the United Kingdom. There could hardly be better evidence of the importance of Monty Python for our national, and international, identity. Would the same thing have happened had she told the "Who Builds Stronger" joke ("What is he that builds stronger then eyther the Mason, the Shypwright, or the Carpenter" [TLN 3230–31]) from *Hamlet*? Perhaps.

There has long been a denial of the importance of Shakespeare to Monty Python studies. Professor Larsen's study will go some way toward ending this division between the two cultures. Just as Shakespeare has so penetrated our language and culture that phrases from his works have been used to sell everything from small cigars to sewing machines, so the Pythons' work has wormed its way into contemporary culture. Saying that something has two important points and then finding that it actually has three will often produce the phrase "No one expects the Spanish Inquisition"; easy cowardice may produce "Run away, run away," from *Monty Python and the Holy Grail*; any sort of odd gait may be identified as being from the Ministry for Silly Walks. In a program presented by Carol Cleveland on BBC Radio 4 (Tuesday, September 14, 1999, 11:30 A.M., BST) called "Long Live the Dead Parrot" the Pythons' career is discussed, and tellingly the question is asked "why the Gumbies should still be popular in Latvia, or killer sheep in Slovakia...?" John Cleese provides a sentiment which, I think, would have been completely understood by Shakespeare: "The nicest thing I ever heard about Python was that people said that after they watched a Monty Python show, they couldn't watch anything else on television that night and take it seriously ... and I thought ... that's a great thing to have achieved." It is certainly the case that when the Pythons presented live shows in the United States they found that members of the audience could complete their lines for them. One is reminded of John Mortimer's story of his blind father's unnerving ability to audibly say the actors' lines a split second early during live Shakespeare performances at Stratford.

What Professor Larsen has discovered and what he presents in this book are not merely examples of intertextuality, but an interpenetration of aspects of culture. On that same Radio 4 program the standup comedian Arnold Brown says of Python:

> It was about types, it was about class, it was about history.... They were satirizing, in a kind of surreal way, what they had been taught, all the educational values— the religion, the attitudes, the middle-class attitudes, and one guy in particular epitomizes this, John Cleese. And I used to be an accountant, and accountancy was being satirized because it epitomized this conformity, and it was a stifling conformity. And John Cleese— this anger welled up in him, and he created all these marvelous anti-establishment, anti-civil servant, anti-accountancy caricatures.

This is not much different from Hamlet's view of things:

> The oppressor's wrong, the proud man's contumely,
> The pangs of despised love, the law's delay,
> The insolence of office, and the spurns
> That patient merit of the unworthy takes... [3.1.71–74].

Professor Larsen sees this similarity and provides the reader with a way of understanding it.

It is odd that the parallels have been so long unnoticed. Shakespeare, a most subversive writer, worked from within the establishment (the King's Men were, of course, minor members of the Court) to expose the various and numerous hypocrisies of his age; the Pythons worked just as subversively, though perhaps more openly, from within one of the greatest establishments of our own day, the British Broadcasting Corporation. *Macbeth* can be seen as a daring exposé of the essentially false and lying nature of witchcraft (equivocation, the use of ambiguity to mislead, is not the same as witchcraft, supernatural power and influence: the Master of the Tiger cannot lose his ship though he may be discomforted, TLN 122–23) presented before a king, James I, who in 1597 had published a book, *Daemonologie*, which forcefully supported the traditional belief in witchcraft (the exercise of supernatural power supposed to be possessed by persons in league with the devil or evil spirits). Similarly, the Pythons were funded from the Licence Fee, paid by all those chartered accountants, government ministers, pet shop owners, travel agents, and mobsters who paid the fee if they owned a television set.

There is, I suppose, one final warning I should offer. Neither Shakespeare nor the Pythons were ever kind to academics. In *Love's Labour's Lost* we have Costard speaking to Moth about the conversation between the latter's master, Don Armado, and the schoolmaster and arch-pedant Holofernes: "O, they have lived long on the alms-basket of words. I marvel thy master hath not eaten thee for a word; for thou art not so long by the head as *honorificabilitudinitatibus*: thou art easier swallowed than a flapdragon" (5.1.39–43). In *Monty Python and the Holy Grail* "A Very Famous Historian" is killed when "A KNIGHT rides into shot and hacks him to the ground. He rides off" (*Monty Python and The Holy Grail [Book]*). London: Methuen, 1977: fol. 29). It may not just be Shakespeare and Python who are subversive; it may be Professor Larsen.

William Proctor Williams
Akron, Ohio
September 2002

Introduction:
"Whither Python?"

Perhaps the most difficult aspect of a study like this might be justifying, to the naysayer or the skeptic, the topic itself. Is academia ready for a book-length study of Monty Python? There have been scattered articles and random mentions— even chapters— in other, longer works, but before now no significant study examining the cultural influences of Monty Python — especially in relation to acknowledged greats like Shakespeare and Jonson — has been undertaken. Are there any ways to discuss English Renaissance drama and the work of Monty Python without falling prey to a reductive fanzine mentality? Admittedly, *Monty Python's Flying Circus* has recently been called "the most influential TV comedy of the post-war era," but does that mean it rates a mention in the same breath as The Bard?[1]

The title of this introduction is cribbed from the title given to the first episode of *Monty Python's Flying Circus* ("Whither Canada?"), and asks the right kind of question.[2] We can fairly ask "Whither Shakespeare?" in an age of cable TV, video games, Internet potentialities, and attention spans that seem to be shrinking at a remarkable pace. The place of William Shakespeare, though, in history and in at least the near future, seems certain. Rising primarily out of the popular, public theaters of the time, Shakespeare was a popular cultural figure whose work was certainly respected because it drew crowds, but whose reputation among the more classical folk ebbed and flowed over time. But he is now "The Bard," an amalgamation of the man, the mythology, and the enduring legacy of written and performed work he left for posterity. Is there, however, another seventeenth-century-type ebb waiting for Shakespeare studies on the horizon? If the Bard can fall out of favor, then whither Python?

Also rising out of the popular, public arena are Graham Chapman,

John Cleese, Terry Gilliam, Eric Idle, Terry Jones, and Michael Palin, whose television (and later film[3]) work at times flustered, angered, and confused, but ultimately became memorialized as the *locus classicus* of Englishness personified for a generation of television viewers on both sides of the Atlantic. Quoting Python has become something of a badge, a certain level of acculturation reached that might mystify the less enlightened. Just being English like the Pythons also conferred a token of pride and belonging that was Englishness. As will be seen in the following chapters, two of the still living and breathing cultural artifacts that defined Englishness and helped renew that same cultural essentialism are Shakespeare and Monty Python.

There are, of course, radical differences between Python and Shakespeare, differences which should be acknowledged and even embraced. Shakespeare worked in the politically charged atmosphere of Elizabeth's late reign more than 400 years ago; Python worked in the late 60s and early 70s under a figurehead monarchy and on public television. Shakespeare wrote for the live theater both public and private; Python wrote for television funded by the government. Shakespeare didn't generally collaborate; Python rarely worked without collaboration (amongst themselves). Shakespeare wrote tragedies, comedies, and histories, as well as hybridizations of all three; Python is a comedy team. Shakespeare has endured, essentially, for 400 years, and his stature today is as high as it's ever been; Python has endured for 30 years, becoming a part of our cultural lexicon. There are many who argue that Shakespeare wrote none of the work attributed to him, giving the nod to Oxford, Bacon, or a host of others. There are many who might argue that serious study of Monty Python is a silly waste of time and resources. These are just a few of the more glaring distinctions that can be made between the author of *Hamlet* and the authors of *Flying Circus*. These particularities and many others will be addressed below.

Chapter 1 will address Shakespeare as England's national poet, as well as Monty Python's more recent elevation to similar status. The cultural assimilation and appropriation of Shakespeare and Python — the quotes, the references, the availability of various productions, the Englishness — illustrate that the status of national poet has been endowed upon both entities.

In Chapter 2, "And Now for Something Completely Different," the various aspects of theatricality are approached, including the troupe configurations, casting and writing choices, and specifically the relationship between Shakespeare, Ben Jonson, and Python, their work and reception. The dramatic unities, the allusions to classical literature, preferred targets of satirical attacks, anachronistic flairs, and the primacy of English (as "the" language) hold our attention in this chapter. Python's signature line heralding its difference is shown to be accurate, often, but the similarities between the English Renaissance dramatists and the later BBC troupe are abundant.

Chapter 3 is a discussion of the uses and abuses of history as exhibited in Shakespeare and Monty Python. This section will examine the place of history and historiography in Renaissance drama (and literature), specifically looking at the sources of history available to the Elizabethan author, and how those sources were used. The special place of Falstaff, Shakespeare's ahistorical character, is especially important as the strictures and structures of "History" — Tudor, Tory or otherwise — are examined. Python's attention to historical characters and the character of history can be seen as defining the absurdist approach to comedy utilized in both *Flying Circus* episodes and the feature films. The result is that neither Shakespeare nor Monty Python were slaves to historical accuracy, shaping history, instead, to their dramatic purposes.

Chapter 4 takes a close look at the various uses of humor, and specifically satire. Python uses satire — direct and indirect — to attack society's hobbyhorses, including politics, royalty, business, television, and the common man, both English and British. Ben Jonson's noted use of satire will be discussed, especially its targets and wordplays, as well as Dekker's *Shoemaker's Holiday* for its significant examples of satirical social leveling — specifically, the elevation of the commoner and the simultaneous lowering of the privileged. This segues neatly into Python, as the Python *oeuvre* features kings treated like commoners, intellectually-elevated peasants, and mentally-challenged "Upperclass Twits."

Chapter 5 will approach the expansive topic of "Other." There are just as many "others" in works of Python as there seemed to be on the Elizabethan stage, including foreigners, women, bastards, homosexuals, and those who would transgress what might be considered Englishness. The specter of anti-theatricality is addressed, especially the effeminization of not only actors but audience members as boys in women's garb are desired. Richard III creates and directs his friends and enemies into the role of Other as he pursues his goals. Falstaff is even transformed by Hal/Henry into an other as the prince becomes the king, marginalizing and finally destroying the once-ubiquitous character. The cross-dressing issue takes center stage in discussing both camps, the Elizabethans doing it out of necessity, while the Pythons chose to don dresses and wigs. There is in Python, as well, the noteworthy occurrence of redemption, or the "bringing back into the fold" of characters and characteristics which may have initially been offered as Other. The visually unattractive but intellectually gifted Pepperpots, and the warmer, often good-natured comic treatment of the homosexual both reclaim Python from the charge of unredeemed satirical scorn.

Each chapter will be structured similarly. After a careful examination of the Elizabethan dramatists and their work in question we will embark on a similarly detailed look at Monty Python. Examples from both sources will be employed liberally. Chapter 2, for instance, focuses first on Shakespeare and Jonson, then Jonson and Python; Chapter 4 takes us from Shakespeare and Dekker to Python, etc. The chapters are meant to be compact studies of one or several key elements found in the works and performances of, especially, Shakespeare and the Python troupe. Along the way, though, significant attention is given to other important dramatists of the period, including Marlowe, Jonson, Dekker and Marston, as well as their twentieth-century counterparts on British television.

Each chapter is also designed to add to the existing knowledge of all concerned, with close textual analysis coupled to more broad cultural elements. The political satire of the Elizabethan theater can and should be appreciated in relation to the political satire of the BBC's Light Entertainment productions, as well as to the incumbent political systems (whether the Elizabethan monarchy or a Conservative government) which supported or just allowed their existence.

Part of the reason for the separable chapter structure is simple practicality. My own research for this study has exposed me to myriad structuring possibilities in journal articles, book chapters, and entire books. I found, not surprisingly, that the more organized resources invariably offered more potentially useful information. My introduction, then, in this work is designed to introduce the reader to the contents as clearly as possible. If a researcher is looking for a particular theme or aspect of, say, Monty Python's work, I would hope that he or she could quickly peruse this text and just as quickly know whether the needed information is offered. If not, then the bibliography will send that researcher on to many other possibilities. One of my goals for the appended bibliography is also nakedly practical. It is as complete a collection of written and recorded (in any format) Python sources as I have seen in any existing text; it is, hopefully, another boon to future researchers.

Finally, the goal of this work is to bring to light the importance and fruitfulness of careful study of a subject like the seemingly whimsical Monty Python. The Elizabethan popular culture entertainments—which included bear- and bull-baiting, broadside pamphleteering, and cock fighting—made room for Shakespeare and Jonson as a part of that culture.

Depending on sources consulted, Philip Henslowe may have even made more money in ventures like the "Royal Game of Bears, Bulls and Mastiff Dogs" than through the laborious work of producing plays.[4] The point, of course, is the relative significance of studying what might be considered "just" pop culture. I hope to prove that such a close textual study is productive in many ways, not only adding to the general body of accepted knowledge, but reinvigorating or reanimating that existing corpus. Each "new" Shakespeare play production generates interest. To a larger but perhaps more disseminated degree, so does each new film production. A new study such as this one generates more than interest, as it promotes and encourages further study, argument, and reappraisal of what had been "known" before. With careful analyses of English Renaissance dramatists and more recent figures like Monty Python, such studies, I will contend, serve to revalidate, refresh, and even create anew an interest in both William Shakespeare and Monty Python.

Notes

1. See Stuart Maconie's "Don't Run Your Flag Up My Flagpole" in *The Times* (25 February 2000). Online. http://www.the-times.co.uk/news/pages/resources/times_searchpage.html. Maconie looks at the current state of British television and its reliance on domestic comedies.

2. All quotations from *Monty Python's Flying Circus* are taken from *The Complete Monty Python's Flying Circus: All the Words*, vols. 1 and 2 (New York: Pantheon, 1989). Since the lines are not numbered, citations are produced as follows: volume number, episode number, page number. For example, a quote from the opening shot of episode 34, "The Cycling Tour," would be indicated as 2.34.148.

3. All quotations from Monty Python's feature films are taken verbatim from videotape versions, with after-the-fact printed Internet versions used for scene delineation. Screenplays with line numbers are not yet available, and the final shooting versions as they are available on videotape are significantly altered from any existing printed versions (including Internet sources). The Internet site used hereafter and featuring the most accurate and complete collection of Monty Python scripts can be found at www.montypython.net. For videotape/DVD versions see Chapman, et al., *Monty Python and the Holy Grail* (1975), *Life of Brian* (1979), and *Meaning of Life* (1983).

4. See Foakes "Playhouses" 1–52 *passim*.

Chapter 1

The Reading(s) of
a National Poet

On January 6, 1663, Samuel Pepys, having attended a revival of Shakespeare's *Twelfth Night*, ostensibly on the occasion of Twelfth Day, wrote summarily that not only did the play seem to have nothing at all to do with the celebrated day, but that it was "a silly play," though well acted (*Diary* 6 January 1663). Two years earlier Pepys had described a similar experience with this Shakespearean revival, perhaps setting the stage for his later opinion:

> ... and [Dr. Williams] and I walking through Lincoln's-Inn fields,
> observed at the Opera a new play, *Twelfth night*, was acted there,
> and the King there. So I, against my own mind and resolution,
> could not forbear to go in, which did make the play seem a burthen
> to me, and I took no pleasure at all in it [11 September 1661].

Did he not want to go in because the King was there? Or was it the specter of watching this old play in the King's presence? Or, was the "burthen" simply the play itself? Pepys isn't entirely clear, but the end result is the same. Pepys also writes that he went home that night and swore to his wife he'd never go to another play without her. He appreciated William Davenant's adaptations of Shakespeare, and he even quotes the Bard often throughout his *Diary*, but there is small praise for Shakespeare's surviving body of work.[1] Eight years later, the Bard's reputation had progressed little further as Pepys attended the last recorded revival of *Twelfth Night* prior to the mid-eighteenth century, calling it "one of the weakest plays" that he'd ever seen (20 January 1669).

Pepys' historical reputation — both real and self-constructed — can and should, of course, be kept in mind when judging these claims. Comments like these are often overtly aesthetic and directed just at the production itself, or its adherence to the playbook Pepys may have purchased, instead of either the play or the playwright. But the general shunting aside of Shakespeare that began not terribly long after his death is apparent and well documented. Pepys in these moments sounds very much like Python's "The Major" character (Graham Chapman), whose role is to mark all the silliness, then stop the sketch and prod the players on to something more erudite, sober, or patriotic. Perhaps it is here that issues of Pepys' epicurean profligacy can be mentioned — again, sometimes extravagant claims made for the benefit of the eventual reader rather than to fulfill any historical calling.[2] But the implications, at least, are clear.

The Major might have been more kind to Shakespeare than Pepys, but another viewer, diarist John Evelyn, confirms and sheds even brighter light on the Bard's diminishing role in the early Restoration period. Evelyn comments on a 1661 production of *Hamlet*: "I saw *Hamlet* Pr: of Denmark played: but now the old playe began to disgust this refined age; since his Majestie being so long abroad" (26 November 1661). This performance was also, most likely, a Davenant-edited production, with "some expurgation of oaths and the diction altered in the interests of clarity and elegance" (Spencer 174–187). Evelyn obviously felt the play had at least some merit at some time, but that time had surely passed. Shakespeare — whom Jonson had described as "not for an age but for all time" — by the Enlightenment's glow was growing old and, having aged over time, could only conjure audience "disgust," it seems.

Python may have commented indirectly on this case of Shakespeare's diminishing stature many years later, when Hamlet complains to a psychiatrist about his condition:

> HAMLET: Yes. All that sort of thing. And I'm just getting really fed up.
> PSYCHIATRIST: *(picking up a skull)* Now do the bit about "Alas poor Yorick."
> HAMLET: No. I'm sick of it! I want to do something else. I want to *make* something of my life.
> PSYCHIATRIST: No. I don't know that bit.
> HAMLET: I want to get away from all that. Be different [2.43.294].

Hamlet then announces that he's decided to be a private investigator. The necessarily silly ending taken in stride, this exchange between Hamlet and his psychiatrist suggests that even Hamlet himself has grown weary of the lot he's been given and the expectations that accompany being a part of Shakespeare's canon. This, of course, is a tension created by Monty Python as the character Hamlet is allowed to step outside his play and comment on the narrative fix he's in.[3] Hamlet will always be, for many, the Bard's greatest character — his soliloquies the most heartfelt, his situation the most tragic, and his role as the man "who could not make up his mind" — accurately or not — cemented forever in popular culture. But the morose Dane wasn't always so beloved.

The coming of the Restoration and the eighteenth century heralded a time of great critical and artistic reassessment *vis à vis* Shakespeare, Jonson, Fletcher, and others. Jonathan Bate notes that when the theaters reopened in 1660, there were essentially three extant Folio editions which constituted available theatrical works; namely, Jonson's *Works* (1616, 1640), Beaumont and Fletcher's *Plays* (1647), and Shakespeare's *Comedies, Histories, and Tragedies* (1623, 1632) (Bate 165). The 1665 edition of *Comedies, Histories, and Tragedies* was also presumably in the works. And, in the estimation of most noted critics of the period, the "triumvirate" of Shakespeare, Jonson, and Fletcher is actually in reverse order of importance. Between 1660 and about 1700, Fletcher's plays were performed more than twice as many times as Shakespeare's plays (165). According to Michael Dobson: "[D]efined as the playwright of neither Art [Jonson] nor Wit [Fletcher], the 'natural,' copious Shakespeare, with small Latin and less Greek, is put into the position of a naïve, perhaps even vulgar, provincial" (*National Poet* 30). Critically, the French court influenced and propagated the "neoclassical aesthetic ideology" (whilst England's aristocracy "waited in exile"), and neoclassically speaking, "Shakespeare's verbal inventiveness and his mingling of kings with clowns were unforgivable 'irregularities'" (Bate 165). The Bard's plays were, in essence, no longer "politically correct," and had to be brought up to date. The Enlightenment, often thought of as a time when Shakespeare was rediscovered, was actually the time when Shakespeare's plays as original texts were experiencing the most dire distress. Wholesale adaptations of Shakespeare's plays appeared and became popular on the English stage, with the amazing paradox that "the revival of every single play in the Shakespeare canon (excepting only *Love's Labour's Lost*)" also featured "the substantial rewriting of every single play in the Shakespeare canon (excepting only *Othello* and *1 Henry IV*)," and those "classics" that remained on the stage, even in "heavily revised versions," were only just tolerated (Dobson *NP* 4). The social values of the Restoration and the eighteenth century in general demanded that the plays, if they were to continue their lives on the stage, be adapted to take into account glaring historical events like the Interregnum and the Restoration, and even address the Commonwealth period in a way which acknowledged its existence while glossing over everything else (3–13). This adaptation was often accomplished by rewritings which reshaped the work in the fashion of a Fletcherian romance, complete with the happy ending, no matter how un-textual or out of place that ending may have been. In *Romeo and Juliet*, for example, the ill-fated couple survive and display the power of heroic love which can pacify even the worst strife, becoming instead a "Tragi-comedy" and a teaching tool for recovery from the Interregnum (27). "Innocent" Cordelia must be now allowed to live, according to *King Lear* adaptor Nahum Tate, and is thus married to Edgar for the happier ending (Bate 166).

Frances Kavenik provides a useful sketch of the relative popularity of the "old" plays versus the new after the Interregnum. In *British Drama 1660–1779* Kavenik lists the "Most Popular Plays" as indicated by the presentation of nine or more performances between the years 1659 and 1685. Of Jonson's plays, three make the transition, but just barely. *The Alchemist* was given ten performances, *Bartholomew Fair* (*BF*) received eleven, and *Epicoene* enjoyed a run of thirteen performances (30). None, interestingly, are listed as being revised, cut, or updated in any way for the newer, more refined sensibility of the Restoration. Shakespeare did not fare so well. Though he did manage to have four plays recorded for performance between 1659 and 1685, two of the plays survived only in greatly rewritten form. While *Hamlet* and *Henry VIII* received eleven and twelve performances each, respectively, it was the revised *Macbeth* (seventeen performances) and *The Tempest* (thirty-two performances) which obviously garnered the bulk of the audience's attention (30). The rewritten *Tempest* must have really been quite popular, outperforming even the newest and most fashionable plays like Dryden's *Sir Martin Mar-all* (twenty-seven performances) and Sir Samuel Tuke's *The Adventures of Five Hours* (twenty-one performances), or, for that matter, any offering from Wycherley, Otway or Lee (30). The very availability of extant Elizabethan plays, rewritten or not, perhaps factors into the higher numbers of their Restoration performances as well, since during the Interregnum performance had been, at least technically, forbidden.[4]

In fact it wasn't until Garrick's Stratford Jubilee in 1769 that Shakespeare would be fully reclaimed as England's own, and "Shakespear's flame" would burn brightly again (Dobson *NP* 105). With Garrick leading the charge and presaging the Bard's return as early as 1747 — "When Learning's triumph o'er her barbarous foes / First rear'd the Stage, immortal Shakespeare rose" — the age of "Bardolatry" was ushered in.[5] The rewriting of Shakespeare's plays (after the Restoration) to satisfy newer, more "enlightened" audiences gradually waned. Michael Dobson writes in *The Making of a National Poet*:

> Once Shakespeare has been abstracted (or even rescued) from his texts by the likes of Pope [1725] and Dennis [1712], and personified

as a true author in Rowe's biography [1709] or the necromantic
prologue to the *Jew of Venice*, the adaptation and appropriation of
Shakespeare's plays begins to decline in importance compared to
the adaptation and appropriation of Shakespeare himself [134].

Actresses appeared on the English stage in a revival of *Othello* in 1660, and
the plays were hence reworked to address the presence of actual feminin-
ity on stage.[6] Marsden indicates that Shakespeare's plays began to be
revived and revised, not — paraphrasing Flecknoe — to weed what was an
otherwise "fine Garden," or even to fit Renaissance sensibilities to Restoration ideals, but to craft Shakespeare into a spokesman for whatever political ideology happened to be appropriating his Englishness (*Appropriation*
3–4). Between Garrick's time and now, Shakespeare has been appropriated
by both extremes of the sociopolitical spectrum, and all points between,
from "Shakespeare as reassuringly counter-revolutionary" to Shakespeare
as androgynous, "able to transcend binary systems" (2). As Dobson noted
above, it was Shakespeare himself who began to be adapted and appropriated, his Englishness defined and embraced.

And as Graham Holderness and Andrew Murphy point out in "Shakespeare's England," the adaptation of Shakespeare "constituted and recon-
stituted, fashioned and refashioned to serve political and ideological ends"
was nothing new and had been practiced, to varying degrees, since the seventeenth century (21). They note that *Richard II* was appropriated in the
Bard's lifetime by supporters of the Earl of Essex as they planned their
rebellion (21). The multiple readings continue today, as we see works like
Stephen Bretzius's *Shakespeare in Theory*; *Shakespeare Among the Moderns*
by Richard Halpern; the multinational readings in emerging European
countries in *Shakespeare in the New Europe* by Michael Hattaway, Boika
Sokolova and Derek Roper; both Marsden's and Dobson's books cited
above; the insightful book in which Holderness's and Murphy's chapter
appears; and John J. Joughin's *Shakespeare and National Culture*. It is in
this context — Shakespeare as National Poet, as the "mythological construct" capable of being read and reread, as proprietarily English — that
we must approach Monty Python's own version of Bardolatry in its often
orgiastic form.

More influential work needs to be accomplished in the area of Shakespeare as cultural icon: specifically, as Marsden notes in her introduction,
in locating Shakespeare in relation not to the Renaissance or the Restoration, but to those who would read the mythological construct of Shakespeare and somehow respond to it. Marsden cites Hans Robert Jauss:
"A literary event can continue to have an effect only if those who come
after it still or once again respond to it — if there are readers who again

appropriate the past work or authors who want to imitate, outdo or refute it" (1). In "Accents Yet Unknown" Michael Dobson echoes this in direct relation to Shakespeare and the eventual canonization of *Julius Caesar*:

> ... conflicting revisions of this play occasioned by the constitutional upheavals which transformed the English state between the Exclusion Crisis and the fall of Walpole, revisions which endow the play with political "accents" certainly "unknown" to its first audiences, ultimately conspired together not to bury *Julius Caesar* but to canonise it, helping to confer a ghostly immortality on Shakespeare in the process [12].

This "ghostly immortality" arising from new "accents" given to Shakespeare's works is the fruit of appropriation, and whether the accents are political, cultural, or historical, the rejuvenation of the Bard continues. We have seen some examples of those who would respond to Shakespeare's work and the legacy of the English Renaissance, and Monty Python must be added to this list. Like grist to the mill Python gathers and then performs outrages on Shakespeare's texts, life, likeness, his cultural standing, and his status as belonging to England and the English — all the while supporting the notion that the process of re-examination breathes life into everything that is Shakespeare. From hospital wards for overwrought Shakespearean actors to the first performance of *Measure for Measure* underwater, from Shakespeare doing the dishes to Hamlet on a psychiatrist's couch, the Bard was appropriated by Python, but this appropriation wasn't limited to textual concerns. We shall see later that Python revived and revised much surrounding this "icon of western culture," including, but not limited to, his writing-to-type technique, the Renaissance's and Shakespeare's use of men in women's roles, his penchant for historical anachronisms and violation of the dramatic unities, his pointed verbal jousting, his relegation to otherness of any language other than English, etc. Python "read" the mythological construct "Shakespeare" and took, piecemeal, what was needed for the television troupe, all the while inflating, deflating, and conflating the iconic status of "Shakespeare" — and, in doing so, revitalizing and introducing Shakespeare afresh.

In *Shakespeare in Theory*, Stephen Bretzius adopts a rather unorthodox approach as he discusses Shakespeare and the Beatles in the same chapter, often comparing their lyrical passages side by side. His assertion that the Beatles "harnessed the tremendous cultural and historical energies that made of Shakespeare's own poetry and plays a kind of living theater" is of interest and supported well throughout the chapter. Curiously, this chapter, entitled "Cultural Studies: Shakespeare and the Beatles," is the final chapter of the book, behind new historicism, multiculturalism, feminism, absolutism, and even "nuclear" criticism. Perhaps the "isms" have made their way into scholarship, and this popular culture scenario isn't yet considered up to critical snuff, though it should be. The contemporary success Shakespeare enjoyed, coupled with the Bardolatry of Garrick and beyond, should show us that reception studies and cultural analyses are rich areas for study, and that the effects of the English Renaissance are still reverberating today, though recent scholarship might be ignoring this fecund area of study. In *The Appropriation of Shakespeare* Marsden bemoans the dearth of scholarship which might "demonstrate the widespread presence of Shakespeare in the theater, the novel, and in the ever growing field of literary criticism" (5). One of the fundamental goals of my study is, of course, to demonstrate the very "widespread presence" of the appropriated Shakespeare in the television and film work of Monty Python. Surveys of more recent literature (since Marsden wrote of this dearth in 1991) indicates that such scholarship remains generally underrepresented. The numbers of critics and audience members who saw a reworked *Hamlet* in Disney's 1994 animated feature film *The Lion King*, or the more obvious use of Shakespeare as a scrap of cultural meat to be fought over by earthlings and Klingons in *Star Trek VI* (1991), illustrates at least Hollywood's continuing fascination with the Bard.[7] But actual scholarship remains scarce, with examples like Graham Holderness's "Illogical, Captain!"— a scholarly look at *Star Trek* and Shakespeare — and Bill Reeves' "Mad Max, Larry, and the Bard" being the exceptions rather than the rule.[8] Marsden sees Shakespeare as the possibility of "appropriation throughout history of a cultural symbol," this cultural symbol being the so-called mythological construct "Shakespeare," the accretion, and not just the texts (5). The accretion that has become "Shakespeare" must include his predecessors and influences, his contemporaries in the theater, his troupe and all his plays, as well as the four hundred years of subsequent scholarship, appropriations, and adaptations. Similarly, Jonathan Dollimore and Alan Sinfield write in *Political Shakespeare* that what is "relevant" to studying Shakespeare as a cultural object is not just the history surrounding the plays' creations, "for culture is made continuously and Shakespeare's text is reconstructed, reappraised, reassigned all the time through diverse institutions in specific contexts" (viii). In "How Will Invented History" Adrian Noble notes that the history plays, specifically, were

> written for an audience listening to and, perhaps for the first time, achieving some sense of its own history. *Shakespeare is telling the*

story of his race. Perhaps it would be more accurate to say that
Shakespeare was *creating* the story of his race [7; emphasis added].

This is the Shakespeare read, adapted, and re-presented by Monty Python,
and is part of the reason why Monty Python has become an English national
symbol, a group National Poet and anglophone[9] itself ripe for appropriation, adaptation, and consumption.

The "living theater" identified by Bretzius, the nexus of powerful "cultural and historical energies" he credits Shakespeare for synthesizing, has
no better twentieth-century visual (television and even cinema) approx-
imation than the works of Monty Python. On a weekly basis beginning
May 10, 1969, *Monty Python's Flying Circus* served up a dizzying farrago of
acid-tipped satire, nonsense, grotesqueries, and general silliness aimed,
often, at the "stuck-up sticky-beaks" of contemporary television. Literally
hundreds of public figures, from Queen Victoria to Edward Heath to Reginald Maudling to moral crusader Mrs. Mary Whitehouse, appeared in
some form in a Monty Python sketch or link, with hundreds more "normal" folk making appearances as well. Rich and poor, powerful and not,
Right, Left, and Center — all were sent up as Python was, according to
Robert Hewison, "always funny *about* something, [but] frequently about
figures of authority" (8). They would wildly deflate these authority figures
or, as was the case with much of Terry Gilliam's animation, tear authority apart, then reconfigure or simply devour it. Hewison, writing of the
difficulties Python experienced with BBC and American TV censors, public crusaders like Mrs. Whitehouse, and even print media like the conservative *Daily Telegraph*, notes that through all the fuss over dirty words
and senseless sketches there was "always a strong thread of contemporary
critical comment in what they chose to be funny about" (8). In fact, Python
was upbraided internally (by the BBC) and from without for some of the
very same reasons Shakespeare suffered during the Restoration.[10] That "the
Shakespearean temperament was seen to match the English temperament
... empirical, sceptical, unsystematic, [and] ironic" cast Shakespeare as a
vulgarian, a coarse native with little connection to the refinement of the
classics (Bate 161).

Python's purposeful venture away from the accepted standards of
British television and dramatic structure sent them afoul of the established
status quo, their lacking of "formal beauty" mirroring Shakespeare's dramatic situations. The works of Shakespeare and Monty Python contain
"loose and episodic scenic form"; are beset with "multiple plots" and track
a "vertiginous course from [mock-]tragedy to comic and back again"; display "motley assemblages of character"; and generally are profligate of

"vocabulary and speech idiom" in a "jumble of prose and verse" (Bate 160). Bate, of course, was describing Shakespeare here, and illustrating Shakespeare's eventuª resuscitation as a genius who "wanted Art," a genius whose "strength" is "of natural parts" (167). He could well have been describing Monty Python, instead, who certainly "wanted Art," but who, like Shakespeare, rewrote the rules of their stage, television comedy. Bate argues that the definition of "genius" that we have come to know — "instinctive and extraordinary capacity for imaginative creation, original thought, invention, or discovery"— is a relatively new definition, and much different from the Latin derivative meaning a "tutelary god" given to everyone at birth (160–161).[11] Bate argues that "'*genius' was a category invented in order to account for what was peculiar about Shakespeare*" (163; Bate's emphasis). The genius moniker is also tied to Shakespeare's Englishness, as he is different from the more classics-bound French and the rest of the Restoration-era favorites; thus the flowering of a National Poet begins. This "capacity for imaginative creation, original thought, invention, or discovery" is reassembled in Monty Python; for, as will be seen with Monty Python — and *is* with Shakespeare — "the plays have held the stage, the poetry is held in our minds, [and] the characters have become archetypes" (158).

The cultural and historical energies employed by Monty Python encompassed all of British history — including prominent names, dates, and events— and literature, the arts, politics and popular culture.[12] The wildly anarchic structure of the show and the often topical satire attracted, at first, a cult following.[13] Soon, though, millions were regularly tuning in, responding to what might be called Britain's newest anglophone — speakers of the Queen's English and purveyors of Englishness. Bretzius asserts that Shakespeare and the Beatles may have actually been "competing for the same audience," that audience being working-class folk feeding on popular culture, the same popular culture which Monty Python plundered, sent up, and ultimately re-created. If, as Andrew Gurr asserts, the offerings on the Elizabethan stage were, for the most part, "bloody and bawdy," then audiences were attending for much the same reasons and seeing much the same spectacle as those who would attend a taping of a *Flying Circus* episode (212). Gurr even connects the two audiences, arguing that twentieth-century television audiences are no more prone to the mindless mimicry of that given them on television than were the groundlings and others who would have regularly attended the Globe and similar theaters. The "basic mentality of the Elizabethan and early Stuart audiences," Gurr asserts, "is not essentially different from that of the majority audiences of today" (212). Audiences attended Shakespeare and still attend today. In fact, with the newest findings surrounding The Globe and Rose theaters, and especially the reconstructed Globe space — where today's audiences can at least get a feel for what an Elizabethan theater-goer might have experienced — one might say a Shakespeare renaissance is underway.[14] In just the last ten years, for example, there have been at least fifty-eight notable television and film adaptations or performances of Shakespeare's work, including (most recently) Ian McKellan's and Richard Loncraine's *Richard III* (1995), Baz Luhrmann's *Romeo + Juliet* (1996), and Julie Taymor's *Titus Andronicus* (1999).[15] It is worth noting that in this recharged environment Taymor's major production of *Titus Andronicus*— a play considered by many to be an inferior example of Shakespeare's dramatic style —can be brought to the screen in a market saturated with other big-budget spectacles. Shakespeare has, perhaps, never been more popular or reached a wider audience than his work and legacy enjoy today.

Audiences also attended Python (in person and via television broadcast) and still attend revivals, videotaped performances, surviving member reunion tours, and fan clubs, visit one of the hundreds of Internet sites, and constantly appropriate the Python construct. The Internet is particularly fluid and potentially difficult for consistent research purposes, since sites "go up" and "come down" constantly, and new sites are added as old ones are subsumed, sold or just abandoned. But at any one time there are myriad sites where the works of Shakespeare and Monty Python can be accessed, discussed, purchased, or just viewed electronically. And if Shakespeare is the National Poet of England, "both symbol and exemplar of British national identity," as Dobson notes, then the critical, cultural, and popular reception of Monty Python must place them in the pantheon as well (*NP* 185). Python reads the National Poet and then creates a new kind of poetry, lending their collective voice to the constant and consistent reassessment of Englishness.

Marsden points out that cultish enshrinements like those found now at Stratford don't exist for the other "greats"— there is no significant "Bardolatry" (outside of academic departments) for Chaucer, Milton, Dickens, nor for any of Shakespeare's more celebrated contemporaries (Marlowe, Jonson, Beaumont and Fletcher), or even for those who would come later and clean up after him like Howard, Cibber, Dryden, and Tate (3). Similarly, many radio and television shows have been mentioned as influential to Python, including *The Goon Show*, *Q5*, *That Was the Week That Was*, and *Beyond the Fringe* (a live stage show), but these shows do not have the cult followings that Python has to this day, more than thirty years after taking to the television airwaves. Only time will tell whether Python's high-water mark will stand, but in an era when fads come and go in a matter of months and even weeks, the fact that Python characters and quotes and "isms" have entered our cultural lexicon is worthy of remark.

Marsden calls the Shakespeare devotion a "culturally inscribed hero-worship," and for those English men and women who today may still culturally possess Shakespeare as their own, but who may not have read or experienced his work beyond the limits of their compulsory education, the biting wit of Monty Python has created for them another hero to possess, another source of pride in their mutual Englishness (2). Accessing the great works of English literature and the figures of English history through Python — however transmuted and filtered — is also a badge of acculturation. This sense of belonging, this national identity credited to Shakespeare, is carried on by Monty Python. To be English or British, then, is to possess Python, as is illustrated by John Diamond in his article "Once I Was British":

> I knew I was British because when I met other people who called themselves British we found we had things in common. They would look at the chicken in my fridge and say, "This parrot is dead!" and I would come straight back there with "It's not dead it's only resting!" and my, but how we would laugh. For I knew that as I was watching Monty Python, so was every other 17-year-old in the country. I knew I could stand at the door of the sixth-form common room the next morning and shout, "No-one expects the Spanish Inquisition!" and only a boy called Kessler, who didn't have a television, would think I'd found Jesus [1].

This cultural collectivism was shaped around the shared culture created by and drawn from Monty Python, the mythological construct. The author's very sense of who he was, his British self (the term here probably used interchangeably to mean "English"), his self-identification during the troubling formative years of adolescence, is placed squarely in his shared National Poet: Monty Python. Jonathan Bate notes that "Shakespeare has survived and has been made to matter as a voice of radical culture, not just of established culture," which seems to translate into the culture which encompasses all points of view (214). In this he is truly the National Poet, able to speak for all viewpoints, English *and* British.

A recent discussion carried out on the editorial pages of *The Sunday Times* illustrates the significance of just what it means to be a neo-anglophone — or a speaker of English culture — and just how far from that Englishness many Englishmen think they have drifted. Writer Jeremy Paxman published chapters from his forthcoming book, *The English* (2000), in *The Sunday Times* on 27 September, 4 October, and 11 October 1998. The loose chapters addressed just what it might mean anymore to be English —from a monarchy infatuation to hooliganism to fear of the euro. His comment — "Once upon a time the English knew who they were"— sets the tone for the collective soul-searching that follows (27 Sept. 1998). He continues:

> There was such a ready list of adjectives at hand. They were polite, unexcitable, reserved and had hot-water bottles instead of a sex life: how they reproduced was one of the mysteries of the western world. They were doers rather than thinkers, writers rather than painters, gardeners rather than cooks. They were class-bound, hidebound and incapable of expressing their emotions. They did their duty. Their most prized possession was a sense of honour. They were steadfast and trustworthy. The word of an English gentleman was as good as a bond sealed in blood.
> ....
> What they are really calling up is a picture of the strength of England [2].

What follows, of course, are the inevitable revisions of this storied history, the "bringing back down to earth" illustrations of England as it is, not as it was or people wanted it to be. Paxman laments the losses— the rural, agrarian society, the red pillar boxes, the pre-war hamlet, the colonies (the "them" to naturally oppose "us"), and even the celebration of St. George's Day (2–7 *passim*). Responses to Paxman from readers were published in *The Sunday Times* on 4 October 1998, under the title "The English Go Out in Search of an Identity." Most seemed to agree, as Sir Roy Strong put it, that "England faces an identity crisis," a crisis he compares to the conditions present just after Elizabeth's death in 1603 ("Letters to the Editor" 4 October 1998). The search for what Elizabeth herself called the state of being "mere English" was being undertaken from one end of the country to the other, and within and between every social class. But in closing his initial chapter Paxman himself offers what it means, to him, to be English, and lists his own reasons for celebration:

> Off the top of my head, mine would include "I know my rights," village cricket and Elgar, do-it-yourself, punk, street fashion, irony, vigorous politics, brass bands, *Shakespeare*, Cumberland sausages, double-decker buses, Vaughan Williams, Donne and Dickens, twitching net curtains, breast-obsession, quizzes and crosswords, country churches, dry-stone walls, gardening, Christopher Wren, and *Monty Python* [27 September 1998; emphasis added].

The anxiety over Englishness in an increasingly global society seems to weigh heavily on the English psyche, but it is apparent that the touchstone still remains. The National Poets—Shakespeare and Monty Python—still speak that cultural dialogue interpretable as Englishness and, judging by the sheer number of avenues through which to access the Shakespearean and the Pythonesque, the message of Englishness is still being spoken and received.

From 1969 to the present, Monty Python has been given status similar to the cultural figure Shakespeare in at least English culture, and is even present at the highest levels of government. In the months following a 1601 performance of Shakespeare's *Richard II*, Elizabeth is reported to have noted that the performance was not about Richard but about herself, concretely identifying the relationship between life and life represented on the stage (Evans 803–04). This incident also serves to illuminate the shared cultural lexicon that exists between the stage and, in these instances, the court and seats of government. In a much-publicized gag (or gaffe, perhaps?) at a 1990 party conference, then–Prime Minister Margaret Thatcher attempted an appropriation of Monty Python to attack the Liberal Democrat party and their "flying bird" symbol. Her speechwriters convinced her to refer to the logo as resembling Monty Python's "dead parrot," and she did, though only after many hours of discussion, several looks at a videotape of the entire "Dead Parrot" sketch, and assurances from her speechwriters that the reference was indeed both funny and apropos (White 1; "Quidnunc" 1). The original sketch—now by the far the most cited of Python's work—features John Cleese as Praline and Michael Palin as Shopkeeper, with Praline trying to return a supine parrot:

> PRALINE: Never mind that my lad, I wish to complain about this parrot what I purchased not half an hour ago from this very boutique.
> SHOPKEEPER: Oh yes, the Norwegian Blue. What's wrong with it?
> PRALINE: I'll tell you what's wrong with it. It's dead, that's what's wrong with it.
> SHOPKEEPER: No, no it's resting, look!
> PRALINE: Look my lad, I know a dead parrot when I see one and I'm looking at one right now [1.8.104].

The Shopkeeper insists that the parrot is just resting, and probably "pining for the fjords," so Praline first shouts at the parrot, then picks it up and bangs it against the counter. The Shopkeeper says that the bird must be "stunned," and then tells Praline that the bird must be nailed or it would escape, still insisting that the bird must be pining:

> PRALINE: It's not pining, it's passed on. This parrot is no more. It has ceased to be. It's expired and gone to meet its maker. This is a late parrot. It's a stiff. Bereft of life, it rests in peace. If you hadn't nailed it to

the perch, it would be pushing up the daisies. It's rung down the curtain and joined the choir invisible. This is an ex-parrot [1.8.105].

The quip had "the party faithful rolling in the aisles" (the "Iron Lady" now an honorary Pepperpot?), but speechwriter John Whittingdale was certain "that when she read it she had not the first idea what we were referring to" ("Quidnunc" 1). Bate writes that "classical quotations are among the most polished badges of the elite," but also indicates that many attempts to "nationalize" Shakespeare are based on misreadings, "risible simplifications" of the sources, and a wholesale disavowal of context (200–201). The Iron Lady may have been the only one within earshot who did not understand exactly what she was saying. Yes, Margaret Thatcher may not have understood Monty Python, but that didn't stop her from appropriating the work to serve, at that moment, the Tories and her conservative cause. And just two years later, in response to the imminent demise of the Maastricht treaty, Norman Tebbit, a former "Thatcherite minister," celebrated the treaty's collapse: "They may try to nail it to the perch again, but nobody will believe that it is still alive" (Phillips 35). The dead parrot lives again, possessed by those at the very heights of power and, importantly, English culture.

Thus Englishmen can have it both ways: access to and possession of the classics, and, simultaneously, the privilege to skewer same. Both Shakespeare and Python have been and can be appropriated by myriad cultural and political sects. The cultural affirmation of both Shakespeare and Monty Python allows for this dichotomous ability to have one's cake and eat it, too. This cultural duplicity (meaning the state of being double or twofold) also allows those who may possess Shakespeare in a more academically significant way (i.e., scholars) to "go slumming" into Monty Python's world as indulging a guilty pleasure, much the same way scholars of the English Renaissance (pausing from their Latin and Greek "classics") would have enjoyed their afternoon at The Globe with a bit of Shakespeare entertainment. Even Jonathan Bate, author of *The Genius of Shakespeare*, wanders momentarily — and perhaps unconsciously — into Python's world as he indulges "in unsubstantiated speculation, looking for nudges and winks on Shakespeare's part" (219). And though the particular sketch to which he refers featuring the endlessly talking and gesturing Eric Idle (as an annoying pub customer) and the somewhat flustered Terry Jones (a bowlered gent) has absolutely nothing to do with Shakespeare, the reference by Bate can't help but be informed, at least partly, by Python, adding a hint of subversion and displaying the cultural badge Bate himself identified earlier (1.3.40–41). The classics informed Shakespeare, as Shakespeare informed Python, and so on.

And where are these cultural allusions being found? Just about everywhere. "Imagine a Monty Python movie as directed by Ingmar Bergman — all British absurdity and discontinuity rendered in the most drawn-out and lugubrious manner possible" (7). This is how one reviewer chose to describe the latest novel from *Remains of the Day* author Kazuo Ishiguro, citing one of film's great achievers, Bergman, and Python in the same paragraph. Fitting, since Ishiguro is also called "British to the core of his soul" in the same review. That Monty Python has truly entered the cultural lexicon can be illustrated by just a quick electronic glance through today's available journals. It might seem that references to a TV show more than twenty years old would be both few and limited to entertainment publications, and that the availability of these same shows would be limited.[16] But, as Marsden also points out, "once established such hero worship becomes self-perpetuating" (2). The trick is to become established. And though there have been hundreds of literary figures and many more recent electronic media figures who all qualify, by their mere existence, for possible enshrinement, the adulatory recognition is, as we've seen, very limited. In *U.S. News and World Report* Anna Mulrine notes Python as the crowning influence on today's comedians who are shrugging off the orthodox constraints of American comedy; a review of Kenneth Branagh's *Henry V* in *The American Spectator* by Bruce Bawer compares Python's "parody of medieval styles" to Branagh's action sequences at Agincourt; in the *New York Times* Ben Brantley reviews the play *The Compleat Works of William Shakespeare (Abridged)* as nearly reaching *Flying Circus*'s "demented level."[17] These are all, as might be expected, entertainment-type citations. But more curious and culturally and politically disseminated citations follow.

In *The New Republic*, Paul Quinn-Judge profiles the Russian nationalist Vladimir Zhirinovsky, characterizing the Russian presidential hopeful as "xenophobic" and his entire candidacy (including his constituency) as reminiscent of Python's *Flying Circus* characters; also in *The New Republic*, writer Henry Fairlie discusses the initial broadcast of the proceedings of the House of Commons on C-SPAN, in an article entitled "Maggie's Flying Circus" (subtitled "And Now For Something Completely Different"); *Discover* magazine features the results of a Rube Goldberg design contest, wherein the contestants must design a machine which performs at least twenty different steps to complete a task, with one of the machines a re-enactment of *Monty Python and the Holy Grail*; in "Clinch That Cliche" from *New Statesman & Society*, Mat Coward, commenting on England's entry into the European Common Market, offers popular stereotypes of Europeans, and while differentiating between "British" and "English," admits that the English are "known chiefly for the Beatles, Monty Python, their mistrust of Europe, their lost empire, their defunct colonies, and for the intense irony with which they manage to imbue the phrase 'our European partners'" (xxviii). (Coward does not mention Shakespeare as an example of well-known British or English cultural artifacts. This could be more a reflection of the author than contemporary Europe, of course.)

These examples, as can be seen, cut across the political and even international spectrum, but with a common theme: these "everyday" situations have reached a Pythonesque proportion of satire, irony, silliness, and even the grotesque, as may be the case with the next example. Rosalind Miles, writing in *Toronto*, examines the royal family (in 1995) and especially the place of young William, heir to the throne. After citing all the silver spoons that William's been provided, she reminds us of the black eyes that his parents have inflicted on the family in their well-publicized indiscretions. William placed tops in a popular poll regarding who should next wear the crown, thus the public is ready to accept William as their next king; this even after all the go-'rounds in the royal family. Miles finds it "interesting that the British want to believe" in the royal family in spite of the royal family, and is somewhat amazed that (here citing Python, among others) "the nation that invented modern satire would go for this guff" (35). Python here, then, is a cautionary tool — a shared, learned experience which, properly appreciated, will help avoid monarchical disappointments. A book review by Colin J. Williams in *The Journal of Sex Research* cited Monty Python when reviewing a new book entitled *Sadomasochism: Painful Perversion or Pleasurable Play?* Python is even used to try to illustrate cultural differences, Anglophilia, and Anglophobia regarding a former colony and its mother state in "Why Americans Feel Inferior to the British ... and Why We Shouldn't" by D. Keith Mano and appearing in *Forbes* magazine. Mano characterizes Americans as essentially unrepressed, and the British as "highly moral and repressed," thus the "gradual disintegration of a moral, repressed character" like Cleese's character in "The Dead Parrot" sketch is hilarious without being silly (124). (If an unrepressed American tried the same comedy, Mano concludes, it could only come off as "foolish and embarrassing" [124].)

Python is additionally cited in a case review article in *Rutgers Law Review*, in *Teaching of Psychology, The Solicitor's Journal, Family Therapy Networker*, and, perhaps most fittingly, Python is acknowledged by the journal *Accountancy* in the article "How Do Students See Us?"[18] There is also the potentially disturbing but perhaps even more fascinating mention of the Python film *Life of Brian* in an article regarding cults and secret societies, two very serious topics (Madigan 12–14). In the film, Brian —

mistaken for a messiah — tells his followers that they shouldn't follow anyone, that they should think for themselves. The crowd agrees whole-
heartedly, then asks what else should they do. And finally, two references
that are perhaps the most telling both have to do with Spam. Python's
"Spam" sketch featured a diner where the menu consisted almost entirely
of Spam, such that nothing could be ordered without the mystery meat:

> WAITRESS: (Jones) Well there's egg and bacon; egg, sausage and bacon; egg
> and spam; egg, bacon and spam; egg, bacon, sausage and spam; spam,
> bacon, sausage and spam; spam, egg, spam, spam, bacon and spam;
> spam, spam, spam, egg and spam; spam, spam spam, spam, spam,
> spam... [2.25.27].

In *The Chronicle of Higher Education*, the most important voice of American academia, authors Gerald Graff and Michael Berube decry the wasteful overlapping and redundancy of courses and requirements at many
colleges and universities. At one university, five different majors featured
the word "culture" in their titles, from "Cultural Studies" to "Literacy and
Culture" to "Literature, Theory, and Culture," with none of the departments having any connection to another (B2). "Perhaps the university was
inspired," writes the author, "by the *Monty Python* show's "Spam" skit to
produce its own version: 'culture, eggs, and Spam; culture, bacon, toast,
and Spam; culture, culture, Spam, culture, and culture'" (B2). And, as an
example of a Python-ism entering firmly the cultural and technological
lexicon, *Time* magazine reported that in Internet lingo, "Spam" has come
to mean "garbage, or junk postings, usually sent in large multiples" (Elmer-
Dewitt 44). One can even be "spammed," in an electronic sense, when
inundated by such garbage mailings.

A quick electronic trip across the Internet landscape displays the fre-
quency with which Monty Python and the Pythonesque are appropriated
in, for instance, prominent English newspapers. A search just for the key
words "Monty Python" at *The Times* website produced sixty-one hits, or
references, to the name just in the previous two and a half months. These
references ranged from television cooking show reviews to political commentary and editorial. Similarly, at *The Guardian* and *The Observer* site,
called "Guardian Limited," 165 hits were found across a broad range of
issues and topics.[19] These hits feature references to Monty Python as a
lasting and embedded part of the English national culture. In no instance
was the reference used to obfuscate the particular article's point or the
author's perspective, but quite the opposite. There was a certain "wink,
wink, nudge, nudge" from the writer to the reader, yes, but a tacit and yet
still somehow expressed understanding based on a shared cultural heritage.
When reporting, for instance, that a recent session of the House of Lords

seemed more like a Monty Python sketch, no explanation was offered to decipher the referent — it was simply understood that the reader understood what "like a Monty Python sketch" meant.

Dobson notes that "changing Shakespeare's words becomes only one among many ways of establishing what their author means, of promoting his authority, and of claiming him as an ally" (*National Poet* 134). One can also say that appropriating these same meanings and authorities— even by just quoting out of context — promotes not only the author as legitimate but the adaptor/appropriator as well. A sense of legitimacy and authority can be created with well-placed Shakespearean quotations, in writing or conversation, conveying a sense of history emanating from the writer/speaker. This seems to be the case when so many varied professions, individuals and cultural strata can and do appropriate both Shakespeare and Monty Python, simultaneously identifying themselves as "cultured" (simply because they can quote, change or appropriate) and as "possessing" the mythological constructs of Shakespeare and Python. Today, the pages of myriad journals are littered with quotes from, comparisons to and a general "in-the-knowingness" (*nudge, nudge*) of Monty Python's *oeuvre*, creating a sort of Pythonolatry that has long outlasted *Flying Circus* episodes and Python movies. The chaotic structure, biting humor, and verbal intricacies which characterize Python's work, according to Roger Wilmut, "do not make their greatest impact at first, but lie in the subconscious like a time-bomb" (207). In this case, a time-bomb of the collective subconscious found in almost every media, a handy grab-bag of ready-made cultural sophistication. And like those who would similarly approach Shakespeare, it is no longer the Python texts which are adapted and appropriated, *per se*, but the construct that has become Monty Python.

A word that has been mentioned above —"Pythonesque"— is actually a fairly recent coining, and seems to be slowly gaining widespread critical acceptance from newspapers to magazines to juried journals by the hundreds. Most often, something is described as "Pythonesque" (or "Python-esque" or "pythonesque") when the situation, event, realization or finished product is absurdly silly, iconoclastic, verbally or visually vulgar and quick-paced, or if, by human intervention, something has been made to defy all logic. The word has even reached something of canonical status, as it has found a place in the most venerable of all reference books: the Oxford English Dictionary. "Pythonesque" now has a dictionary meaning, and is formally a part of the cultural lexicon:

> **Pythonesque** *a.* [-ESQUE.] Of, pertaining to, or characteristic of *Monty Python's Flying Circus*, a popular British television

comedy series of the 1970s, noted esp. for its absurdist or sur-
realistic humour.
1975 *Guardian* 18 Oct. 8/1 A range of comic methods that stretches
from Pythonesque funny walks ... to comedy of manners. **1977**
Time Out 17 June 9/1 It veered from the Pythonesque, mostly due
to the presence of the Cleese-like Julian Hough, to the twee. **1979**
Listener 28 June 873/2 It is doubtful if anyone looked up a dictionary for a definition of 'python,' but it is certain that future com-
pilers of dictionaries are going to have to append a new meaning to
"Pythonesque," for the word is now common English usage on both
sides of the Atlantic.... It describes a set of events that are more
than bizarre, yet less than surreal. **1986** *Financial Times* 28 Feb. 19/1
Everything from classically slapstick scenes to Pythonesque non
sequiturs [948].

"Pythonesque" cuts across all social and political boundaries, and is
attached to politics, culture, entertainment and people just behaving in a
ridiculous manner. Just as one might say a piece of writing, the turn of a
phrase, a plot structure, a subject or a certain viewpoint is "Shakespearean," one now may also describe as Pythonesque a silly, bawdy or
loquacious act or utterance. The "Pythonesque" moniker has been attached
to reviews of children's theater, newly staged and innovative operas, newly
staged but still torpid dramas, especially bad Shakespeare adaptations
(which had serious intentions), and even a new "how-to" billiards CD-
ROM. Also recently characterized as Pythonesque are highlights of the
Conservative Party conference in Glasgow; the exploits of the Prince of
Wales Company as they guard a police station on the Irish border; the violence in a play set in a pig sty; the sufferings a food critic must endure to
be culinarily honest; the one-upmanship escalations of an argument
between two Frenchmen who are suffering through a transit strike; an
opera seria based on Shakespeare's *Midsummer Night's Dream*; a new and
celebrated novel from deceased author Georges Perec, written without
using the letter E; the interpretation of a ballet; and the poor interview-
ing techniques of various ITV personalities.[20]

"Pythonesque" is even becoming a sort of catch-all phrase which can
mean either banal and deadpan in one instance or loony and outrageous
in another. In other words, a certain cultural and historical awareness is
necessary for the allusion to make complete sense, much like the allusive
references in Shakespeare (i.e., the multiple explanations for one word,
"innovation," in *Hamlet* [2.2.333], or the complete appreciation of the
topicality of Hamlet's questions regarding boys' theater in London
[2.2.319–368]). But, just as getting all the in-jokes isn't necessary for
an appreciation of the genius of *Hamlet*, Monty Python's humor can be

appreciated without knowing anything about Luton, a blanc mange, or Reginald Maudling.[21] Monty Python "is by nature sympathetic to states of incomprehension and confusion," writes Veronica Geng in *The New Republic*. "That's why its special references and high-culture allusions don't intimidate Americans or other ill-educated or out-of-it English-speaking people ... [as] the audience will hear how ignorance and knowledge are being deployed" (34). Jeffrey Miller notes that the American *Monty Python* audience wasn't actually the *Masterpiece Theatre* crowd. They were instead:

> college-age viewers — an audience that, in acquiring educational
> capital, might have some appeal for public television stations
> already defining themselves, through their relationships with Mobil
> and other "sponsors," in terms of just such an elite audience [129].

This is an audience, whether in Iowa or New York City (where *Flying Circus* appeared on public television stations), that possessed the appropriate level of acculturation to "get" much of the Python humor, and just enough college-level immaturity to revel in the accompanying absurdity. This was also an audience which sponsors could hope to attract as future and long-term customers, another attractive incentive for the support of Python on American television.

One of these in-jokes which recently has attracted much attention is the appearance of a bit of Python work in 1997's *As Good As It Gets*, directed by James Brooks and starring Jack Nicholson, Helen Hunt and Greg Kinnear. In the film, Nicholson plays an obsessive-compulsive who struggles to have any kind of a normal relationship with a world and people he finds so untidy and unkempt. At one point he is forced into caring for his neighbor's dog, and in an effort to entertain the dog (like the animal was some sort of bored child), he sits at the piano and plays and sings "Always Look On the Bright Side of Life," a song which originally appeared as the finale for Python's *Life of Brian*, and was penned by Eric Idle. The song was sung by Idle's character and others as they all hung on crosses, and was meant to lift Brian's spirits. *Life of Brian* and Monty Python were castigated in the media by those who saw the film as sacrilege ("...blasphemous, sacrilegious and an inducement to possible violence"[22]), especially this scene, wherein the sanctity of the crucifixion was supposedly trammeled with irreverent satire and flippancy. The song itself is actually engagingly nihilistic ("You were born with nothing, you die with nothing. What have you lost? Nothing!"), acknowledging life's problems but calling for a cheerful outlook. *As Good As It Gets* composer Hans Zimmer, faced with appropriating a song from a film which, to many religious adherents of many faiths, was a "vilification of their faith and the debasement of culture represented by this sick enterprise," chose to adapt the song anyway as an affirmation of the Nicholson character's change in attitude about his own life (Hewison 67). This is indeed a recontextualization.

Again, these are but a few examples from many, all of which support Monty Python as cultural hero, and what we are witnessing is the self-perpetuation of hero-worship that Marsden noted earlier in regard to Shakespeare. The genius of Shakespeare and Monty Python demand their Englishness, their common discordant structures and rabble-ish characters, their disavowal of classical modes and methods, and their appropriation and exportation by diverse groups and beliefs that cut across and through culture. This appropriation of Shakespeare as mythological construct — as National Poet, especially — revitalizes the Bard via Bardolatry from Shakespeare figurines in Stratford shops to the Beatles' "Billy Shears" to Shakespeare falling in love with one of his players.[23] The enshrinement of Python as anglophone — the English cultural speaker — allows for the appropriation of Python as a mythological construct, as well. Thus "Pythonesque" can enter the cultural lexicon as a broadly-used descriptor, from entertainment to culture to politics, even making its way into scholarly journals and texts. The readings of Shakespeare by Monty Python and the subsequent appropriation of Python as cultural hero will constitute the remaining chapters, from Shakespeare and Python's abuses of history to their disavowal of many accepted dramatic structures to their use and treatment of female characters and, in the case of Python, of actual women. The following chapter will look closely at Shakespeare, Jonson and Monty Python, and their significant (and often shared) employments of theatricality as each further defines what it is to be English. The readings of the National Poet by Monty Python include revitalization, revision, and re-historicizing, and further defines the genius of both anglophones as their "plays have held the stage," their "poetry is held in our minds," and their "characters have become archetypes" — from commingling "kings and clowns," from Falstaff to Ken Shabby.

Notes

1. A handy index has been included for Pepys' *Diary* by Robert Latham in *The Shorter Pepys* (Los Angeles: U of California P, 1985). An avid theater-goer and seeker of entertainment, Pepys' mentions *Hamlet, 1 Henry IV, Henry VIII, Macbeth, The Merry Wives of Windsor, Midsummer Night's Dream, Othello, Romeo and Juliet, The Tempest,* as well as *Twelfth Night* in his diaries (as well as the plays of many other playwrights, both past and present). Pepys often would buy the playbook, then go and see the play, and compare the two. See Latham's *The Shorter Pepys* for the index.

2. Pepys' self-aggrandizement is somewhat legendary, and his cryptic short-hand might have just been used to insulate himself during and just after his nat-ural life. Since deciphering and publication were inevitable, the boasts—especially those of a sexual nature, but perhaps everything else — have to be taken with a grain of salt. See Harry Berger, Jr.'s "The Pepys Show: Ghost-writing and Docu-mentary Desire in *The Diary*" (*ELH* 65.3): 557–591.

3. Shakespeare himself performs this "stepping out" from the play's pre-scribed action in *Hamlet*, in a way, as he allows Hamlet, Rosencrantz and Guilden-stern to discuss the contemporary state of the London stage. Specifically, Shakespeare is attacking the then-fashionable use of boy troupes, and describes them, via Rosencrantz, as "an aery of children, little eyases, that cry out on the top of question" (2.2.339–340). Interestingly, the narrative action of the play almost completely stops here, which Shakespeare must have appreciated, so that his short diatribe can be voiced. This pregnant pause would most certainly be understood by the contemporary audiences for what it was, and the artifice of the play would then have been forwarded.

4. See Kavenik; Dobson *National Poet*. Recent scholarship has overturned an earlier belief that no public stage performances occurred during the Interregnum. Dale Randall notes that the very presence of an edict forbidding performance attested to the power and presence of the theater, and that,

> [f]urthermore, throughout the ensuing official hiatus in playing, dramas continued to be composed, translated, revived, transmuted, published, bought, read, and even acted.
> ....
> [T]he larger fact [to] be explored here is that drama, which had so inter-ested the English in earlier years ... continued to interest many and to pro-vide English writers, readers, and sometimes audiences with many forms of expression, whether for persuasion or pleasure or both. The very recurrence of prohibitions against playing attests to the persisting life of drama [*Win-ter Fruit* 1–2].

For other studies of Interregnum theater see also William Nelles' "Cosmo Manuche's Castle Ashby Plays as Theater Pieces" (*ELN* 27.4 [June 1990]) and Wil-liam Proctor Williams' "Evidence of Performance" (*ELN* 30.1 [September 1992]). For a comprehensive look at all aspects (in great detail) of the English stage dur-ing the period, see Van Lennep's *The London stage, 1660–1800; a calendar of plays, entertainments & afterpieces, together with casts, box-receipts and contemporary comment. Compiled from the playbills, newspapers and theatrical diaries of the period* (Carbondale, Southern Illinois UP, 1960–68).

5. George Bernard Shaw is credited with coining this term in 1901. See Mars-den, *Appropriation* 3.

6. See Jean Marsden's excellent article "Rewritten Women: Shakespearean Women in the Restoration" which appears in the equally strong book *The Appro-priation of Shakespeare*, also edited by Marsden (New York: St. Martin's P, 1991). The rewriting of women's roles for women rather than men led, according to Marsden's social analysis, to "radically revised" roles which tended to portray females who were more virtuous, meek, passive, and best suited for domestic life (43–45).

7. See Roger Ebert's review of *Lion King* on the *Chicago Sun-Times* website,

www.suntimes.com/ebert/ebert_reviews/1994/06/927167.html, or in the *Sun-Times* (24 June 1994).

As for the cultural appropriation of Shakespeare as National Poet, *Star Trek VI* features a meeting between Klingons and the Enterprise crew wherein Shakespeare is quoted and claimed by both parties: "You should read him in the original Klingon," says one participant. See *Star Trek VI* (1991), written by Leonard Nimoy and Lawrence Konner, and directed by Nicholas Meyer. There are also numerous Shakespearean references in the various *Star Trek* television series.

8. The few other examples of forays into the "Shakespeare" appropriation and influence field include: Lorne Buchman's *Still in Movement: Shakespeare on Screen* (New York and Oxford: Oxford UP, 1991), a look at the spectatorial process of Shakespeare as adapted to cinematic language; a neo–Marxist approach to Bard appropriation in John Collick's *Shakespeare, Cinema and Society* (Manchester and New York: Manchester UP, 1991); and a look at the earliest cinematic adaptation of Shakespeare, "The First Shakespeare Film: A Reconsideration and Reconstruction of Tree's *King John*" by B.A. Kachur and found in *Theatre Survey* 32.1 (May 1991), among others. A more recent article looks at Shakespeare's influence on the novel: H.R. Harris's "Jane Austen's Venture Into Tragedy" in *Contemporary Review* 272.1589 (June 1998): 314–18, which looks at Austen's appropriation of *Lear* for her novel *Mansfield Park*.

9. I mean "anglophone" in a special sort of way. The dictionary might describe an anglophone as an English-speaking person, especially in a country of two or more languages. My assertion will be that Shakespeare and Monty Python speak and convey an "Englishness" that includes a shared cultural history. The utterances then become definable as Englishness, and are appropriated and shared by others who are also English. This Englishness is evident in the histories plumbed for drama, the otherness of anything and anyone non–English (even the British), etc.

10. In December 1970, for instance, after the broadcast of a *Flying Circus* episode which featured Chapman and Cleese discussing the eating of the Cleese character's mother, a BBC planners meeting convened. Various heads of BBC divisions "found parts of this edition disgusting" and "over the edge of what was acceptable," while others argued that "the programme had contained some dazzle" and "it would be very sad if the BBC lost the programme" (Hewison 21). Not just upset at the "cruel" and "nihilistic" humor, the fact that the show seemed to wander into other BBC shows, namely *Late Night Line-Up*, "bothered the BBC heads of the Light Entertainment Group, Features Group, and even the Programme Controller, BBC 1, and Director of Programmes, BBC 2. The forms of television had been tested, expanded, and even done away with. This show, episode 26, the last show in the second series, was not shown again by the BBC, and was not made available when the series went overseas. This may, as Hewison surmises, have had as much to do with the fact that the entire show is based on the premise that the Queen might be tuning in, and the royal family as a whole is sent up (see Hewison's *Monty Python: The Case Against*. London: Eyre Methuen, 1981: 22).

11. See *The Oxford English Dictionary* for both the classical and "English" definitions of "genius."

12. The terms "British" and "English" are used as other authors cited have used them in their various works, but for my own purposes I must acknowledge Willy Maley's important article "'This sceptred isle': Shakespeare and the British

Problem" found in John J. Joughin's *Shakespeare and National Culture* (Manchester and New York: Manchester UP, 1997). Maley's differentiation between English and Englishness and British and Britishness is marked by the colonialism of the Empire's past. In short, the "English" include those actually in (most of) England, while "British" brings in the Scots, Welsh, Irish, and peoples inhabiting the surrounding islands. Those living or from beyond the "Anglo-Celtic boundary" fall into the British category, and have been (and still are, to some extent) under the political and cultural influence of England, and relegated, often, to "other" status. It should be noted that for the most part, Python seems to have taken great pains to barb just about everyone, even their own Englishness.

13. Despite the BBC's rather slack attention to the solidity of the show's time slot (*Flying Circus* originally appeared in the place of a religious rebroadcast; at other times the show was preempted without notice in favor of, for example, an interview with the Duke of Edinburgh), the show's audience share increased to three million, and once to as many as four-and-a-half million (Hewison 17).

14. The Globe Theatre information can be found online at http://www.shakespeares-globe.org/; Rose Theatre information at http://www.rdg.ac.uk/Rose/. Also, see *Shakespeare's Globe Rebuilt* (Cambridge: Cambridge UP, 1997) edited by Gurr, Mulryne, Mulryne, and Shewring.

15. See the Internet site www.IMDb.com (Internet Movie Database) for listings of Shakespeare productions. The listed productions also include those appearing on public and commercial television, as well as those produced for feature film release.

16. This is especially noteworthy in today's media-drenched society. With hundreds of cable and satellite outlets/channels, the market for reruns of televisions shows long off the air is booming. These shows, like American television's *Petticoat Junction* (1963–70) and *Green Acres* (1965–71), may be able to be seen in just about any television market with the proper equipment. The fact that these shows are available but still have not created lasting appropriations to the cultural lexicon indicates the special place that Monty Python must occupy.

17. See Colin J. Williams' "SM in the Sceptred Isle" in *The Journal of Sex Research* 32.2 (1995): 170–171; "Guide to the Ways and Words of Cyberspace" in *Time* 145.12 (Spring 1995): 42; Gerald Graff and Michael Berube's "Dubious and Wasteful Academic Habits" in *The Chronicle of Higher Education* 41.23 (Feb 17, 1995): B1–B4; Rosalind Miles' "Will Power" in *Toronto* 110.3 (Apr 1995): 32–37; Mat Coward's "Clinch That Cliche" in *New Statesman & Society* (May 26, 1995): xxvi–xxviii; Jeffrey Kluger's "Rube Awakening" in *Discover* 16.8 (Aug 1995): 78–83; Anna Mulrine's "Off to the Flying Circus" in *U.S. New & World Report* 124.11 (Mar 23, 1998): 64–65; Ben Brantley's review of *The Compleat Works of William Shakespeare* in *New York Times* (Feb 27, 1995): C11–C12; Paul Quinn-Judge's "Flying Circus" in *The New Republic* 205 (Nov 11, 1991): 20–21; Bruce Bawer's review of *Henry V* in *The American Spectator* 23 (Mar. 1990): 30; Henry Fairlie's "Maggie's Flying Circus" in *The New Republic* 202 (Jan. 1, 1990): 22–25; Timothy J. Madigan's "Opus Dei and Secret Societies: The Open Society and the Open Mind" in *Free Inquiry* 15.1 (Winter 1995): 12–14; and D. Keith Mano's "Why Americans Feel Inferior to the British ... and Why We Shouldn't" in *Forbes* (Mar. 13, 1995): 123–126.

18. The accountancy profession takes a great deal of ribbing in Python's *œuvre*. In episode 15, a Civil Service meeting discusses a possible new tax on all

sexual acts, ensuring that "chartered accountancy" would become a "much more interesting job" (Chapman, et al., 1.15.196). In the Monty Python film *The Meaning of Life*, chartered accountants are pictured as pirates commandeering vessels and wrecking investment banks and multinational conglomerates.

19. Find *The Times* website and search functions at http://www.the-times. co.uk/news/pages/Times/frontpage.html?1124027; and the Guardian Unlimited network at http://www.guardianunlimited.co.uk/. Note that these numbers of references—and even the website addresses—can and do change over time, and many times over a period of days or weeks. The numbers quoted are from 15 March 2000.

20. See Gerald Warner's "Conservatives on the Cusp: Issues: Scotland" in *The Times* (May 14, 1995): 1; Nancy-Banks Smith's "Television: Woman Among Men" in *The Guardian* (Oct. 20, 1995): T.009; Mark Cook's "A Place with the Pigs Traverse" in *The Guardian* (Aug. 15, 1995): 008; A.A. Gill's "Sugar and Spice: Table Talk" in *The Times* (Oct. 22, 1995): 1; Ben Macintyre's "Metros Pampered Pests Bite Dust in Paris Siege" in *The Times* Dec 6, 1995; Allan Kozinn's "Opera Satire Revived with English Eccentricity" in *The Oregonian* Oct 16, 1995: D06; Robert Boyd's "Author's Challenge: Avoid 'E'" in *St. Louis Post* (Jun. 11, 1995): 05.D; Amy Sutherland's "Ballet's Gift Guest Artists Imported" in *Portland Press Herald* (Nov. 26, 1995): 1.E; and John Henderson's "Soft Touch on the Touchline" in *The Guardian* (June 4, 1995): 21.

21. Luton is an English city now best known for its "Vauxhall cars, hats, and London Luton Airport" (see http://www.lutononline.co.uk/), though in Python it was a haven for strange party candidates; the blanc mange is featured in episode 7, the "Sci-Fi Sketch," where Earth and Wimbledon are threatened by giant alien dessert creatures; and Reginald Maudling was made Heath's Commonwealth spokesman in 1965, and also served as Home Secretary.

22. See Robert Hewison's *Monty Python: The Case Against*, p. 67.

23. A reference to the Academy Award–winning 1998 film *Shakespeare in Love*, directed by John Madden and starring Gwyneth Paltrow, Joseph Fiennes, and Judi Dench. The film won awards for Best Actress, Art Direction, Costume Design, Music, Picture, Supporting Actress, and Original Screenplay.

Chapter 2

"And Now for Something Completely Different(?)" Shakespeare, Jonson and Monty Python

This simple phrase, uttered in nearly every episode of the BBC's landmark comedy series *Monty Python's Flying Circus*, alerted the viewer that the television show was about to begin, end or abruptly veer off onto some unforeseen tangent. Though *Flying Circus* originally aired only from 1969 to 1974, and the Python troupe's official film collaborations included just five feature films[1] (two of which were compilation films), as mentioned in the previous chapter Monty Python–isms have entered our cultural language and Python characters and humor have become abiding elements of late twentieth-century popular culture. The Pythonesque influence is especially apparent, according to Kim Johnson, in America, where the members of the Python troupe today still enjoy celebrity status, and in such popular American television shows as *Saturday Night Live* and *Cheers* (xv).

The Monty Python troupe — Graham Chapman, John Cleese, Terry Gilliam, Eric Idle, Terry Jones, and Michael Palin — broke the mold of the television stage by writing and performing their own material — material suited for themselves and no one else. They were their own resident poets and playwrights, but more playwrights, since their "stream of consciousness" material — both visual and oral — was meant to be performed and not just read (5). They practiced both repertory acting and type-casting in their troupe, trading parts seemingly at will, while casting to type for many others. And though their signature line heralded "something completely different," the Pythons were actually upholding (or reviving) a tradition in British performing arts that can be traced back more than three hundred years. Following this theatrical pedigree brings us back to two other English playwrights of some repute: William Shakespeare and Ben Jonson.

The mention of the "Swan of Avon," or of his colleague and competitor, the so-called "Bricklayer of Westminster," and of the Monty Python troupe in a single breath seems an untenable — even unforgivable — claim, at best.[2] But with relative cultural significance aside, it's probably a fair bet that many Americans of the baby-boomer era and beyond can more easily quote a *Monty Python* line (whether they know its derivation or not) than anything from Shakespeare and especially Jonson, Marlowe, Marston, et al. (This is not a brag, but a sure indicator of prevailing popular culture.) The question that must be addressed herein, then, is one of legacy. Beyond the acknowledged National Poet status of both Shakespeare and Python, what possible connection can there be between the masters of English Renaissance drama — the creators of the characters Hamlet, Lear and Volpone — and the purveyors of "Silly Walks" and "Naughty Chemists?" For this chapter and this study overall, the answer lies in the relationship between the playwrights, their players and audience, and the plays themselves.

This chapter specifically will examine a particular notion of "theatricality" and its multiple and varied ingredients. These ingredients include the kind of troupe Shakespeare, Jonson, and the Pythons wrote for, the method of employing (or deploying) actors (repertory or casting to type?), the writing styles and intended audiences, as well as the preferred objects of comic attack and the nature of satire utilized by each. The appearances and uses of anachronisms — which Shakespeare allowed, Jonson decried, and Monty Python embraced — as well as the humor arising from both visual and verbal incongruities will be addressed. Both the "historical" aspects of the works and authors, including anachronisms, as well as the structures of humor used will be expanded and covered in greater detail in Chapters 3 and 4, respectively, but will be broached in this chapter *vis à vis* the pertinent aspects of theatricality and *mise en scène*.

Much has been written concerning the relationship between Shakespeare and Jonson. And while the jury is still out on whether they were cheerful competitors or pointed opponents, Gerald Bentley's studies of Elizabethan literature "make it quite clear that Shakespeare and Jonson were generally accepted as the two greatest dramatists of England" (13). They were comparable in reputation among their contemporaries, but the similarities become rare beyond. Shakespeare wrote for and acted with one company for most of his career, while Jonson went from company to company, both adult and children's troupes (Gurr 20). Shakespeare was a company member — and actor, dramatist, and sharer — while Jonson was not. Gurr writes that "Jonson was incapable of maintaining good relations with any one employer for long," roaming from Henslowe to the Chamberlain's Men to various boys' companies and elsewhere (20). Jonson never completely depended on popular theater for his livelihood, either, often ridiculing his audience for their tastes in popular plays and all manner of popular fashions (Bentley 8). Bentley juxtaposes Shakespeare and Jonson, arguing that "Shakespeare's connection with the theatre was not the slightest — it was the most complete … [h]e was not an amateur dramatist … [h]e was completely professional" (4). Bentley concludes that Shakespeare "made his living from the theatre" as other professionals did — Jonson not included (4).

The audience for whom Shakespeare and Jonson respectively wrote certainly deserve attention. Shakespeare wrote primarily for the public theater (though the King's Men did appear regularly at court), specifically the Globe and the Rose, where "the admission price was cheap enough for almost anybody in London" (9). Jonson presented his dramatic works almost exclusively at private theaters like the Blackfriars and to the court of James I (9). Ultimately these very different venues signify undeniable differences between the playwrights. Shakespeare most often "[took] his audience and his theatre as he [found] them," whether writing for court or commoner, he was actually writing for the King's Men. Jonson, imagining himself the *cognoscente*, "[longed] to address only those souls akin to his own," and directed his efforts toward a questionably cultivated audience of English court *literati* (8–9). Perhaps the intended audience had something to do with subject matter selected by either playwright, as well. Shakespeare, writing for the "groundlings" or the commoners, the merchants and the tradesmen, dealt with those subjects which might have fascinated his audience and been appropriately foreign to them: the antics and machinations of the upper class. Jonson, writing for those whom he considered were his intellectual peers, often dealt with the common man and relied heavily on sustained satire. Shakespeare often discarded the unities of time and space as well as historical accuracy, while Jonson preferred real time and space and was "pedantically" accurate in regards to dramatic structure, history and geography (12). Where Shakespeare plumbed the classics and the ancients for material, Jonson may have felt it his responsibility to uphold the classical tradition. The list of differences and similarities between Shakespeare and Jonson is much larger and more complex than appropriate for this study, and is covered in great detail in other works listed in the bibliography. An identification and analysis of differences and similarities between Shakespeare, Jonson, and Monty Python does not yet exist — examining this new area must now secure our attention.

Ben Jonson's *The Alchemist* is set in a London residence abandoned during a time of plague. The master, Lovewit, is away and his house has been left in the care of Face, the housekeeper; and, according to Jonson's "argument," the house fell prey to assorted "Coz'ners at large ... only wanting some / House to set up" (1.1.6–7). In 1969 the BBC called in the six young writers and performers who would become Monty Python, gave them thirteen episodes in the late-night slot, and then essentially left the house. Not unlike alchemists just waiting for some "house to set up" to perform their unnatural conversions, Monty Python set out to create popular comedy from unlikely combinations, to convert randomly chosen base metals into gold. Python attempted an unheralded amalgamation of high and low comedy, of burlesque and political satire; they lampooned the monarchy, the aristocracy, the middle-class, and the base commoner; they wrote razor-sharp dialogue and nonsensical visual fluff; they threw everything into the pot and concocted a tantalizing witch's brew of sarcasm and irony and silliness that took British (and eventually American) television by storm. Producer Barry Took remembers that there were many established performers and producers— and many at the BBC, even — who were certain that Python's unorthodox approach could never succeed because it hadn't been tried before (Johnson 4). Took's (and Python's) attitude was that they "must do it because it's never been done before" (4).

That the Pythons were aware of the works of Jonson and Shakespeare is a given, being Oxford and Cambridge educated.[3] And Shakespeare, at least, was and is still required reading from the early years in England's schools. What Jeffrey Miller calls "the irruption of high culture and philosophy into the commonplace norm" was Python's *métier*, the brandishing of their "Oxbridge" educations which could produce a seemingly unending flow of historical, theoretical, philosophical and cultural quotations, allusions, and hyperbolic metaphors (131). Shakespeare's own probable attendance at an institution like the Stratford King Edward VI Grammar School would have exposed him to a broad curriculum which, as noted by Irvin Matus, would have included Latin, the writings and translations of Erasmus, Ovid, "Terence, Mantuan, Tully, Horace, Salust, Virgil, and such other as [were] thought convenient" (36). Jonson's educational experience would have been similar, beginning at the admittedly more distinguished Westminster, and including a lack of university training, but both obviously read widely and were exposed to a great deal of classical knowledge from an early age (32–34). Like Shakespeare, the

Pythons wrote their own material and wrote it for themselves. There were no staff writers or buying of material from outside sources; they didn't even have to shop their work around to other venues, as Jonson did.[4] For Shakespeare, the benefits of writing for a single company with known players are evident. The familiarity that was naturally bred within the King's Men — among players and with their playwright — spread to the audience who came again and again to see their favorite actors perform their favorite Shakespeare plays, and perhaps even to see Shakespeare, the actor. Andrew Gurr notes that it is reasonable to presume that Shakespeare's plays had "been tailored to the company's personnel and particular talents at the time of writing" (104). Gurr even mentions surviving cast-lists which seem to confirm this presumption (104–6). "Casting to type," then, might be a misnomer in the case of Shakespeare and the King's Men. "Writing to type" may more accurately describe the situation which prevailed for Shakespeare's company.

T. W. Baldwin's much-argued characterizations regarding type-casting within the King's Men are useful here in their limited applicabilities. Gurr outlines Baldwin's categories ("hero," "tyrant," "smooth villains," "dignitaries," etc.) and those actors whom Baldwin believed fit those roles and played them consistently (Burbage, John Lowin, Eyllaerdt Swanston, and Robert Benfield, respectively)— though Baldwin's assigning of specific "lines" to specific actors is not a part of this example (104–105). Jonson was never employed by one company for long enough to build the writing to type association that Shakespeare enjoyed.[5] The Python troupe wrote to type to some extent, but there was also a great deal of sharing of roles. In this they were perhaps unique and a product of their time. Not only were they not consistent in assigning roles, though the roles often arose from everyday life (soldiers, lawyers, MPs, housewives, BBC announcers), they often reprised the same role more than once and with more than one player in a single episode. Like Elizabethan audiences of Shakespeare's works and players, *Flying Circus* audiences quickly came to appreciate and expect certain performances from particular Python performers. In the later *Monty Python and the Holy Grail* (1975) and *The Life of Brian* (1979), Graham Chapman would assume the "lead" roles in the films, playing Arthur and Brian (and many other smaller parts, of course). In many *Flying Circus* episodes, Chapman played the "hero" or "The Colonel," who interrupted sketches which had grown too silly. In the fourth season he played Mr. Neutron, a super-man:

> VOICE OVER: Mr. Neutron! The most dangerous and terrifying man in the world! The man with the strength of an army! The wisdom

of all the scholars in history! The man who had the power to
destroy the world [2.44.312].

Chapman, however, did not fit neatly into any particular role or type. In
"The Architect's Sketch," Chapman begins as a very respectable (and certainly typical) buttoned-down Chairman of the Board, Mr. Tid, who introduces visiting architects as they display their respective designs. The
respectability quickly deteriorates as it is revealed (through elaborately
contortive and silly handshakes) that some of the architects are also
Freemasons; and the remainder of the sketch (which is played out outside
the studio and shot on film) features various Freemasons and instructions
on how to recognize them. Chapman, wearing only a diaper, black shoes
and socks, and a bowler with protruding antlers, stands at a bus stop as
the voice-over narration details the essentials of capturing these types and
curing their "unfortunate Masonic tendencies."[6] Moments later Chapman
plays a very staid and normal insurance customer (complete with the
superimposed caption "Straight Man") who eventually leaves the sketch
when he finds out he has no more lines to speak. Graham Chapman's next
appearance in this same episode is a bit part as a vicar who explodes while
at the pulpit preaching. And finally, Chapman is Mrs. Potter, a woman who
actually lives out on the street and has Alfred, Lord Tennyson, in her bath-
tub.[7] Though Chapman may often have been written or cast as an authority figure, he very often strayed from that role to share in the nonsense.
    Terry Jones took on some meaty female roles in *Holy Grail* (Peasant
Woman); *Life of Brian* (Brian's Mother); and *The Meaning of Life* (the
amazingly fecund Catholic Mother; the wife in "Live Organ Donor"); but
Jones doesn't hold the lion's share of the cross-dressing roles. In episode
17 mentioned above, Terry Jones plays a Gumby (as all the members do),
a City Gent, "The Bishop," a housewife with a poet problem, and one of
the Naughty Chemists. That the men played almost all of the women's
roles isn't surprising — it is well-known that all the players on the Elizabethan stages were men and boys. Monty Python may have inadvertently
revived this older tradition as they instituted their boys-only club in 1969,
perhaps hearkening back to their Oxbridge revue days.[8] And with the
exceptions of Carol Cleveland and Connie Booth, no females made more
than irregular appearances on *Flying Circus*. In the first episode of *Monty
Python's Flying Circus* the "Pepperpots" (described as "four middle-aged,
middle-class women"), played by Chapman, Cleese, Palin, and Jones, make
their debut. The Pepperpots, whether as a group or singly, became a staple in the Python diet, appearing in literally every episode over the next
four seasons. In this same episode Eric Idle appears as the mother of a man

who has written the funniest (and most lethal) joke ever. The second episode (actually shot second, chronologically, but aired first) features a filmed appearance of the Pepperpots discussing the French philosophers (Johnson 48). In this episode Carol Cleveland makes her first appearance, here as a wife who leaves her husband for their marriage counselor. Perhaps this early in the troupe's career there may have been more misgivings about a man in drag undressing behind a screen with another man. Or perhaps they feared the BBC might not look too kindly on this homoerotica and pull their plug in the first season. Whatever the reason, it didn't take long until sexuality was no barrier in scenes between a man dressed as a man and a man in drag. By episode 17, Terry Jones as the Housewife and Michael Palin as the Poet Reader are fraternizing like Romeo and Juliet or Henry and Katherine:

> SHE: Oh, Wombat. Wombat Harness! Take me to the place where eternity knows no bounds where the garden of love encloses us round. Oh Harness!
> INSPECTOR: All right, I'll have a quick look at yer Thomas Hardy[9] [Chapman, et al. 2.17.230].

Including the division of "women" roles, Python was more likely to avoid type-casting in favor of sharing. Perhaps exemplifying their departure from Shakespeare and Jonson, in "The Naughty Chemist Sketch" the part of the chemist is played by Cleese, then Jones, and finally Palin. The scene is, essentially, played three times with three different actors. The same motif appears again in episode 11 as a host of police inspectors attempt to unravel a drawing room shooting, each falling victim to his own description of the crime (1.11.137–43). Real time is fractured here beyond what even Shakespeare would have attempted.

With careful analysis of the written scripts and visual performances of *Monty Python's Flying Circus*, a reasonably accurate diagram can be completed regarding an updated version of Baldwin's list of roles. Remembering that Baldwin's analysis of Shakespeare's players stands as uncertain scholarship, this reapplication of the model is by no means the final word on types and roles within and beyond the works of Shakespeare, Jonson, and Python. For Python, the hero might be Cleese (Dennis Moore, Attila the Hun); the smooth villain is Palin (Spanish Inquisition, Dinsdales); and the dignitary is most often Chapman (The Colonel), etc. The role of "tyrant" isn't even on the list, since Python is completely comedy and doesn't allow for a hero's foil. If anything, the role of tyrant is assumed by the narrative itself, as it constantly intrudes upon sketches, characters and themes already in progress. There is a state of constant usurpation —

narratively speaking — as the tyrannical narrative elements consistently replace or refresh the narrative trajectory. The sheer number of roles and the rapidity with which the Pythons switch roles almost precludes this rigid paradigm, and certainly calls for a possible rethinking of Baldwin's thesis if we are to attempt a thorough structural analysis within *Monty Python*.

Instead of casting to type, Shakespeare and Monty Python wrote to type, taking advantage of the familiarity within the King's Men and the Python players. Significantly, while Shakespeare wrote primarily alone, collaborated less often (with Fletcher, at least, on *Henry VIII* and *Two Noble Kinsmen*), or touched up extant playscripts, the Pythons wrote as teams or even singly, then workshopped the material in front of the entire group. Commonalities arose within the troupes—familiar characters and types that were born and flourished with consistent players, specifically written roles, and audience identification and approval (i.e., Shakespeare's Falstaff and Python's "Vox Pops" or "Gumby" characters). As mentioned at the outset, Monty Python wrote material that was specifically intended for performance and nothing else. In this they reclaim the legacy of Shakespeare, who, as Bentley somewhat testily mentions, "wrote for the theatre and not for the study" (4). Taken out of context, Polonius' false moralizations to Laertes ring out like Bentley's "moral maxims": "This above all: to thine own self be true" (1.3.78). Similarly, when former Prime Minister Margaret Thatcher attempts to quote from Python's "Dead Parrot" sketch to make her own obscure point, that point is lost or missed entirely.[10]

Jonson, conversely, wrote his plays specifically "to combine instruction with the pleasure they gave" (Gurr 25). He viewed his plays as meriting careful study, while Shakespeare and Python often seemed to almost go out of their way to simply entertain. Considering the venues of Shakespeare and Python as opposed to Jonson — the more public forum versus, often, the insulation of the court — this elevation of entertainment over instruction by both Python and Shakespeare isn't surprising. In fact, it most certainly made good financial sense.

The question of subject matter has been broached with regard to Shakespeare and Jonson, but what of Python? With half the troupe educated at Cambridge and most of the other half at Oxford, they were certainly aware of the classics and classical traditions, just like Jonson and Shakespeare. Armed with that knowledge, Python lampooned both the upper class and the common man, sparing neither their silliness. With sketches like "The Upperclass Twit of the Year," "Ministry of Silly Walks," "The Queen Will Be Watching," "The Secretary of State Striptease," and characters like The Colonel and Pantomime Princess Margaret, Python satirized authority and the upper class much as Jonson had with Sir Epicure Mammon in *The Alchemist* and Sir Politic Would-Be in *Volpone*. But perhaps most noticeable in Python's work is the "leveling" effect imposed by balanced attacks on all elements of society (to be discussed in more detail in Chapter 4), an effect which Jonson certainly anticipated and achieved in his *Bartholomew Fair* (1614).

If Jonson has come to be remembered for his attention to detail and the unified, often singular narrative arc of his stageplays, then *BF* is the exception to his own rule. The alchemical metaphor utilized so well in *The Alchemist* is given added significance here: change and transformations on many levels can make for good theater. *BF* is constructed like the experience of a fair — multiple plot lines given nearly equal weight — attractions or events one can visit, turn away from, then visit again. It might even seem as if the spectator is given more autonomy than is really available — a testament to both its structural flexibility and integrity. Norman Rabkin notes that Jonson was actually painting a very conceivable and realistic picture of the metropolis during holiday, wherein he offers "a coming together of citizens of every class, gulls, pickpockets, avaricious tradesmen, con-men, gawkers, whores: a cross-section of the city..." (*BF* 191). Over this cross-section he drapes a seemingly random but actually highly orchestrated narrative structure which highlights in glimpses each of the characters and social castes.

BF is indeed a difficult first read, as Rabkin points out, perhaps because the reader might be expecting a more conventionally structured Jonson piece, and perhaps because this work lends itself to performance, much like a multi-voiced opera (191). The multi-vocal bustle is perpetual and understandable, an accomplishment which Rabkin lauds: "[Jonson] has daringly founded the oneness of the action rather on the harmony of innumerable interacting elements than on a plot dominated by a single character operating a comprehensive scheme" (191). These "innumerable interacting elements" are transcribed much later in the fair-like *Flying Circus* episodes, though most often without the completely unifying "oneness of action." If there is a unifying Python theme, though, it is most often based on the generic and aesthetic elements of "television." Rabkin calls the fair itself in *BF* the "magnetic core of the play and its final meaning," which we can easily transmute to television for the Python core. The Prologue invites the King to experience the fair, reminding him, though, even warning him, of the setting's necessary accoutrements: "Your majesty is welcome to a Fair; / Such place, such men, such language and such ware, / You must expect" (Prologue 1–3). Python's fair trots out the myriad interviewers, quiz shows, hosts, sitcom settings, and every format of televised matter. This invitation is reinvoked over and over again in the television fair(e) of *Flying Circus*.

Also following Jonson, Python relied heavily on contemporary popular culture and politics as ample fodder for their comedic bursts. They satirized contemporary television (their tele-theatrical peers, to some extent) with sketches like "Wishes" (a quiz show), "The Money Programme," "Probe-around," "Face the Press," and "It's a Living." Politicians and political parties came under fire in "Election Night Special," "Today in Parliament," and "How Far Can a Minister Fall?" In episode 32, politicians and television take it on the chin as a newsreader (Palin) delivers the "Nine O'clock News," where various ministers are characterized as closet sexual perverts, thieves and "easily frightened by any kind of farm machinery" (2.32.127). This long-winded diatribe is followed later in the show by a BBC apology which also turns into an attack, characterizing politicians in general as "squabbling little toadies" and "crabby ulcerous little self-seeking vermin" (2.32.128). The episode goes on, of course, to further castigate politicians (especially those of the Conservative Party) for all manner of villainy, debauchery and silliness. And just as Shakespeare plumbed the classical depths for his mythological references (whether accurate or not), and Jonson studied the sciences for correct alchemical reactions, Python scavenged the historical grab bag for their own historical and literary allusions. In "The Poets" sketch Alfred, Lord Tennyson, has been installed in a bathroom, while nearby, Wordsworth is under the stairs reading about "bloody daffodils" (1.17.228). In the same sketch, Shakespeare is included as a necessary kitchen appliance and Thomas Hardy is murmuring in the bedroom. Episode 22 features "The First Underwater Production of *Measure For Measure*," wherein Shakespearean actors bob and dive reciting blank verse. The feature performance film *Live at the Hollywood Bowl* (1982) offers a world-class football match ("The Philosophers' Football Match") between famous German and English philosophers, including characteristic quotes (and footwork) from each.[11] Ben Jonson may have been certain that his audience would be familiar with his historical allusions and included them as accurately as possible; Shakespeare wrote for the public and still referenced the classics throughout his works; and Monty Python created a furious mish-mash of contemporary culture and historical allusion to form a frenetic pastiche for their audience — the television-viewing public.

Monty Python had the luxury of being employed by the state; they were completely funded by the BBC and had access to the BBC's enormous resources (recordings, props, costumes, equipment, stock photos, film footage). John Cleese describes the working relationship implied by BBC employment, having left the practice of law:

> ... I took the BBC job. I wasn't at all sorry to say good-bye to the law; it was easy to convince my parents that it was okay because this was the BBC so there was a pension scheme — it was almost like going into the entertainment branch of the civil service [Morgan, *Speaks* 13].

Jonson wrote masques for performance at the court of James I, and depended on the good graces of his monarch for continued patronage; the Pythons, however, took every opportunity to "bite the hand that had been feeding them" (Johnson 6). With panache that belied their position they lambasted the curmudgeons of the established and stodgy BBC in sketches like "The BBC Is Short of Money" and "BBC Programme Planners," in which BBC planners are successfully replaced by penguins. The BBC "world" symbol was often inserted after sketches had been "halted" or sidetracked, the "Beeb" announcer apologizing, offering silly information, and introducing the next (more respectable) sketch. The financial success or failure of their theatrical ventures was not directly connected to a paying audience, even though the BBC was mainly funded by license fees paid by viewers. In Jonson's case, his first order of business was pleasing his monarch and frequent benefactor, James I (Bentley 9). In 1616 Jonson even began to receive a royal pension, and would have been named to the Office of the Master of Revels if the holder of the office hadn't outlived him (Brock 134–35). Shakespeare's allegiances, at least officially, were also necessarily monarchical, as displayed by the name of his company: the King's Men. Monty Python did suckle at the state's teat, though, sure of at least the thirteen episodes that they had been promised, no matter the popular reception, or what kinds of irreverences were committed.[12]

Monty Python and Ben Jonson also share a similar taste in at least one object of satire: the church. In *The Alchemist* Jonson attacks the Puritans as money-grubbing hypocrites who practice a sanctimonious double standard toward alchemy when they smell a profit. Tribulation Wholesome is not unlike Python's "The Bishop" (Terry Jones), a chain-smoking tough guy with a bishop's miter. Even though Tribulation is an Amsterdam-based Puritan, he isn't above mucking about with the likes of Subtle if there's a profit to be had. Ananias, a deacon, argues that they must steer clear of evil if they are to remain spiritually pure: "the sanctified cause / Should have a sanctified course" (*Alchemist* 3.1.13–14). Tribulation disagrees, his argument sounding very much like Subtle's alchemical jargon:

Trib.   Not always necessary.
The children of perdition are oft times
Made instruments even of the greatest works.
Besides, we should give somewhat to man's nature,
The place he lives in, still about the fire,
And fume of metals, that intoxicate
The brain of man, and make him prone to passion.
Where have you greater atheists than your cooks?
Or more profane, or choleric, than your glass-men?
More anti–Christian than your bell-founders?
What makes the devil so devilish, I would ask you,
Satan, our common enemy, but his being
Perpetually about the fire, and boiling
Brimstone and arsenic? We must give, I say,
Unto the motives, and the stirrers up
Of humors in the blood. It may be so,
Whenas the work is done, the stone is made,
This heat of his may turn into a zeal,
And stand up for the beauteous discipline
Against the menstruous cloth and rag of Rome.
We must await his calling and the coming
Of the good spirit.
....
And so a learned elder, one of Scotland,
Assured me; *aurum potabile* being
The only med'cine for the civil magistrate,
T' incline him to a feeling of the cause;
And must be daily used in the disease [3.1.15–44].

Tribulation seems to be arguing that getting dirty is all part of fighting sin, though his analogy that the most corrupt men can always be found working in the most "devilish" confines inevitably tends to include himself amongst the ranks of the fallen. This unwitting irony on his part is, of course, Jonson's very point. And how helpful would it be to "the cause" if the alchemist were to transmute his evil in zeal, taking his booty-producing talents into the fold, so to speak? While Jonson vents his spleen almost solely at the Puritans (though more good-naturedly in *BF*), Python satirizes Catholics ("The Spanish Inquisition," "Italian Priests in Custard"); Anglicans ("Restaurant"); Puritans ("The Money Programme"); God ("Salvation Fuzz"); and just about every example of authority available, whether ecclesiastical or secular. The Pythons diverge from Jonson, however, and move closer to Shakespeare when the unities are discussed. Where Jonson generally kept his action limited to one location and a twenty-four hour period (*Volpone, The Alchemist, BF*), Shakespeare felt free to cover days, months, even years in his plays and move from location to location as the historical plot dictated (*Henry V*). Python (partly, at least, because of the freedom of the television medium) utilized the so-called "stream of consciousness" structure wherein one sketch (or play) could intrude upon another, then finish or not, and, with editing, the unity of place and time was completely upset. Brock points out that even Jonson never completely embraced the unities—allowing subplots to creep in and even disrupting locations (285). It can be said here that perhaps, of the three, only Shakespeare was able to further deny the unities by combining tragic and comedic elements in efforts like *Hamlet* and even *Much Ado About Nothing*. Python, to this date, has yet to try anything resembling tragedy.

In styles of writing Python and Jonson seem to share a great deal. *Monty Python's Flying Circus* built a reputation on wild wars of words, with the "Argument Clinic" ("Shut your festering gob you tit!") leading the way (2.29.86). In *The Alchemist*, Jonson's second line seems almost an answer: "Thy worst. I fart at thee" (1.1.2), which becomes an insult adapted to the screen in *Monty Python's Holy Grail*. An old woman is being accosted by Arthur and Bedivere and she responds: "Do your worst!" In the same film, a rude Frenchman yells, "I fart in your general direction!" Jonson's choice of insult has been lightly translated into modern English and used with equal effectiveness. A later exchange in *The Alchemist* between Face and Subtle contains a terrific rally of insults worthy of any Python sketch; including "cheater," "bawd," "cow-herd," "conjurer," "cutpurse," and "witch" (1.1.106–107). While Shakespeare was no slouch when it came to lobbing insults, the crudeness and rhythm of the language of Jonson seems much more comparable to that offered by Python. It may be that the language of heavy satire was best realized by Jonson and emulated much later by the writers and performers of Monty Python. Bentley mentions that Jonson excelled at sustained satire because he wanted little else in his plays; he was, after all, trying to "appeal to a sophisticated and literate audience," and not Shakespeare's groundlings (12). More and more we can see that the work of Monty Python was not, after all, so "completely different."

The larger issue of language figured importantly in the works of Jonson, Shakespeare, and Python. Jonson was so concerned with accuracy of language (with an eye, perhaps, to his place in the future pantheon of great literary artists) that in *The Alchemist* he demanded (and received) black letter type in the printed book when Subtle, the Alchemist, speaks in German to Face: "𝔘𝔩𝔢𝔫 𝔖𝔭𝔦𝔢𝔤𝔢𝔩" (2.3.32–33).[13] Jonson does so again as Subtle tells Dol Common, a prostitute, that in order for her to play her part in his swindle with the Puritans she must "bear" herself "𝔖𝔱𝔞𝔱𝔢𝔩𝔦𝔠𝔥," or simply remember to affect a stately manner and bearing (2.4.6). This attention to the *printed* details of his dramatic texts has little or no effect on how the work or even the specific line might be performed; Jonson was more concerned with how the printed book would be read after the fact. Performance was just one aspect, then, of the potential life of Jonson's creative work, and he was determined to control that life as meticulously as possible. This compulsion for perfection in the details of printing separated him from Shakespeare and, for the most part, from Monty Python as well.[14] Later in that same act Ananias, a Puritan Deacon, visits Subtle and Face, the housekeeper and Subtle's assistant, for the purpose of ascertaining Subtle's alchemical skills. Speaking to himself, Subtle plans to utilize a "new tune, new gesture, but old language" to confound Ananias, and Subtle promises himself "[I]n some strange fashion now, to make him admire me" (2.4.27, 32). The "strange fashion" will be an "old language" which is unintelligible to Ananias—the language of alchemy—which Subtle will use to subvert any meaningful communication, thus overwhelming the unsuspecting Deacon:

> [*Sub.*] Where is my drudge?
>   [Enter FACE.]
> *Face*   Sir!
> *Sub.*   Take away the recipient,
> And rectify your menstrue from the phlegma.
> Then pour it o' the Sol, in the cucurbite,
> And let 'em macerate together [2.5.1–4].

Here Subtle is tossing the alchemical jargon around, knowing full well that Ananias has entered the room and should be suitably impressed. Subtle finally notices the Deacon, who identifies himself:

> *Anan.* A faithful brother, if it please you.
> *Sub.*   What's that?
> A Lullianist? a Ripley? *Filius artis?*
> Can you sublime and dulcify? Calcine?
> Know you the sapor pontic? Sapor stiptic?
> Or what is homogene, or heterogene? [2.5.6–11].

The first misunderstanding here, then, is purposeful. Subtle knows full well that Ananias is a member of Tribulation Wholesome's flock; to confuse the issue, when Ananias says "brother," Subtle pretends that he must mean a fellow alchemist, and so quickly tries to discover Ananias' alchemical affiliation and knowledge. Ananias, of course, cannot understand the foreign language:

> *Anan.* I understand no heathen language, truly.
> *Sub.* Heathen! you Knipperdoling! Is ars sacra,
> Or chrysopoeia, or spagyrica,

Or the pamphysic, panarchic knowledge,
A heathen language?
Anan.   Heathen Greek, I take it.
Sub. How! heathen Greek?
Anan.   All's heathen but the Hebrew [2.5.12–16].

Jonson here is attacking both the greed of the Puritans who seek after alchemical riches, as well as the ignorance associated with those who would attempt such fallacious and greedy enterprises. Rabkin notes that Jonson was ultimately satirizing the "inflamed ... imaginations of Englishmen and Europeans who coveted gold and believed that God had created the world to serve them with its riches" (143). Ananias alludes to this just before he and Tribulation make their final, forced exit, as he blasts Lovewit for denying them the spoils of Subtle's cellar: "I ask thee with what conscience / Thou canst advance that idol against us / That have the seal?" (5.5.98–100). The "seal," in the language of Jonson's Puritans, is the mark of God and thus the mandate to do just about anything. The Puritans here are, of course, not understood nor are they heeded. This overall lack of communication, ultimately, serves to subvert the plans of the Puritans. Jonson may even be condemning the Puritans for their uncompounded notion that "All's heathen but the Hebrew," or their single-mindedness when it comes to the language of the chosen. If this is the case, Jonson, who is no slouch when it comes to defending his own language beliefs (to the extent, certainly, of sitting with the typesetter as his manuscripts are set for printing[15]), may be undermining himself as he attacks Ananias and Tribulation Wholesome and the zealous Puritans. In either case, it is the primacy of language that determines much in this play. The Puritans suffer because they see every tongue as inferior to Hebrew, and Subtle is eventually undone as, in part, a factious manipulator of understandable English.

As Jonson upheld English as the essential language of his peers, Shakespeare and Monty Python often fractured other languages in their attempts to create either true-to-life or comical foreign characters. Again, the butt of these linguistic jokes is most often the French. A somewhat silly comparison (and where better to attempt this?) can be made by looking at the "dialect" in which Shakespeare wrote dialogue for the French Princess Katherine, and Python's similar take on the dialect of foreigners. In *Henry V* Shakespeare illustrates Katherine's "foreigner-ness" by skewing her English, reducing her lines, often, to nearly baby-talk. She asks: "Is it possible dat I sould love de ennemie of / France?" (5.2.169–70). After he gives her his much longer response, she counters with "I cannot tell wat is dat" (5.2.177). Her last words in butchered English (she does have one more speech in French) come soon after: "Den it sall also content me" (5.2.250).[16]

Her woman Alice is painted with the same brush, and though Alice is able to translate Henry's English into French, her accented English is nearly indecipherable; "*Oui*, dat de tongeus of de mans is be full of deceits: dat is de Princess" (5.2.119–20). Katherine thinks she hears that Henry compares her to angels, which he does, and asks Alice if that is the case. Alice answers that he did indeed say such a thing, and Henry, obviously understanding the French quite clearly, betrays that understanding: "I said so, dear Katherine, and I must not blush to affirm it" (5.2.113–14). That Henry speaks French shouldn't be a shock, since it was the official court language for many years in London and he would have almost certainly been well-schooled in French. It is perhaps a simple mistake or just a dramatic choice made by Shakespeare to create a more interesting, actable wooing scene. What is key here seems to be Henry's English entitlement—his speaking of English and his demand, obviously, that Katherine speak it as well. The primacy of English is certain, even as Henry plays down his talents at wooing, and highlights his lack of eloquence (5.2.121–130). He speaks French only when he sees she might not understand any other language, but she just as quickly tells him that his French is better than her English, and he returns to English. English becomes, then the language of love *and* conquest, for if she understands "Canst thou love me?" then the day is won. A comparable section within the Python world for more contemporary comparison is the "Fraud Film Squad" sketch (episode 29), providing a terrific example of the willful deconstruction of languages—and especially French—perpetrated by Python.

A Messenger (Palin) rides his motorized bicycle into Elizabeth's palace hall and near the throne of Queen Elizabeth I (Chapman). A fanfare greets him, and the superimposed caption "The Almalda" is seen as he approaches a clerk (Idle):

MESS: I bling a dispatch flom Prymouth.
CLER: Flom Prymouth?
MESS: Flom Sil Flancis Dlake.
CLER: Entel and apploach the thlone [Chapman, et al. 2.29.77].

The writers here have done nearly the same thing that Shakespeare did three hundred years earlier—contorted English pronunciations to proclaim the presence of a foreigner. What is different here is that we find out this "play" is being directed by a man (Jones) who claims to be Italian film director Luchino Visconti, but who is actually "Slit Eyes" Sakamoto, a Japanese Visconti impersonator. The Messenger approaches the throne of Elizabeth, who is surrounded by courtiers, including Leicester (Idle), who are all astride motorized bicycles:

MESS: One hundled and thilty-six men of wal.
LEIC: Broody herr.
QUEEN: Is Dlake plepaled?
MESS: He has oldeled the whore freet into the Blitish Channer.
QUEEN: So we must to Tirbuly. Reicestel! Sil Wartel Lareigh! Groucester!
   We sharr lide to…
(*Enter Japanese director.*)
JAP: Groucestel! Groucestel! Not Groucester! Come on, ret's get this light!
   Reicestel! [2.29.77–78].

The "l" for "r" and "r" for "l" suddenly make some sense — in an adolescent, derogatory, and even ignorantly racist way — and yet another Shakespearean tradition is carried on. Katherine and Alice butcher the English they speak, and so do the actors in this film directed by an accented Japanese man. There are many examples of miscommunication, of messages being sent and not received, in Python. In episode 5 a police inspector raids a flat looking for, well, something:

YOUNG MAN (Idle): Well, what sort of certain substances?
POLICEMAN: Er, certain substances of an illicit nature.
YOUNG MAN: Er, could you be more specific?
POLICEMAN: I beg your pardon?
YOUNG MAN: Could you be "clearer."
POLICEMAN: Oh, oh … yes, er … certain substances on the premises. To be
   removed for clinical tests [1.5.60–61].

Just what the policeman's after is never made entirely clear, and the sketch is interrupted by several letters from angry viewers before any conclusion can be reached. This scene is somewhat incongruous, as well, since the young man — contrary to much of the "hippie" generation of the time — is not only polite to this ultimate authority figure, but helpful and well-spoken. In episode 12 there are two instances of misunderstood language and miscommunication, the first of which involves a Man (Jones) at a police station desk trying to report a crime. The First Sergeant (Cleese) can't understand the man, asking him to speak in a higher register. The Second Sergeant (Chapman) must be spoken to in a low voice, the Inspector (Idle) must be spoken to very, very fast, etc. Each of the policemen seem to know how to talk to the other, but the man reporting the crime is completely befuddled, as all seem to be miscommunicating, including one who sings to all squad cars (1.12.154–55). This sketch has been preceded by one wherein Hitler, Himmler, and von Ribbentrop are able to live and work (in full Nazi regalia) in North Minehead without being noticed simply because they've changed their names to Hilter, Bimmler, and Ron Vibbentrop. Their plans to invade Stalingrad are confused for a day's outing at Bideford, and they are rendered narratively impotent and satirized for their misguided (and many years delayed) world conquest plans. (1.12.150–51). No one seems to notice their outrageous German accents, either, which may be just as much a swipe at North Minehead as the Germans.

These sketches are actually perfect lead-ins to the "Upperclass Twit of the Year" sketch, scenes where the perhaps misunderstood upper class are satirized on the basis of language, appearances, dress, intelligence, etc. Other examples come from the film *Monty Python and the Holy Grail*. King Arthur (Chapman) and his knights have reached a castle where they seek shelter for the night and assistance in their quest. After arguing with the sentry (Cleese) above them, the sentry finally points out: "I'm French, you silly English pig-dogs! Why do you think I have this outrageous accent?" This is, of course, spoken with a truly outrageous French accent, and the point is well-hammered home — again. The brutalization of the English language, as we see, is another commonality linking the Pythons to the Elizabethans.

The second point to arise from this same scene (and which is repeated in a similar scene near the end of the film) has to do with the efficacy of the French language itself. On several occasions the French guards speak to each other in French, and each time they must repeat themselves to be understood. Or, instead of repeating in French, they translate into English to be understood. Either way, the primacy of English as the language of civilization is an ensign raised by both Shakespeare and Monty Python. In discussing stylistic differences in language use in films depicting medieval times and settings, Richard Osberg and Michael Crow search specifically for the "collision of modern and medieval worlds" in these films (Harty, *King Arthur* 40). Focusing on the Arthur-Dennis conversation, the authors here find an essential "incomprehensibility" in Python's medieval language, and that the "language collapses into incomprehensibility in an endless deferral of meaning" (40). The language thus loses its effectiveness, its efficacy, made manifest by Bedivere's constant lifting of his face mask to speak (40). They see other "medieval" films like John Boorman's *Excalibur*, Steven Spielberg's *Indiana Jones and the Last Crusade* and Terry Gilliam's *The Fisher King* as retaining the power of the word, where "the signifier and thing signified have a hieratic, sacerdotal relationship" (40). While this last may be true, Python's work proves over and over again how powerful words can be. If mysterious knights can simply say "Ni" to prevent anyone from passing, and those same knights are similarly afflicted by a word as simple as "it," then words have power in Python. At the Bridge of Death the correct answer means life, and the wrong answer means death. Launcelot is drawn to Swamp Castle by a written note. Also at Swamp Castle, Herbert's father marginalizes him by constantly calling him "Alice," rather than Herbert.

There do exist incomprehensibilities, though, within the texts, moments which define characters and are meant to be humorous. In *Life of Brian* Brian's mother misunderstands the Three Wise Men, certain that "homage" is something "disgusting" and indecent, that myrrh is actually deadly, and a balm is a biting animal of some kind. But there also exists the finality of language, as well. As Mandy and Brian go to the stoning, Brian asks why women aren't allowed to participate in stonings, and she answers: "Because it's written, that's why." At the stoning, the word "Jehovah" becomes an accepted word of power, insomuch that one man is to be executed for uttering it, and the administrator of that execution is himself stoned for accidentally saying the word. The Knights Who Say "Ni" cannot utter, or bear to hear, the word "it," though no reason beyond the pronouncement of its mystical, taboo-like power is given in the film text. (KNIGHT: (Palin) "I cannot tell, suffice to say is one of the words the Knights of Ni cannot hear!"). Words and attendant meanings—denotative or connotative—can hold great significance for Shakespeare, as well. Hamlet takes umbrage with his mother's use of a word as simple as "seems" as she confronts him about his father's recent death:

> *Queen*.... Thou know'st 'tis common. all that lives must die,
>   Passing through nature to eternity.
> *Ham*. Ay, madam, it is common.
> *Queen*. If it be,
> Why seems it so particular with thee?
> *Ham*. Seems, madam? nay, it is, I know not "seems" [1.2.71–77].

What Hamlet means when he says "common" is very different from what his mother means when she says the same; she's referring to death in general, while he comments on the lowness, the baseness of the acts of murder and adultery. Hamlet is particular to attach intended meanings to his own words and actions, his complete theatricality, so that he might appear mad, thus creating the setting and atmosphere for his revenge.[17] In a later scene in *Life of Brian* where Brian is painting an anti–Roman slogan on the palace wall, the meaning of words and phrases takes a back seat to the correct linguistic structure of those words. Intended meaning is thrown out in favor of proper syntax.

The phrase "Romans go home" becomes a pedantic lesson in Latin grammar rather than a punishable offense:

CENTURION: (Cleese) What's this, then? "Romanes Eunt Domus"? "People called Romanes they go the house"?
BRIAN: (Chapman) It — it says, "Romans, go home."
CENTURION: No, it doesn't. What's Latin for "Roman"? Come on!
BRIAN: "R — Romanus"?
CENTURION: Goes like…?
BRIAN: "Annus"?
CENTURION: Vocative plural of "annus" is…? [Scene 8].

And on and on until the phrase is properly spelled on the wall. When Brian is finished, of course, he has correctly painted "Romans Go Home" all over the temple walls, and the two sentries set to watch him tell him to leave and not do it again. This is, of course, undercut as two new sentries walk around a corner, see Brian and what he has done, and try to arrest him. The primacy of language, especially its structures, seem to outweigh whatever might be actually said, painting a picture of a rigorous, blinded authority figure. This satiric deflation of the Roman authority figures is continued throughout the film, and can also be seen as Python's continued fun-poking at the BBC, the Conservative government, and the properness of their own English society. Deferrals of meaning do occur, as new powerful words overcome other powerful words, but language — betraying knowledge — in *Holy Grail* and other Python works, often overcomes both rank and status.

Bernard Beckerman addresses the language of Shakespeare in a way that invites comparison to the Monty Python troupe:

> Theatrical and even melodramatic as his situations are, they are couched in words and sentences that invite detachment: detachment of speech from scene, of image from action, of sentiment from character. The readiness with which readers have lifted speeches from his plays and recited them as poems testifies to the seductive autonomy of Shakespeare's language [397].

As mentioned above, Python material has entered the cultural lexicon, as well. That more post–Baby Boomers can probably recite an entire scene from Monty Python before any from Shakespeare (and especially Jonson or Dekker or Middleton) not only outlines Python's place in our cultural milieu, but trumpets the "quotability" of Pythonisms as the phrases leap from television sets to the pages of quote books, into political speeches, and into video fossilization, instantly ready for refreshed enunciation. The "seductive autonomy" of Shakespeare's language, then, is shared — if certainly at the popular culture level and in a scattered, pastiche manner — by Monty Python.

While William Shakespeare and Ben Jonson will not be unseated from their (well-deserved) positions as masters of English drama, especially by television upstarts like Monty Python, the areas of commonality are definable and comparisons can fruitfully be made. The structures of their respective troupes were different but did contain significant similarities, including some casting to type, writing to type, and repertory acting elements. Generally, Python and Shakespeare wrote for somewhat similar audiences, the viewing public, while all three shared varying levels of state sanctioning, and — with at least Jonson and Python — the desire to deflate authority figures both temporal and spiritual. All three relied on popular culture to some extent: Jonson castigating it, Shakespeare working within it, and Python feeding off and often even creating it. All three at some point disregarded the classical unities, but each to a varying degree: Jonson wandered rarely, Shakespeare rarely did not wander, and Monty Python took full advantage of their medium and rendered the unities almost obsolete.

Similar to Shakespeare's disavowal of the necessity of time and place unification was his equally casual attitude regarding historical anachronisms. If time can be bent and real space ignored to allow for Shakespeare's drama, then the devices and persons and ideas of a particular era can become subject to this same manipulation. The structure of history, then, to Shakespeare, is not as firm and unyielding as the strictures of time might indicate. It is the structure of the drama, the smooth telling of the story, that takes precedence over any historical truth. These excursions from verisimilitude weren't just casually brushed off by all, though. Even Ben Jonson — himself a "self-professed and professing classicist" who "deride[d] past and contemporary dramatic usage in favor of the decorum of his beloved ancients" — addressed the historical license that Shakespeare took, condemning it, though not vociferously (Cartelli 152). The conflict was truly engaged much later, though, as Alexander Pope in 1728 responded to Lewis Theobald's response to Pope's edition of the works of Shakespeare. Pope took Theobald to task for what the poet saw as excessive pedantry, enshrining the critic/theorist in the pantheon of "Dulness" in *The Dunciad Variorum*. But where Theobald may have been picky and overly concerned with accuracy, he might not have been so injudicious towards the "incomparable author" as Pope implies.[18]

In *Lewis Theobald and the Editing of Shakespeare* (1990), Pete Seary outlines the critic's approach to Shakespeare and his editing practices in general as pedantic, and notes that Theobald had a "complacent belief in the rules" (29). In this, according to Seary, Theobald (as a theorist) was much like Dryden in the 1670s, "when Dryden was rebelling against the neo–Aristotelian constraints" of critics of his time (29). Seary writes that

Dryden believed, first and foremost, in pleasing his audience, and the "English audiences delighted in character as revealed through language," and not necessarily historically accurate settings (29). In a moment of enlightened foresight coupled with perspicuous hindsight that would be re-engaged by the Monty Python troupe almost four centuries later, Dryden, in his "Of Dramatic Poesy," identifies the French version of neo–Aristotelianism as denying the "soul of poesy."[19] For Dryden, it was Shakespeare who employed a "more masculine fancy and greater spirit in the writing than there is in any of the French" (29). The French took it on the chin at the quill of Shakespeare, relived the affront through Dryden, and continued to suffer during the run of *Monty Python's Flying Circus* and the Python feature films.

So Theobald is akin to Dryden, who supports the violation of the unities by Shakespeare as being necessary to the furtherance of the dramatic structure. But Pope condemns Theobald as having a lack of reverence toward Shakespeare, doesn't he? Theobald's own words can help clear the muddied waters here. According to Geoffrey Bullough in "Theobald on Shakespeare's Sources," Theobald was well aware of Shakespeare's anachronisms, but "regarded them with a kindly eye as 'Liberties taken knowingly by the Poet and not Absurdities flowing from his ignorance'" (17). Theobald, then, did not attack Shakespeare, as Pope suggests, but merely pointed out the anachronisms inherent in the poet's work and offered emendations beyond what Pope might have considered either necessary or reasonable.

The anachronisms are well-documented, but more than likely go unnoticed by the modern reader, and, as has been written, "we have all been instructed that neither Shakespeare nor his original audience was troubled by such inconsistencies" (Rackin, "Temporality" 101). In fact, without the help of an annotated, carefully glossed version of his works, most readers wouldn't even think twice about the irregularities listed below. To mention just a few examples: Theobald points out Hector's mentioning of Aristotle in ancient Troy (*Troilus and Cressida* 2.2.167); Pandarus' "goose of Winchester" allusion (5.10.54); Menenius' allusion to Galen (*Coriolanus* 2.1.117); Edgar's mentioning of the Curfew (*King Lear* 3.4.116); cannon references prior to the fourteenth century (*King John* 1.1.26); and an allusion to Machiavelli in *1 Henry VI* (5.4.74) and *3 Henry VI* (Bullough 17). G. Blakemore Evans' *Riverside Shakespeare* corroborates many of these anachronisms, but leaves others unmentioned. Some Evans treats as anachronisms, pointing out the discrepancy and identifying its possible reasons for inclusion, while others he treats as examples of Shakespeare's poetic license. The Aristotle allusion is treated anachronistically, while Evans mentions nothing about "the Curfew" except to say that it was probably nine o'clock (1277n). Significant, though, is that, whether Theobald or Evans, a reason or excuse is offered as to why an anachronism was included and, occasionally, even necessary. In *1 Henry VI*, the well-known Niccolo Machiavelli was used to sum up in a single word what the Duke of York thought of Alanson; "Alanson, that notorious Machevile?" (5.4.74). In *King John*, the specter of destruction by cannon is meant to frighten the Chatillion of France; "For ere thou canst report, I will be there; / The thunder of my cannon shall be heard" (1.1.25–26). An audience of the time, as well as an audience of today, would respond to these fleeting anachronisms as parts of a unified whole and react to what Dryden later called the "dramatic poesy" of the entire work: the "mistake" would probably be ignored and the play enjoyed.

As mentioned above, the ever-meticulous Jonson even took time to note, in his "Conversations with Drummond," that "Sheak∫pear jn a play brought jn a number of men ∫aying they had ∫uffered Shipwrack jn Bohemia, wher y^r is no Sea neer by∫ome 100 Miles" (Herford and Simpson 138). In *1 Henry IV*, there is a reference to pistols (2.4.234–46) which had yet to be invented; and, as pointed out by Phyllis Rackin, the "conspirators in *Julius Caesar* wear anachronistic hats and Antony's Cleopatra lived too soon to play at billiards" ("Temporality" 102–03). Dr. Samuel Johnson explains Shakespeare's lack of historical accuracy rather simply: "Shakespeare never has any care to preserve the manners of the time" (Variorum 157n). Herschel Baker was later even more succinct, simply noting that when the subject was history, Shakespeare "did not tie himself to facts" (Evans 930). He gave landlocked Bohemia a sea coast in *The Winter's Tale* (1584n), and in *Richard III* offered confusing travel directions from Northampton to London: "Last night, I [hear], they lay at Stony-Stratford / And at Northampton they do rest to-night. / Tomorrow, or next day, they will be here" (2.4.1–3). Following these directions it certainly would not be tomorrow or the next day; one would find the Irish Sea quicker than the city of London. Rackin offers that Shakespeare's dubious geography was certainly "careless," but "only because he had better things to do with his settings than plot their locations on a map..." ("Temporality" 102).

Bernard Beckerman attempts to sum up the creative genius of Shakespeare as it pertained to his source material, including historical facts and geography:

> Throughout his plays the degree of faithfulness to the original
> varies; sometimes it is close, sometimes remote, often modulated.
> No one principle of adaptation seems to have existed for Shake-

speare; he copied and altered stories and characters as he saw fit
[402].

Beckerman goes on to identify Shakespeare's habit of "contaminating" his
source by wedding it to other source material of a different time or place
(402). The story of Gloucester is combined with the tale of Lear and his
daughters, for example. Again, a disavowal of the unities. Beckerman also
mentions Shakespeare's proclivity for "liberally modifying established
sources with the products of his own invention" (402). The tone of the work
could be comic, tragic, or historical, but the tone could easily be "modified
by new invention or by adroit infusion of contrasting matter" (403). Johnson rebuts those "neoclassical critics" who clamored for more accurate
Romans and kings as he reminds us that Shakespeare's "story requires
Romans or kings, but he thinks only on men" (101). And Shakespeare's
sources, it must be remembered, were wildly uneven in their attention to
historical verisimilitude, favoring instead political considerations and
mythology (see Chapter 4). It is at this point that the techniques of the
Monty Python troupe can again be approached.

Monty Python's television shows, feature films, and sketch films teem
so animatedly with anachronisms—they are so "contaminated," to borrow Beckerman's term—that Ben Jonson might have dismissed them
entirely as completely nonsensical. Here again, though, the anachronistic
items have a purpose, a usefulness. A *mise en scène* is constructed using
elements from across time, using perhaps unrelated happenings at a fair
not locked into a single era. If, as Jonson believed, Shakespeare wrote about
men and not kings, then Monty Python shares this legacy. Jonson may
have written with the peerage and his monarch in mind, but the
groundlings composed much of Shakespeare's audience, and Monty
Python's, as well, and theatricality for this audience meant entertainment,
not verisimilitude. Rackin identifies what she sees as the "crucial Shakespearean strategy" in regards to historical and spatial accuracy as

> the manipulation of the temporal relationship between past events
> and present audience ... Shakespeare uses this strategy in his his-
> tory plays to dramatize the distance and the intersection between
> past and present, eternity and time, and to ponder the problematic
> nature of history itself [103].

The creators and actors behind the Monty Python *oeuvre*, as will be shown,
certainly manipulate temporal relationships, drawing from the well of
English history with abandon as they combine the past and the present for
a purpose: to laugh at society. Where Shakespeare may not have intended

a comic effect from most of his anachronisms and Jonson scrupulously avoided them, Python depended on the incongruous and the anachronistic to fuel its humor. John Morreall identifies incongruity as a definable area of humor wherein our expectations of the world as it is presented to us can be subverted by an incongruity. If the pattern we have seen before and expect to see again is somehow manipulated, altered, or skewed, then that manipulation "violates our expectations" and we laugh (130). Morreall cites Pascal: "Nothing produces laughter more than a surprising disproportion between that which one expects and that which one sees" (130). Morreall traces the theory forward through Pascal, Kant, and Schopenhauer (130). Most of Shakespeare's anachronisms would not fall into this category, since he didn't use them to make obvious the incongruities within his plays but to facilitate his dramatic structure. But the simple fact is that Shakespeare did use them, and so would Monty Python. Python made a healthy career out of violating expectations. Examples are myriad and include both the *Flying Circus* episodes and all Python's feature films. We will first look at some instances from the television series, and then venture into the film *Monty Python and the Holy Grail* (1974).

In the first episode of *Monty Python's Flying Circus*— entitled "Whither Canada?"— the Python penchant for anachronistic humor exhibits itself from the first scene. As an Announcer welcomes us to the program there is a cut to Mozart as he sits at a piano. Mozart, apparently, has his own television show, *It's Wolfgang Amadeus Mozart*, on which famous deaths are performed and judged. Genghis Khan is the first to die, and, to double back on the anachronism, judges hold up scorecards to rate his performance. We then see that St. Stephen, Richard III, Marat, and King Edward VII, among others, have already performed their death scenes (Edward [1841–1910] rating only a 3.1 combined score). Later, the Announcer at the desk is replaced, in a quick cut, by a Viking in full regalia. Following this, Pablo Picasso is said to be involved in a bicycle race, during which he will paint a "specially commissioned painting" (Chapman, et al. 1.1.8–10). After following Picasso for a moment, another cut reveals that the same Viking seen previously has been joined by a Knight clad in full battle armor. The anachronisms continue to pile up as we learn that painters Kandinsky, Braque, Mondrian, Chagall, Klee, and many others (including Toulouse-Lautrec, who rides a tricycle) are also involved in the bicycle/painting race (1.1.8–10). What should be obvious in just this short description from one episode is the repeated use of humor not only based on incongruity, but a constantly iterated incongruousness bordering on the absurd.

Shakespeare and Jonson employed incongruous humor to a certain extent, viz., characters of noble birth or stature not acting their station, or characters in disguise who can act like another, as Benedick (as a masker) in *Much Ado About Nothing* (2.3.125–154). A strong argument can also be made for humor arising from the incongruities of characters. The entire constructed affection between Beatrice and Benedick in *Much Ado*—fostered by Don Pedro, Leonato, and Claudio for Benedick's side, and Hero and Ursula on Beatrice's side—creates terrific humor for the audience as the two would-be lovers interact thereafter, each certain that the other is the one in love. The incongruity lies in what Beatrice and Benedick do not know, what they think they do know, and what the audience knows.

Python's version of incongruous humor doesn't rely on the situations as much as the visual and aural properties of particular characters and scenes. In the "Whither Canada" episode, the anachronistic characters and props are often used for their shock value — "the orderly world where we have come to expect certain patterns among things" is upset, and we laugh (Morreall 130). As mentioned above, just the fact that Mozart would be hosting a television show is funny, as is the spectacle of the bloodthirsty Genghis Khan performing for judge's scores. The humor is compounded by the distinguished list of other participants (including Richard III and Abraham Lincoln). The Viking actually participates as a linking element as he finishes the sentence of an Interviewer, and the ridiculous image of Toulouse-Lautrec on a tricycle adds yet another layer to the already multivalent incongruity (Chapman, et al. 1.1.9–13).

Other episodes yield similar anachronisms, all introduced to "upset patterns" of expectations. In episode 20, stock film footage of "huns thundering around on horseback" is accompanied by narration which describes the atrocities committed by Attila and his "barbarian hordes" (Chapman, et al. 1.20.264). There is then a cut to Attila the Hun (Cleese) running in slow motion, smiling and laughing to the theme from *The Debbie Reynolds Show*. Attila is portrayed as a devoted father who lives in a comfortable house, and responds to his wife's query as to his day at the office by mugging for the camera: "Another merciless sweep across Central Europe" (1.20.264). Canned laughter erupts, and Attila goes on to give his children, Jenny and Robby, a present of a severed head: "I want you kids to get a-head" (1.20.264). Moments later animated titles announce a new segment, "Attila the Nun," in which a nun who has taken a "vow of eternal brutality" crashes a motorcycle and fights with her hospital attendants (1.20.265). The episode continues with the Secretary of State for Commonwealth Affairs (Jones) doing a strip tease (spinning his propeller-like tassels) as he lectures on the Common Market (1.20.266); killer sheep soon threaten London, news especially for parrots is read, and a village idiot (Cleese) discusses why the idiot has such "a vital role to play in a modern rural society" (1.20.268–73); furniture and appliances play cricket and run the three o'clock race at Epsom, and the final scene involves three bishops jumping on a "sexily-dressed" girl, played by Graham Chapman (1.20.274–78). This "stream of consciousness" approach offers one image after another without pause for reconsideration or appraisal; there may be a common theme that is followed for a time (Attila the Hun, then Attila the Nun), but more often than not Vikings and Knights and Killer Sheep are just connected end-to-end-to-end.

These kinds of *visual* incongruities didn't play a large part in the work of either Shakespeare or Jonson. Perhaps, short of the "wholeness of sensibility" which Beckerman attributes to Shakespeare's writing, Monty Python's appeal is the very outrageous nature of their anachronisms, the sheer memorability of a patch-eyed sheep using a rifle and using it well, or a blanc mange nearly winning the Wimbledon title, for example. A case can be made, though, if not for the purposeful incongruity generated by humorous anachronisms, then certainly for verbal incongruities in Shakespeare's work, particularly in *Much Ado About Nothing*. The characters of Constable Dogberry, his partner Verges, and the Watchmen combine to misspeak themselves and misunderstand each other with verbal gymnastics which — in silliness and loquacity — rank alongside any that Python created.

Dogberry and Verges routinely create verbal incongruities as they either say one word when they mean another, or mangle a word almost beyond recognizability. Verges begins by offering, instead of damnation for potentially untrue men, a warning that they will "suffer salvation, body and soul" (3.3.3). G. Blakemore Evans identifies several incongruous moments in Dogberry's response following the "salvation" line: "Nay, that were a punishment too good for them, if they should have any allegiance in them, being chosen for the Prince's watch" (3.3.4–6). To "suffer salvation, body and soul" is, in Dogberry's fractured language, a "punishment," and Evans also sees "allegiance" as being used in a manner opposite its true meaning (347n). Dogberry later praises the watchmen as being "senseless and fit" for their task, and rather than apprehending any suspicious men, the watchmen are to be "comprehended" (3.3.23, 25). Dogberry's incongruous logic is betrayed as the second watchman asks how they are to treat any who refuse to heed them during their watch. The Constable responds: "Why then take no note of him, but let him go, and presently call the rest of the watch together, and thank God you are rid of the knave" (3.3.28–30). Dogberry continues his linguistic creativity as he warns that "for the watch to babble and to talk, is most tolerable, and not to be endured" (3.3.35–36). Dogberry substitutes "decerns" for concerns, "odorous" for odious, "comprehended" for apprehended again, "aspicious" for suspicious, and "suffigance" for sufficient (3.3.3–52). Could Shakespeare here be taking a poke at local constables or lawmen as he lampoons Dogberry and Verges? The mounting evidence would seem to support the hypothesis.

Dogberry's circumlocution begins to tire Leonato, the governor of Messina:

> *Leon.* Neighbors, you are tedious.
> *Dog.* It pleases your worship to say so, but we are the poor Duke's officers' but truly, for mine own part, if I were as tedious as a king, I could find in my heart to bestow it all of your worship.
> *Leon.* All thy tediousness on me, ah? [3.5.18–22].

Continually, what is said and what is meant are two completely different things, and everyone surrounding Dogberry and Verges struggles to make any sense of their speech. Shakespeare here puts characters like these in charge of keeping civil order, the same kinds of characters Python would later lampoon as representatives of authority (like the policeman in a tutu and carrying a wand in *Flying Circus* episode 13). Also worth mentioning is the fact that no matter how addled these representatives of the law might be, they actually do "out" the criminals and allow the narrative to move to its successful conclusion. The incongruity here then emanates from at least two distinct areas: Dogberry and Verges not only speak what is not expected to be spoken, thereby disrupting a pattern, but they are also the representatives of civil authority as they offer their gibberish. And the fact that Shakespeare then doubles back on expectations and allows these characters to figure so prominently in the successful resolution of the narrative is yet another incongruous element.

Dogberry's final speeches act as the ultimate evidence to his incongruous nature. Don Pedro asks just what the two malefactors (a title Dogberry and Verges answered to earlier) have done, and Dogberry offers his answer:

> *Dog.* Marry, sir, they have committed false report; moreover they have spoken untruths; secondarily, they are slanders; sixt and lastly, they have belied a lady; thirdly, they have verified unjust things; and to conclude, they are lying knaves [5.1.215–19].

Dogberry has managed to somehow say the same thing six times, though the careless listener might mistake the list of charges as longer than it truly is. Don Pedro's response is fascinating. He finds a way to communicate with Dogberry that others have missed: "First, I ask thee what they have done; thirdly, I ask thee what's their offense; sixt and lastly, why are they committed; and to conclude, what you lay to their charge" (5.1.220–23). In mimicking Dogberry's speech pattern Don Pedro has added a level to the incongruity — what is humorous now is the prospect of a nobleman like Don Pedro speaking as if he were the eccentric Constable — and another pattern is disrupted.

Claudio is able to see the clever nature of Don Pedro's response to Dogberry's circumlocutive answer, and sums up the conversation: "Rightly reason'd, and in his own division, and by my troth there's one meaning well suited" (5.1.224–25). Though Shakespeare did not regularly engage in the sight gag anachronisms that Monty Python found so useful, favoring instead more subtle anachronisms, the National Poets Shakespeare and Monty Python did write cleverly incongruous characters and dialogue for similarly humorous effects.

Monty Python's first feature narrative film, *Monty Python and the Holy Grail* (1974), is resplendent with anachronistic visuals and dialogue that disrupt the pseudo-historical air of the story and act, at times, as self-reflexive elements. Phyllis Rackin notes the power of the anachronism, writing that

> ... anachronisms that disrupt the historical context to create direct confrontations between past and present are more radical in their effect. The very essence of history is that it deals with the past, with events that have already taken place. Therefore, any invocation of the present in a history play tends to create radical dislocations: it invades the time frame of the audience, and its effect is no less striking than that of a character stepping off the stage to invade the audience's space or addressing them directly to invade their psychological space ["Temporality" 106].

Rackin cites Sigurd Burckhardt's "brilliant argument" regarding the clock in *Julius Caesar* as an example of Shakespeare deliberately using an anachronistic device to drive home a point, Burckhardt argues that Shakespeare intended the effect to "signify to the audience that 'time is now reckoned in a new, Caesarean style'" (119n). Monty Python takes the further step, purposely trying to create the "radical dislocations" of time frame, to the point of actually stepping off the (sound)stage to address the audience directly, or playing directly to the camera. This disavowal of the "fourth wall" is not, however, a Python creation, since Shakespeare himself allowed his Prologue in *Henry V* to bow and scrape to the audience as he apologized for the "unworthy scaffold," and implored their "imaginary forces [to] work" as he asks their "humble patience pray, / Gently to hear, kindly to judge, our play" (Prologue 10, 18, 34–35). Jonson, the playwright, even steps slightly out of character as he brings *The Alchemist* to a close, creating a dislocation which may have been something of a surprise to audiences who were familiar with his unified work. He takes the liberty of asking his characters to act the part of Chorus or Epilogue, speaking both as characters and as actors on a stage, and addressing the audience directly:

> *Love.* Whiff in with your sister, brother boy.
>   [*Exeunt* KASTRIL *and* DAME PLIANT.]
>   That master
> That had received such happiness by a servant,
> In such a widow, and with so much wealth,
> Were very ungrateful, if he would not be
> A little indulgent to that servant's wit,
> And help his fortune, though with some small strain
> Of his own candor. [*To the audience*] Therefore, gentleman,
> And kind spectators, if I have outstripped
> An old man's gravity, or strict canon, think
> What a young wife and a good brain may do:
> Stretch age's truth sometimes, and crack it too.—
> Speak for thyself, knave.
>   *Face.*   So I will, sir. [*To the audience*]
> My part a little fell in this last scene,
> Yet 'twas decorum. And though I am clean
> Got off from Subtle, Surly, Mammon, Dol,
> Hot Ananias, Dapper, Drugger, all
> With whom I traded; yet I put myself
> On you, that are my country; and this pelf
> Which I have got, if you do quit me, rests,
> To feast you often, and invite new guests [5.5.145–166].

The stepping out here is performed both by the characters as they bring the story to its conclusion, and the actors as they close the play. Both Love-wit and Face acknowledge the constructedness of the play with this delivered epilogue—words like "kind spectators," "scene" and "decorum"—a practice that would reach its full flower in later Restoration and eighteenth-century drama. Shakespeare also self-reflexively drew attention to his plays as plays, as constructed artifices, a tactic Monty Python assumed many years later in both *Flying Circus* and their feature films, like *Holy Grail*.

Holy Grail begins well enough, with hauntingly fitting music that heralds the dark ages, a time of mystery. This mood is quickly subverted, though, as a printed subtext in broken Swedish runs beneath the credits, offering a running dialogue concerning the beauty and wildlife of Sweden.

The credits themselves include multiple references to moose actors and moose technicians, and various Hollywood and political figures, both living and dead, creating another subversion/diversion. The credits are stopped and started, the music changed, and the flow interrupted several times before the film actually begins. A title in uncial letters tells us it is A.D. 932, and that we are in England. We hear the sound of approaching horse's hooves, and we see a hilltop shrouded in mist. The sound of hooves draw nearer, and over the hill comes a man (Chapman) wearing a crown and mail armor with an heraldic surcoat (bearing the image of the sun). The man is not riding a horse, merely trotting along as his servant (Gilliam), who trots behind him, bangs two halves of a coconut together. The incongruity of the scene is twofold: The sound of the horse's hooves turns out to be coconut-produced, and this obviously kingly person is pretending to ride a horse.

The crowned man and his servant approach a castle, where he announces that he is "Arthur, King of the Britons," and that he is seeking knights to join him at Camelot. The castle guards (Palin and Cleese) end up being far more interested in how Arthur came by the coconuts, since Mercia — where Arthur says he found them — is a "temperate zone," as the sentinels point out, and not tropical. Their conversation includes air speed velocities of various types of swallows and how these swallows could have carried the coconut to England. They decide that by stringing a strand of creeper under the "dorsal guiding feathers" of two European swallows— not African — the feat is at least possible. And how do two lowly castle guards in the Middle Ages know anything about avian physiology, the physics of air travel or even the particular climactic zone they happen to live in? They are once again the seemingly inconsequential purveyors of knowledge so immanent to the Pythonesque. Here the knowledge seems truly idiot-savant-like, as Arthur and his man can get no useful information about the castle or its occupants from the prattling guards. These learned idiots people the Python landscape, providing often useful, always funny, and almost always frustrating narrative information. What is less apparent than the verbal incongruities, though, is the question of actual history. Python constantly offered anachronisms and incongruities to upset previously-held patterns of expectation; but did they ever commit an accidental anachronism? Michael Palin later said that they set out to make a film that looked "real," which was also historically accurate and humorous:

> I was more keen on keeping the narrative in the Arthurian world than making jokes about Harrods. I was interested in creating this world and making the convention, the background setting, so con-

vincing that you don't have to defuse it, you don't have to apologize
for it, you don't want to leave it! [Morgan, *Speaks* 148].

But in their rush to create such visually and verbally funny historical farces,
did they ever unintentionally present anything out of its proper place or
time? In this "convincing" world they'd created, were there Bohemian
coasts and Caesarean clocks? As in Shakespeare's worlds, there certainly
were.

   First, the clothing for Arthur and all of his knights falls under our
scrutiny. Historians have identified the types of armor worn at the time
this film is supposed to depict (the early tenth century), and heraldic surcoats were not yet in style (Grancsay 276). In fact, surcoats bearing heraldic
patterns (including Arthur's "sun," the Black Knight's "boar's head,"
Lancelot's "griffin," Bedivere's "oak tree," Galahad's "cross," and Robin's
"chicken") were not worn until the beginning of the thirteenth century
when helmets covered the combatants' faces, necessitating some other
means of individual identification (277; Nickel iv). Warriors of the period
would have typically been wearing chain mail with protective undergar-
ments, or even metal plating. Secondly, Arthur announces himself as "King
of the Britons." In A.D. 932 England (Northumbria and south of Hum-
ber) was actually ruled by Athelstan (A.D. 925–929), the son of Edward
the Elder. That Arthur is a shadowy historical figure at best is a given, so
his place on the historical timeline is dubious, but certainly still debatable.[20]
Even the title at the beginning of the film, "England A.D. 932," deserves
some scrutiny. Printed in uncial letters meant to evoke and "reinforce the
alterity of the 'medieval' content that the film mediates," this type of lettering was used from about the fourth to the eighth century, and then primarily in Latin and Greek manuscripts (Osberg and Crow 46).

   The verbal incongruities continue as Arthur and Patsy meet a peasant husband and wife (Palin and Jones) who engage them in a sort of Ur-
Marxist political discussion. Dennis and his wife bandy about phrases like
"outdated imperialist dogma," "working class," and "supreme executive
power" that derives "from a mandate from the masses," as if they were left-
ists discussing politics over black coffee. In "Monty Python and the
Medieval Other" David Day comments on the incongruity of this oft-
quoted scene:

> The political coloring of the scene's visual presentation, portraying
> an expected typical condition of the medieval worker, is surrealisti-
> cally juxtaposed with the socialist construct that at least in part
> produced such preconceptions—the Marxist model of history,
> which with its insistence on the linear progressivity of human

achievement toward socialist perfection requires as a starting point a view of the feudal economy as exploitative. The effect of putting Marxist rhetoric into the mouths of medieval peasants is again to undermine this modern construct of medieval economic realities [87].

Later, as a suspected witch is about to be burned, the alleged witch (Connie Booth) says, "That's a fair cop," a phrase from twentieth-century British culture and from multiple *Flying Circus* episodes. She also happens to say the line in direct address to the camera, a sort of aside to the theatrical audience which immediately re-acknowledges the artifice of the presentation. While Rackin pointed out the immediate connection between past event and present time in Shakespeare's anachronisms, the connection between *Flying Circus* and the film is made just as efficiently. So not only is *Holy Grail* a fictional historical film made by a team of noted comedians, but this same generically oxymoronic film supports Palin's earlier-mentioned assessment and has been called "one of the most authentic-looking films ever made about the Arthurian legend" by contemporary critics (Hertzberg 69). The "authentic-looking" filth and British settings must be the reason for such a glowing assessment, especially as the dialogue and many of the anachronistic characterizations and moments belie that authenticity.

"The Book of the Film" section offers a woman's hand turning the pages of a gilt-edged manuscript volume, each page containing some period lettering (as if from some ancient tome one might find in the Bodleian Library) and a color photograph. The photographs—mostly head shots of the main characters—illustrate the incongruity between the medieval story and the modern telling. There is even a further time disruption here, as the series of photographs of Sir Robin (Idle) cowering under his shield depict the "attack rabbit" section of the film, which the audience hasn't yet seen. Like a temporal anachronism in a Shakespeare text, this small moment may escape most viewers, and it certainly shouldn't distract those who do notice it from the established narrative trajectory (however fractured that trajectory may be). That the photographs are anachronisms merely adds to the visual effect. As the knights approach Camelot, its beauty is praised, and Patsy mumbles, "It's only a model." He is quickly "shushed" by other characters. This seems an echo of the Chorus offering the unreality of the "unworthy scaffold" that is the stage and set for *Henry V*: "Can this cockpit hold / The vasty fields of France? Or may we cram' / Within this wooden O the very casques / That did affright the air at Agincourt?" (1.1.10–14). The sentiment is the same: acknowledgement of the artifice of the production, of the representation of historical material. As if to fully subvert the spectacle of reality, the Knights of the Round Table in Camelot then sing a nonsense song with anachronistic elements in the lyrics like "Clark Gable" and "Spam," often addressing the camera directly.

As the quest for the grail continues, the knights approach the Cave of Wonders where a vicious rabbit guards the entrance. The rabbit attacks and kills one of the knights, then sets on all of them, scattering the entire party. This certainly upsets patterns of commonly-held expectations. Rabbits that kill? Sounds like *Flying Circus* episodes wherein sheep happen to be crack shots ("Killer Sheep"), or giant, marauding hedgehogs threaten otherwise brutish gangsters ("The Piranha Brothers"). As the rabbit attacks, Arthur cries, "That rabbit's dynamite!" and he of course is prognosticating, since dynamite would not be invented by Alfred Nobel for more than 900 years. To combat the rabbit they call forth the Holy Hand Grenade of Antioch, which, according to the Book of Armaments, will "blow [their] enemies into bits." Needless to say it does just that. The perils in the cave are interrupted by the death of the animator (Gilliam), and "the cartoon peril was no more." This full self-reflexivity reminds the audience that what they are witnessing is not reality but a staged, fractured version of reality, and a reality that can be undercut or interrupted at any time. Rackin points out that Shakespeare takes pains in *Richard II* (5.2.23–40) to remind his audience that they are just that, an audience, as he comments on the similarities between the theater and the history of the fourteenth century (112–16).

The penultimate anachronism can be found at the Bridge of Death, where three questions must be answered by the knights "ere the other side they see." One of the questions (also anachronistic) concerns, of course, the "air speed velocity of an unladen swallow," which finally finishes off the long-lived gag. The anachronistic question is, "What is the capital of Assyria?" Phrased as it is, the inference is that Assyria is still a viable state in A.D. 932, the film's announced timeframe, though history records that Nineveh, Assyria's centuries-old capital, had been destroyed by the end of the fifth century BC (Finegan 231). Long before the tenth century, Nineveh was only mounds of grassy rubble, and Assyria was no more.

The final anachronism, which eventually ends the film, is the massive police raid as Arthur and Bedivere attempt to storm the Grail Castle. Lancelot has been arrested earlier, as we saw him being patted down, and both Arthur and Bedivere are disarmed and hustled into paddy wagons. One police officer finally puts his hand over the camera lens, blocking the shot and ending the film. This very abrupt quashing of the film's seemingly fluid narrative authority is perhaps the troupe's nod to the ultimate authority of the society they are lampooning, a society of which they must remain a part of and within. But it's more likely just another attempt at overt, bare-faced theatricality. The camera as a physical object is acknowledged, and as an extension of the implied viewer (our eye equals the camera lens), the action is terminated, and it's the police squad who actually, physically and even forcefully end the film. If T. W. Baldwin's role of the "tyrant"— the type of character mentioned previously as possibly missing from the Python *oeuvre*— is actually present, then he is the narrative tyrant, the controlling and uncontrollable influence of a character or narrative impetus that does not adhere to the prescribed limits of the story, plot or even the text. This tyrant is an influence, like the constables who enter the film's historical narrative, follow the historical characters as in pursuit of criminals, and finally bring about the film's surcease in a most self-reflexive and artificial way. Shakespeare acknowledged the theater setting— the stage, the audience, the unreality of a staged performance — adding to the theatrical experience another dimension of understanding and experience. Python breaks the rules of performance and, in so doing, helps create new rules, or at least new levels of theatrical experience for the television and film-going audience.

Notes

1. The five films are: *And Now for Something Completely Different* (1971); *Monty Python and the Holy Grail* (1975); *The Life of Brian* (1979); *Monty Python Live at the Hollywood Bowl* (1982); and *The Meaning of Life* (1983).

2. See Bentley 3.

3. Johnson points out that Chapman, Cleese, and Idle attended Cambridge; Palin and Jones hail from Oxford, and Gilliam was given honorary Oxford status. See Johnson, *20 Years* 7–13 *passim*.

4. It should be noted that Python did, on occasion, sell material they felt didn't represent the *Flying Circus* or was just somehow inappropriate. Terry Jones specifically mentions that skits which weren't "funny enough" were farmed out to friends on other BBC radio and TV shows. See Morgan, *Speaks* 37. Also before, during and after the *Flying Circus* run various Python members (especially Cleese and Chapman) would write material for other venues, but always as distinctly non–Python material. See Miller 111–138.

5. It may be argued here that Jonson did "write to type" in as much as he was often writing for one man— James I. He was not writing a part for a particular player, but a masque for presentation at court, thus demanding a certain particularity from Jonson in regards to his monarch, his intended audience. It seems logical to conclude that he would have known and catered to his monarch's particular theatrical tastes as he wrote. William Proctor Williams makes the noteworthy distinction between Shakespeare writing for his company and then having those works performed at court, as well as in the public theaters, and Jonson writ-

ing for the court, though those same plays might be also performed in theaters. Intended audience and actual audience becomes the distinction. For a list of Jonson's court masques see Brock 134.

6. The "look" of the sketch in regard to Python's overall approach to comedy is evident here. The visual juxtapositioning of four "City Gents" wearing bowlers and pinstripes, yet still hopping along Threadneedle Street with their pants about their ankles, speaks volumes— authority is lampooned, made to look silly, and deflated. A respectable fraternal organization, the Freemasons, bears the brunt of Python's wit, much like the Puritans suffered at the pen of Jonson. It is the very elaborate ritual that makes Freemasonry what it is that Python satirizes (and which they later make a mock "apology" for).

7. This is episode 17 (recorded as Series 2, Show 8 — Production No. 61964) from Sept. 1970.

8. Roger Wilmut makes an arresting point as to the theatrical acceptability of women at Cambridge, noting that since the founding of the Cambridge University Footlights Club in 1883 — where Cleese and Chapman worked together and the Oxford Pythons attended as audience — there had been a "no women" member policy. The club had been originally created in a sort of robust athletic environment, and featured satirical musical comedy productions. Roger Wilmut describes the charged dramatic atmosphere:

> Since membership of the club was limited to men, female impersonation
> was a necessary performing art until 1932 when "real women" were
> included in the cast for the first time. The result was felt to be such an
> unmitigated disaster that the following year's show was called *No More
> Women* and it was not until the early 1960s that female membership of the
> actual club was allowed, although a few women appeared in the revues
> from the late fifties onwards [1].

It would seem, then, that women as *performers* became at least the admitted issue, a theatrical consideration, though not explicitly linked to performance, but perhaps reception. The men-only audience in what had been historically a men-only club obviously responded poorly to the infiltration of women into this secure environment. Monty Python, it seems, saw no reason to change this. For a more thorough look at cross-dressing and both the Elizabethan stage and Python, see Chapter 5 and its accompanying notes.

9. Hardy was, of course, both a novelist and a poet, producing eight volumes of poetry which were somewhat tepidly received during his lifetime, though greatly appreciated after. Hardy's admitted dislike of flowery speech, or the "jeweled line," perhaps accounts for why the housewife disdains her Hardy and seeks the "garden of love" with Wombat.

10. This reference can be attributed to a conversation the author had with Dr. William P. Williams at Northern Illinois University, DeKalb, IL, on September 30, 1994. Also, the public uproar over the attempt at appropriation by Thatcher can be found in the English newspapers of the time. See White 1 and "Quidnunc" 1.

11. "The Philosophers' Football Sketch" was a film made for Bavarian TV and shot completely in German. The Pythons made two such films for the German market. See Johnson, *20 Years* 161–5, 190.

12. *Monty Python's Flying Circus* originally aired on British television from Oct. 5, 1969 through Dec. 5, 1974. Forty-five shows comprised this original BBC series. See Johnson, *20 Years* 46.

13. Till Eulenspiegel (Jonson's "𝕌𝕝𝕖𝕦 𝕊𝕡𝕚𝕖𝕘𝕖𝕝") is a character originally found in Low German folktales. He is a trickster and a commoner, and his pranks tend to be directed at the nobility, clergy, and well-to-do townsmen. A Eulenspiegel prank is "broadly farcical, often brutal, sometimes obscene," but features a "serious theme" (*Encyclopædia Britannica*). He is the peasant character who can "get back" at society through trickery. First translated into English from the Low German by about 1520, with a later popular version appearing in 1560. See www.britannica.com/bcom/eb/article/0/0,5716,33799+1+33215,00.html.

14. In what would become something of a landmark copyright protection action (a concept probably quite alien to both Jonson and Shakespeare), Python would exhibit a similar attention to detail as the American television network ABC aired a compilation of some of the *Flying Circus*'s fourth (and final) season episodes in October 1975. Knowing the restrictions of American television would demand at least some censoring of the more "naughty bits" in various *Flying Circus* episodes, Python only agreed to the deal if ABC would air the episodes in their entirety. ABC simply assured the Pythons that the three thirty-minute episodes (originally aired on BBC without commercials) would run back-to-back. It would seem, though, that at least the Python representatives, including the BBC, would have realized that there was almost no chance ABC would or could air the shows without commercial interruption, but this is hindsight. The end results were, of course, significantly edited versions with space made for commercials, and Python sued to stop a second compilation from airing, and to regain its distribution rights to the entire series. Their suit was successful. See Miller's *Something Completely Different* pages 137 and 225; also Hertzberg's "Onward and Upward," 69–85; and Hewison's *Monty Python: The Case Against* (London: Methuen, 1981): 41–58.

15. This information is at least partially anecdotal, arising during discussions at Northern Illinois University, Sept.–Dec. 1994. Douglas M. Lanier cites Jonson's *Workes* (1616), which Lanier identifies as "the first printed edition of an author's works supervised by the author himself" (253). See Lanier's "The Prison-House of the Canon: Allegorical Form and Posterity in Ben Jonson's *The Staple of News*."

16. The wholesale slaughter of English as forced from the mouths of foreigners is by no means confined to the works of Shakespeare. For a very funny example of this affliction see Marston's *The Dutch Courtesan*, wherein Francischina can be heard to utter: "O mine aderliver love, vat sall me do to re- / quit dis your mush affection?" (1.2.87–88). It should be noted that Francischina's accent seems to come and go as the play moves on.

17. Richard III also uses language to define his friends and enemies, or transform his friends *into* enemies, including Hastings and the simple but fatal word "if." See Chapter 6 of this study, and *Richard III* 3.4.73–76.

18. Theobald's response was entitled *Shakespeare Restored: or a Specimen of the Many Errors, as Well Committed, as Unamended, by Mr. Pope in His Late Edition of This Poet* (1726). See Tillotson, et al. 682.

19. See Dryden's *An Essay of Dramatic Poesy* 45–49.

20. For a fascinating look at the latest in (at least semi-popular) Arthurian research, see Britannia's website, http://www.britannia.com/history/h12.html. For more on the armor used in the film, see Helmut Nickel's "Arms and Armor in the Arthurian Film" in Harty's *Cinema Arthuriana*, 188–89.

Chapter 3

"Is Not the Truth
the Truth?"
(Ab)uses of History

Falstaff asks about the nature of truth in *1 Henry IV*, changing and adapting his version of recent history even as he tells it.[1] In *Monty Python and the Holy Grail*, a group of French soldiers taunt Arthur and his knights from the walls of an English castle; this is history turned about on itself, since Shakespeare writes of Englishmen controlling Burgundy, and France as a part of England, rather than vice versa. In *Holy Grail*, it seems, Arthur has lost Britain (or at least parts of it) before his quest has even started. Shakespeare also, however, telescopes time, creates non-historical characters in his histories, and delivers anachronisms without hesitation or apology, all of which combine as the warp and woof of Shakespeare's very believable and influential history of the English civil wars, or the Wars of the Roses. One can also pursue Shakespeare's history beyond the tetralogies, examining the historical curiosities of the comedies or tragedies with a similar discovery: Shakespeare was not a slave to history.

The purpose of this chapter is to discuss Shakespeare's uses and abuses of historical fact as he created his history plays, and to approach other plays and their various submissions of history to the service of dramatic efficacy. Shakespeare's historiography — his valuation of sources like Hall, Holinshed, popular culture and myth, and the demands of contemporary political influences— is also key as certain histories are used and others ignored in the quest for effective drama. Specifically, Falstaff as a fictional character in historical settings and surrounded by historical characters will be treated, as Shakespeare utilizes Falstaff for the special, "metahistorical" character that he is. Monty Python's appropriation of Shakespeare's fre-

73

quent disregard for the unities of time and space will also be examined; their ahistorical and textually-challenging "unconformities" will become significant as time and space are collapsed into an ever "present"; and Python's methods of historiography — the constant assessing and weighing of the relative value of historical texts, whatever those "texts" might be — will also be considered as comedy in relation to British history is constructed. And as comedy is constructed by Monty Python, so too is another history.

Historian Charles Ross reminds us, notably, of the great influence of Shakespeare's versions of history: "Shakespeare, the great Duke of Marlborough once remarked, was the only English history book he had ever read" (8). This is a very telling comment, especially when considering the level of education the Duke must have achieved in contrast to the groundlings who flocked to Shakespeare's plays. To the commoner and to at least some of those higher on the social ladder, Shakespeare's popular entertainment *was* history. An afternoon at the Globe, eating hazelnuts and viewing *The Second Part of Henry the Fourth*, was a chance to be entertained with a lesson — albeit, perhaps, a euhemeristic one — from English history. Perhaps even more so today, however, the mythology surrounding Shakespeare and the relative distance of required secondary school curricula by which most people (at least in the United States) are introduced to Shakespeare forwards the notion of euhemerism with unprecedented vigor. He is after all The Bard, the National Poet of Englishness. Shakespeare, then, *is* history.

Shakespeare, of course, should not stand alone when the massaging of history is discussed. He was pursuing staged, theatrical history, whereas the "histories" available to him as he wrote his own dramatized versions were perhaps no more historically veritable than the politicized, narrationally-related "facts" from available history books. A short list of these Tudor "histories" include the fairy tale-like *Poly-Olbion* by Michael Drayton (1612); Edward Hall's Tudor paean *The Union of the Two Noble and Illustrate Families of Lancaster and York* written in 1548 for Henry VIII; and Raphael Holinshed's *The Chronicles of England* (1587). These were just some among the many ostensibly historical works to hold influence as Elizabeth's reign came to an end.[2] As late as 1612 Drayton mined the legends of Brut and Arthur to "fill in the dim beginnings" of the history he was constructing, in essence following the model of Tudor historians already in place.[3]

Ronald R. MacDonald writes that "there has always been uncertainty about what we call Shakespeare's 'histories'" (22). He is referring specifically to the tetralogies, but the word he's chosen — "histories" — can be read as not only the history plays, as such, but Shakespeare's multiple and often fluid versions of history which serve the ends of all of his plays. "Shakespeare's history plays," Catherine Belsey writes, "are not commonly taken seriously as history" (24). The anachronisms peppered throughout his collected works (like the clock in *Julius Caesar*), as well as the malleability of time offers a sort of transcendence or purposeful reconfiguring of time and history in the quest for the play and specifically its eventual performance. "No one has ever dreamt of condemning the playwright for adding some ten years to the age of Richard of Bordeaux's wife in *Richard II* or for subtracting some twenty from that of Hotspur in *1 Henry IV*," writes Paola Pugliatti (21). No one outside of the late seventeenth or early eighteenth century, she may mean. Clarence may have actually preceded Edward in death by as much as five years, and while Sir Thomas Grey's "scarce current" title as the Earl of Dorset was at least eight years old by the time portrayed in *Richard III*, Shakespeare isn't called to task for theatricalizing history (Evans 720n; *Richard III* 1.3.255). The pursuit of this dramatic historicity is, according to Shakespeare in *The Taming of the Shrew*, "a kind of history" (Induction.2.141). This "kind of history" has recently been described by Adrian Noble, artistic director of the Royal Shakespeare Company:

> We contend that far from developing a single ironic view of English
> history, Shakespeare's real view is fragmented, kaleidoscopic, highly
> complicated, even random at times; it reflects as much his own
> development as an artist as it does a considered view of history, and
> almost certainly says as much about the politics of his own age as
> that of the period he was writing about [7].

Perhaps Shakespeare was New Historicist before the moniker had been coined, acknowledging at least the possibility of multiple histories as he created a dramatic history his characters— historical and fictional —could populate with at least the appearance of historical veracity. He certainly understood that there were at least two histories— that set of historical events resulting in and thus approved by Elizabeth and the Tudors, and any other historical possibility. "He must have found a challenge in shaping the English history play," Jonathan Hart writes, "in condensing the flow of historical time into a play about the past with a beginning and end as well as a middle" (13). The flow of time has no concise, four- or five-act dramatic structure with carefully placed moments of high drama; this structure was brought to history by Shakespeare and other playwrights of the era like Peele (*Edward I*; *The Battle of Alcazar*) and Marlowe (*Edward II*). Or, as may be more the case now that Shakespeare is The Bard and

National Poet, history came to Shakespeare to be ordered as he saw (dramatically) fit. Hart admits the complexity of a history play, and identifies the "external pressures" brought to bear on those dramatists and performers of the public theaters (13). History, then, consisted of those events and characters which the prevailing power deemed appropriately historical, or which lent themselves to acceptable interpretation in light of the current political process.

Pugliatti writes that censorship rarely if ever arose from the mangling of history; rather, "plays were often condemned for telling the truth, obviously when this truth was in some way in contrast with the official political perspective" (22). When the Chamberlain's Men became the King's Men in 1603, did Stuart history become "the" history? Oldcastle became Falstaff in response to a hue and cry from a politically-connected William Brooke, 7th Lord Cobham. And with the history plays starting so close on the heels of the Armada, is there a whiff not only of nationalism but of court favor in these plays?[4] Such motivational questions are myriad, and must be added to the generic mutability of Shakespeare's genres (including the histories), creating multifaceted works which continue to reward examination. Writes Hart: "Shakespeare also represents mutability in history by showing that history itself is mutable" (212). History is as mutable as the varied sources are distinct. When Edmund Bolton cautions historians to avoid the corruptive influences of "Addition, Mutilation, Substraction, Distraction, or otherwise" he nearly exhausts Shakespeare's (and Python's) uses of history as an engaging narrative tool (Pugliatti 21). Without such mutilations there would be no dramatic structure, no genre (outside of history), and very little Shakespeare.

MacDonald continues, calling into question the generic stability of Shakespeare's "genres":

> The genre (if it is a genre) seems inherently unstable under critical scrutiny, always threatening to become something else, to slide over into other generic modes about which there is firmer agreement, to become simply tragedy (*Richard II*), or comedy (*1 Henry IV*), or dramatic satire (*2 Henry IV*). Yet, with the possible exception of early work like *The Comedy of Errors*, Shakespeare seems never to have been willing to accept the traditional genres quite as he found them, and the evidence of impurity, even in the lighthearted romantic comedies, is well known. We will never find in the Shakespeare canon the kind of generic purity that a more strictly classical temperament would consider indispensable [22].

This sort of moving target provided by Shakespeare becomes somewhat more fixed, according to MacDonald, in the histories, where Shakespeare expresses a scrupulous concern for history, for by "history" I do not mean a narrative of events, the "story" of the past, but a concern with processes and the inner necessities of historical change, the mechanisms of transition, the deep and nearly invisible shifts in thinking and assumptions that form the basis of what we call in retrospect, and partly for interpretive convenience, "epochs" [22].

This "historical change" that so interested Shakespeare and which he so adeptly transferred to his play structures is termed "adjustment" by Robert Ornstein and, according to Dennis Burden in "Shakespeare's History Plays: 1952–1983," is another "view of the disintegration of the Tillyard thesis" in regard to the order, coherence and "dignity" of Shakespeare's history plays (1). Tillyard's thesis of the "Tudor myth" brought a "new significance" to Shakespeare's plays and, perhaps more pointedly, to Shakespeare studies (1). Tillyard's well-known assertions of Tudor "order" and his overall thesis regarding Shakespeare's history plays has become, "whether one agrees or disagrees with it ... the traditional interpretation of the history plays" (Bergeron, *Guide* 56). So either agreeing with Tillyard or disagreeing with him, the critic has at least begun there since the publication of Tillyard's work in 1944. The history plays are England's great "epic" of nationalism, which are carefully crafted so as to be "a linked and integrated series, revealing a broad and complex panorama of national life, unified and balanced into a coherent aesthetic 'order' mirroring the political order of the Elizabethan state" (Holderness, *Recycled* 21). The plays are then "parables of political order," and Tillyard was merely identifying this self-same, inalienable characteristic (21).

Tillyard's assertions of order and English unity shortly prefigured Laurence Olivier's film version of *Henry V*, touched-up by Winston Churchill. Shakespeare's history plays as histories may have mirrored existing policy, and Olivier's wartime government-sponsored version of Henry's trials and triumphs adapted that struggle for order, especially in regard to treatment of Henry's enemy (and England's World War II–era ally), the French. As Shakespeare reshaped history to suit the Tudor court and tastes, Olivier and Churchill would later create a Henry who treats as comical England's claim to the French throne, "reinforcing the clownishness of the claim itself" (Manheim 122). Also, the portrayal was "intended to strengthen the morale of a Britain which had been at war with Germany for five years."[5] Tillyard was also fairly certain that his view of order was the final, appropriate view, as he admits that "it is not unlikely that anyone will question the conclusion that Shakespeare's Histories, with their constant pictures of disorder, cannot be understood without assuming a larger principle of order in the background" (319–21). Tillyard continues:

> In the total sequence of his plays dealing with the subject-matter of
> Hall [Shakespeare] expressed successfully a universally held and
> still comprehensible scheme of history: a scheme fundamentally
> religious, by which events evolve under a law of justice and under
> the ruling of God's Providence, and of which Elizabeth's England
> was the acknowledged outcome [321].

Holderness questions (without indictment, of course) Tillyard's ignorance
or disavowal of the possible immediacy of this same argument in relation
to "war-time Britain" and the existing political realities of an England at
war with the Axis powers (*Recycled* 23–24). The quest and, indeed, need
for order during the horrific Battle of Britain and as the war stretched into
the middle of the decade seems the more likely genesis for Tillyard's orderly,
providential thesis, Holderness and others claim. Burden examines the
subsequent answers to Tillyard's scholarship, and a general freeing of
Shakespeare from the confines of artistic, political, and even historical
orthodoxies can be seen as a developing trend in critical studies from 1952
even to the present day. In Ornstein's view, "adjustment is the art of drama
as well as of politics; and Shakespeare, like his characters, calculates, impro-
vises, experiments, achieves dazzling success and … makes mistakes" (3).
Ronald R. MacDonald notes that history was not an ordered "compilation
of events" which Shakespeare then decorated with his "brilliantly conceived (if fundamentally ahistorical) dramatic characters" (22). History
was, then, an "extra-personal — if not quite impersonal — phenomenon,
playing itself out in different registers in the huge cast of characters that
peoples the tetralogy" (22).

History was beyond (but included) the characters and situations and
events available to Shakespeare. Paola Pugliatti writes of the differing
expectations for history and theater, as the "history plays practised all the
forms of corruption" that were anathema to Elizabethan-era scholars (21).
Shakespeare violated the rules, but his violations were never "judged an
'impiety'":

> Admittedly, then, the requirements were looser in the case of
> drama, and playwrights were granted the right to invent because
> the expectations connected with theatrical entertainments were
> different from those connected with the more "serious" history
> books. After all, drama was the most marginal of intellectual
> expressions; it was a sort of "third world" of culture striving for
> emancipation and therefore, as happened with other forms of mar-
> ginality, it was granted some freedom of speech [22].

And while it may be more true that Shakespeare was allowed free historical dramatic reign because he was simply a dramatist (though those who

exist on society's margins might argue the "freedoms" granted by the society which marginalizes them), Pugliatti is at least certain (and correct) that Shakespeare was, indeed, approaching history in his dramatic works, striving for historicity as "a consciously pursued effect" (22). Graham Holderness approaches the subject in *Shakespeare Recycled: The Making of Historical Drama*, with his subtitle already identifying the essential conflict in the perhaps uncomfortable coupling of "historical" and "drama." That history, or simply events accomplished, and drama, or accomplished events represented (with all the vagaries and potential incumbent discourses acknowledged), should ever reside together comfortably is arguably uncertain. Catherine Belsey notes, even, that "the term 'history play' is something of an oxymoron ... *real* history, stands outside literature as its binary antithesis, fact as opposed to fiction" (24). This held true, she mentions, until the "postmodern condition" allowed for a more "sympathetic" reading of history plays as— possibly and even "perversely"— history (24). Holderness argues that the disturbances and controversies generated by these confrontations are inevitable and, finally, fruitful:

> But what we call literature is not merely the effect of a cause, and historical drama is not a mere reflection of a discourse which can claim greater authenticity by virtue of its proximity to the "real" of history. Shakespeare's historical plays are not just *reflections* of a cultural debate: they are *interventions* in that debate, *contributions* to the historiographical effort to reconstruct the past and discover the methods and principles of that reconstruction. They are as much locations of historical controversy as the history books: they are, in themselves and not derivatively, historiography [*Recycled* 13].

The interventions of Shakespeare's histories become contributions to the search for historiographical verisimilitude then, rather than anomalous and anachronistic or even damaging to it, if the viewer takes Shakespeare's history as History. The plays are, to Holderness, "major initiatives of Renaissance historical thought" (13). The Duke of Marlborough's admission, then, of Shakespeare as his historical keystone, seems as valid as the dramatist's, or the chronicler's, or the historian's claim to History.

In much the same manner, the television groundlings of today may know more (or think they know more) about the Spanish Inquisition — including the fact that red-clad Inquisitors appear whenever the words "Spanish Inquisition" are uttered — and rely on this version of history for lack of any other remarkable reference. The Monty Python troupe can mix medieval knights and coconuts, while Shakespeare mixes Mortimers; Python creates humor from the resulting incongruities, while Shakespeare creates his own historical dramatic flow. Using history to their own ends, both William Shakespeare and the Monty Python troupe identify, send-up, comment upon, and finally confront the larger social and political forces that exist around them. Distilling the problem down to "ends" and "means," essentially, leaves us with Shakespeare's and Monty Python's ends—or motives—for such cultural confrontations as being discrete, which will be shown; but the means—the narrative paths traveled: the structures of history, the characters, time, etc.—the paths traveled within their respective mediums to reach the social/political/historical end that is the finished play and performance; these paths are comparable, and William Shakespeare as National Poet and a maker of history as read by Monty Python can then be pinpointed and studied.

David Bergeron identifies Shakespeare's ubiquitous character Falstaff as "the special artifice of Shakespeare's construction of history, the one who brings narrative history and narrative fiction face to face" (231). Appearing in *1 Henry IV*, *2 Henry IV*, and *The Merry Wives of Windsor*, as well as dying ignominiously offstage in *Henry V*, Falstaff is a created (ahistorical) character within works (the histories, that is) pertaining to real historical figures, places, and events. But it is precisely because he is not attached to history, per se, that he has the freedom to become, in Elizabeth Fox-Genovese's words, "something more" than the confines of historical verisimilitude would ever allow (216). A question that seems pertinent at this point must be directed at the Falstaff-Oldcastle persona: What if Falstaff never existed? It is well-known that Shakespeare originally named this character Sir John Oldcastle, presumably after the Protestant knight executed for both his Lollard leanings and his eventual claim that his liege-lord was actually Richard II (of Scotland). If Shakespeare hadn't felt the political pressure to change this historical character into a contrived character by a mere name switch, thus creating a powerful ahistorical character amongst the "real," would there be such an abundance of scholarship surrounding the drunken lout Sir John Oldcastle? He would still be the funny, roaring, lying braggart so endeared to audiences of the time and even today, but he would not be the ahistorical, enigmatic entity invested with such inter-, intra-, and extratextual power. And would this character, a more historical Oldcastle, have been as influential as Bergeron and others have concluded: would he have been able to bring together "narrative history and narrative fiction," as Falstaff managed?

At least some of the restrictions of history must have constrained Oldcastle, if only his name as an anchor in the real world, and subjected him to the same historical forces as every other "real" character. Would Oldcastle have been treated differently—meaning, with more respect and given to less villainy — as Oldcastle and not Falstaff in *The Merry Wives of Windsor* and *Henry V*? Falstaff is certainly a different, less resourceful and more "degraded" character in *Merry Wives* than in either of the *Henry IV* plays, and he is dispatched ungraciously in *Henry V*. If Shakespeare felt compelled to write a romance for Falstaff (at Elizabeth's behest) or create an occasional piece for the Garter Feast of 1597, then either situation might account for the "lesser" Falstaff presented in *Merry Wives* (Evans 287). Whatever the case, it may be that Shakespeare scholarship was given an unexpected plum by virtue of Lord Cobham's reaction to the unflattering (though popular) portrayal of his ancestor. Oldcastle is a part of history, thus at least somewhat answerable to it; Falstaff is above history, and able to transcend it, to our critical delight.[6] Borrowing and expanding upon Bergeron's depiction of the metahistorical Falstaff, I will argue that the work of Monty Python in *The Holy Grail* is a "special artifice" of their own creation, a metahistory; and, like Falstaff, this artifice brings a self-consciousness to both the history and the art form. This self-awareness exhibited in Shakespeare and Monty Python draws on "narrative history and narrative fiction" to break down boundaries between texts, often highlighting the artificial nature of the presentation to create a "history" that is never far removed from the present. In fact, through metahistorical characters like Falstaff and Arthur and his knights, the past and the present can and do exist simultaneously. But first, to Falstaff.

In *1 Henry IV* 2.2, Falstaff and his gang have set upon four purse-heavy travelers and, with plenty of bluster, relieved them of their money. Prince Harry and Poins watch the goings-on and then — donning disguises— proceed to rob the robbers. As they all later gather back at the tavern, Henry and Poins prod Falstaff for his explanation of the night's events. Falstaff describes the murderous band of villains that beset them, the number and ferocity of the attackers increasing with every verbal poke from Harry. The prince listens, then describes what actually happened, contradicting Falstaff, calling his own version of the incident a "plain tale" (2.5.258). Harry's "plain tale" pares the exaggerated numbers back down, from hundreds of villains to just two, and recites the incident almost as it happened (2.5.256–268). Almost.

Even Harry's self-professed plainness cannot escape scrutiny here. When Harry recites the scene, he adds a flourish or two of his own. Shakespeare's stage directions (as identified in Taylor and Wells' 1987 Oxford edition) merely say that "Gadshill, Russell, and Harvey run away [severally], / and Oldcastle, after a blow or two, [roars and] / runs away too, leaving the booty behind them" (2.3.12–14). Harry describes Falstaff's roar, however, as a cry "for mercy" (2.5.262) when it could just as easily have been an expression of frustration, anger, or sheer exertion, taking Falstaff's girth into consideration. The stage directions are oblique, and become especially troublesome when the editorial brackets around "roars and" are taken into consideration. Harry also casts aspersions on Falstaff's bravery: "What a slave art thou, to hack thy sword as thou hast done, and then say it was in fight?" (2.5.264–265). Remember that the sparse stage directions only mention that Falstaff offers "a blow or two" before running away, with no reference as to whether he was afraid, holding his own, or just out-numbered (2.3.13). So we are left with what we read in the playscript as "truth": we have Falstaff's version of that truth; we have Harry's recount-ing of a more "plain" truth; and, finally, our own reading of the text with all three versions of the incident — of this history — in mind. In perfor-mance, we would have to add "staged truth," which is inevitably inter-pretive, and another truth as received or interpreted by a particular audience. Events that occur within the text are then suspect, and depen-dent upon various sources, including the reader, for interpretation. This history, recent as it was for the participants, is as colored, twisted, added upon, and generally misread as events that happened ages ago.

The reading or "ciphering" of history is acknowledged from the out-set of *Henry V* by the Chorus. He has already admitted that the "unwor-thy" stage he occupies cannot truly represent the "vasty fields of France" (Prologue 10, 12). The first and second lines of the play introduce this his-tory by invoking a Muse who will "ascend / The brightest heaven of inven-tion" (Prologue 1–2). History, then, is about to be invented, or given poetic life and will thus be subject to the whims of dramatic structure and not to historical verisimilitude. The Chorus essentially apologizes, and more than once, for the inability of the stage to reenact history, asking that his-tory be taken in relation to theatrical economy. This seems a carefully crafted way for Shakespeare to be granted historical license, as the Cho-rus assumes what Herschel Baker calls a "deferential stance":

> The second speech of the Chorus regrets "abuse of distance" in the rapid shifting of the scene; the third suggests we "work" our thoughts to compensate for imperfections in the presentation of a siege; [and] the fourth ... superbly comments on the eve of Agin-court [Evans 934].

All these are essentially asking for the same thing: Can and will the audi-ence surrender its historical beliefs for the duration? R. A. Foakes in "Play-houses and Players" (found in Braunmuller and Hattaway's *English Renaissance Drama*) stresses the importance of the Elizabethan audience: "However uneducated, and however much they may have preferred fights, noise, and clowning to serious drama, the groundlings remained an important part of the audience, and the arena theatres continued to cater to them" (9). Paola Pugliatti concurs, noting that Shakespeare's audiences did know a version of history, arising as it did from "the established corpus of facts and problems that concerned national history" (23). And just what constituted "established" is arguable, and certainly based on inherent political and cultural biases. Pugliatti also mentions that the Chorus is aware of the audience's knowledge and expectations:

> *Chor.* Vouchsafe to those that have not read the story,
> That I may prompt them; and of such as have,
> I humbly pray them to admit the' excuse
> Of time, of numbers, and due course of things,
> Which cannot in their huge and proper life
> Be here presented [5.Prologue.1–6].

The nation's recent past would have been known to many, if not most, and a striking historical omission would not only have been noticed but could have drawn the wrath of audiences who were known to throw at least eggs and apples when dissatisfied with the performance (Foakes 9). And if, as Alfred Harbage notes in his introduction to Bluestone and Rabkin's *Shakespeare's Contemporaries*, the "prime of Elizabethan drama fitted a span no longer than the prime of a single human life," then the Elizabethan audience would have had ample opportunity to sample Jonson's attention to the unities as well as Shakespeare's inattention (xi). Simply put, a forwarding of the artifice of the constructed play and its attendant "histories" was necessary so that Shakespeare could fashion his history as he saw fit. Further, the "ciphers to this great accompt" will figure or reckon the worth of Henry's story, a description that goes beyond the mere retelling of history, but implies adding, subtracting, and even multiplying to reach a sum or product that is Henry V and *Henry V* (*Henry V* Prologue 17). This historical inexactness carries over to the comedies and tragedies, as well, but is probably most noticeable in the tetralogies just by their claimed historical nature.

Moving even closer to the text for a moment, we see that the problem can be compounded by various versions of the "same" text. There is history as presented on the stage, and there is history as it is presented on the page. Textually speaking, Shakespeare can be incredibly frustrating. The lack of playscripts or promptbooks known undoubtedly to be of Shakespeare's own creation — in other words, penned by his own hand — opens the door for all sorts of authorial and editorial possibilities that can distract from any careful analysis. There are entire books and now Internet sites devoted to debunking the "Shakespeare as author" claims, forwarding other authors in his place, and the disagreeing extant Shakespeare manuscripts don't exactly argue for The Bard's singular, unadulterated authorship. Again though, like the Falstaff-Oldcastle debate, it is the uncertainty that spurs so much worthwhile critical discussion. One passage, for instance, taken from *1 Henry IV* and spoken by Prince Harry, will help illustrate this point:

> We two saw you four set on four, and bound them, and were masters of their wealth.— Mark now how a plain tale shall put you down.— Then did we two set on you four, and, with a word, outfaced you from your prize, and have it; yea, and can show it you here in the house. And Oldcastle, you carried your guts away as nimbly, with as quick dexterity, and roared for mercy, and still run and roared, as ever I heard bull-calf. What a slave art thou, to hack thy sword as thou hast done, and then say it was in fight! What trick, what device, what starting-hole canst thou now find out to hide thee from this open and apparent shame? [2.5.256–268].

The version quoted above is taken from the 1987 edition of *The Complete Oxford Shakespeare* by Wells and Taylor. The reference to "Oldcastle" instead of "Falstaff" should be immediately obvious, as this is the first major collection of the plays to make that change. However, *The Riverside Shakespeare* (1974) by G. Blakemore Evans could have been used instead, and the scenes would have read in a slightly different manner. In the thirteen lines (as printed in the Wells and Taylor edition) during which Harry exposes Falstaff and his exaggerations, there are no fewer than eleven textual differences between the *Oxford* and the *Riverside* editions.

The differences aren't earth-shattering, but tremendously important to, say, a textual bibliographer, much as evidence of metathesis and assimilation might be to a phoneticist. Editors of both texts argue their cases for textual emendations with equal fervor, but the fact remains that the texts, though very similar, are not identical. Critical choices were made as to what to leave in (a comma, an apostrophe, etc.) and what to take out (in the case of the *Riverside*, the Falstaff character's probable original name: Oldcastle). In the case of the thieves' battle scene, the *Riverside* stage direction omits "roars and"— there is only Harry and Poins' later mention of Falstaff's vociferousness to tell the reader anything about what might have been heard during the scuffle. The Wells and Taylor edition, on the other hand, includes "roars and." Add to just these two editions the many extant printed editions (Penguin, Arden, etc.) and the possibilities for textual variety broaden exponentially. The recent wave of Internet-based editions of Shakespeare's collected works must also be considered. Some editions, such as the version of *1 Henry IV* at an Australian university website (www.gh.cs.su.oz.au) is based on a popular web version of Shakespeare called "Complete Moby Shakespeare," and both the University of Sydney site and the MIT site (one site where Moby can be accessed) admit to textual irregularities but insist these so-called "editorial differences" are the norm. With critics, scholars, and performers wrestling over even a comma versus an apostrophe, "the norm" hardly seems an adequate explanation for dissimilarities. These critical choices were made by modern editors working with several versions (many of dubious textual validity[7]) of the earliest surviving texts of Shakespeare's work. Also, the multiple electronic and manual transfers of Shakespeare's works to these web archives leave open room for many and varied typographical errors, a service which will confound the careful textual bibliographer for years to come.[8] But even considering just the more well-known printed collections of Shakespeare's works: what to leave in and what to leave out; what is important and what isn't; in short, what will offer the "best" (most valid and readable) version of Shakespeare's history plays was central to these critics. This textual tinkering is yet another aspect of the "histories" of Shakespeare's plays, for authority can be argued in many ways.

Without much of a stretch we can see that Shakespeare himself faced an actual, historical dilemma as Elizabeth's reign began to wax long and he searched the available histories of the civil wars, the struggle for the throne between the Lancasters and the Yorks, for his own version of history as it would appear on the stage. What to leave in? What to leave out? Which history would best serve the court, the stage, and the groundlings? Or what about writing a history that would satisfy the abilities, whims and structure of his own company? History plays relating to the Wars of the Roses became fashionable after about 1580, after everyone involved in the actual skirmishes (on the battlefield and elsewhere) had safely passed away. Were the history plays an attempt to reinforce the importance of clear succession while presenting the awful specter of civil war before the people of London? If not an outright examination of succession, the plays were at least a reflection of the piqued interest in matters of the monarchical succession. Marie Axton writes that "[f]rom the death of Henry VIII to the accession of James I dispute over the succession to the English crown was a principal focus of political debate" (ix). Charles Ross goes further, pointing out that the real fear of the "horrors of civil war" arose from Elizabethan Englishmen's "deep-felt need for order and unity" (8). Dennis Burden writes that Shakespeare "reflects the age's fear of rebellion which was what helped most to keep order" (2). This order and unity could only be made manifest in a clear succession. L. C. Knights (1962) described what Tillyard might have called the "Elizabethan world picture of history":

> History, for all its immediate appeal to the human interest story, in character and action, was essentially the record of a moral process: it taught lessons that could be applied to the understanding of the present and the conduct of affairs [9].

The too-recent civil wars may have loomed large in the minds of Elizabeth's subjects, who "were impatient with their Queen whose disinclination for matrimony and childbearing was becoming notorious" (Axton 1). A series of historical plays which both reminded Englishmen of the "horrors" of civil war and promoted the concept of clear succession might have seemed the perfect answer to these troubling times, and the number of such plays—including but not limited to Shakespeare's—almost supports this assumption.[9]

What Shakespeare intended, though, is both arguable and truly unknown; what remains is the "history" he has constructed in his plays—the acknowledged history plays as well as those plays which might feature or treat historical subjects or events. The history Shakespeare was writing was not literature, but drama. These were works meant to be performed, not read. This is a point that is often overlooked by critics who approach the history plays as history, but not as plays, as entertainment for a paying audience. This bifurcation of purpose must have occurred to Shakespeare as he wrote, and must be kept in our minds as we explore his writings. He certainly commented on the theatrical aspects of his work often enough.[10] His adherence to the details of history depended upon the dramatic situation within the play. Irving Ribner described Shakespeare's history plays as "an adaptation of drama to the purposes of history" (29). In reading the plays and the histories, it seems more likely that Shakespeare adapted the available history to suit his dramatic needs. In *Divine Providence and the England of Shakespeare's Histories*, Henry A. Kelley establishes the existence of more than one "Tudor myth," another avenue down which dramatists and historians could pursue the past (Burden 2). The Yorkist myth involves the punishment of the house of Lancaster, but there is also the Lancastrian myth which "justified the overthrow of Richard II because his corrupt government did not serve the welfare of the kingdom" (2). Not only are we studying Wars of the Roses, then, but Wars of the Myths. The vagaries and political agendas (or just historical ignorance) of Shakespeare's sources are also fodder for reconsideration. Sixteenth-century historians engaged in "hesitancy, inconsistency of interpretation, [and] more off-the-cuff judgment" than scholars like Tillyard may have accounted for, lending a similar variety of interpretations available to and subsequently found in the works of these historians (2). Shakespeare — working with the chronicles of Hall and Holinshed, existing plays such as *The Famous Victories of Henry V* (for his *1* and *2 Henry IV*), Marlowe's *Edward II* (for *Richard II*), and Daniel's *Civil Wars* (1595) — appropriated these historical figures and "so-called facts," which he then "artfully or ruthlessly deployed to tighten up the action and reinforce the theme" (Evans 843). In *1 Henry IV* Falstaff, when Harry has thoroughly "put" him "down," immediately changes his story, arguing that he could instinctively feel the presence of royalty behind Harry's disguise, and thus refused to be engaged. "I was now a coward on instinct," he announces, adapting his previous story in light of new and possibly troubling information (2.5.275–276). The "History" that had been created by Falstaff and his cohorts out of very recent events was suddenly transmutable — it became "history" — then just a flawed story. Louis O. Mink would much later write that "narrative form in history, as in fiction, is an artifice, the product of individual imaginations" (199). Falstaff produced his own history as he narrated events, and Harry his own as he emended Falstaff's history. But Shakespeare as creative author of these characters — one literal, one literary — must be included with Falstaff and Harry as history-maker.

According to David Bergeron, Shakespeare "reshape[d] history to suit [his] artistic purposes" (232). These histories were a product of his "individual imagination." This echoes Evans' assertion of Shakespeare's artfulness with regard to the dramatic adaptation of "so-called facts," as well as that of John Turner, who highlights the "value of the blend of drama and history in the plays" of Shakespeare (Holderness, *History* 4). Falstaff's pleading question, "Is not the truth the truth?" brings us to the consideration of what Bergeron calls the "ahistorical" (or may be termed the "metahistorical") character of Falstaff, and his function in Shakespeare's histories; following that, the similar role of Monty Python's metahistorical and historical characters in *Monty Python and the Holy Grail* and several *Flying Circus* episodes will be examined as they bring together the threads of narrative history and narrative fiction.

David Bergeron's "Shakespeare Makes History: *2 Henry IV*" follows its title and explores the artful history-making that exhibits itself in at least three versions. These three lead to Falstaff, the "special artifice of Shakespeare's construction," through whom Shakespeare "examines and constructs history" (231). The three "different but related strata" are "ahistory," "national" history, and "literary" history (233).

"Ahistory" is explored through Falstaff himself. Since Falstaff is a fictional character interacting with historical figures and experiencing "happened" events, any "history" he associates with can automatically become suspect, and, to Bergeron, lessens the likelihood that a "single 'historical truth' can be attained" (232).[11] The tavern scene discussed above exhibits Falstaff's propensity for falsifying history, and a jaundiced eye must be cast on any "history" that is possibly tainted by his association. Bergeron identifies Falstaff with Rumour, or the spreading of false history. Bergeron notes that "the appearance of Rumour, 'painted full of tongues,' invites a consideration of how one can know what even happened in the past" (233). History, then, is immediately called into question. Rumour, in 2 Henry IV, is concerned with national history, as seen when Prince Hal is reported dead at Shrewsbury (1.1.16). Rumour is supplanted, though, by eyewitness testimony, and true history begins to prevail. Falstaff, as we have seen, has done his own part in falsifying history, but it isn't until he becomes a former associate of the new King that he is a part of national history. "Rumour" is overthrown when Falstaff suffers "rejection, expulsion, and imprisonment," and a "'correct' historical discourse can be inscribed in national life" (233). So Falstaff is the ahistorical catalyst (or lightning rod) to whom nothing can be ascribed historically, but without whom Shakespeare has no history; and Prince Hal "and the royal party" function as national history (233).

For literary history, Bergeron sees Shakespeare as drawing upon himself, his own work, aware of a literary history and accessing it in a very self-conscious manner (237). Bergeron points out that Hal's and Falstaff's memories of events at Gad's Hill (2.2.310–314) cannot both be "actual history since Falstaff is essentially ahistorical; rather, he recalls 2.2 of Shakespeare's 1 Henry IV, the Gadshill robbery scene" (237). Bergeron also notes that Shakespeare has the Duke and Duchess of York rehearse the shame and disgrace heaped on Richard as he returned to London, and the rehearsal is in detail found only in Shakespeare's own work (237). Shakespeare, then, creates history "out of his own artistic history, providing thereby an intertextual construct" (237). This intertextuality was penultimately made possible by Falstaff, the ahistorical character who survived from play to play without ever actually being; who, because of his lack of historical constraints, was able to falsify history and bring the narrative fiction which he represented closer to the narrative history in which he moved; becoming answerable only to the needs of literary history (namely, Shakespeare's writings) as it served to create, uphold, and make certain a stable national history. The stable national history was the rise of Prince Hal to King Henry V, which Shakespeare probably meant to translate into Elizabethan terms as the country struggled with yet another prickly succession.

The popularity of Falstaff as a character, coupled with his unique "ahistorical" situation, created a double-edged sword for Shakespeare. Bergeron concludes of Falstaff: "Despite his size, he functions like a moving target, impossible to pin down and possessing elusive, ahistorical qualities: *a fiction that threatens the making of history*" (241; emphasis added). The last thing Shakespeare would have wanted for his nationalistic *Henry V* was the literally (and literarily) uncontrollable Falstaff tainting the history he was creating for Henry and England, and by metaphorical extension Elizabeth and the future of the Tudor dynasty. The metahistorical had to be sacrificed for the merely historical. Perhaps this explains Falstaff's ignoble, off-stage demise as recounted by the Hostess in *Henry V* 2.3. But even here, since Falstaff is at least ephemerally involved, the question of truth in the retelling (of his death throes) must be taken with a modicum of skepticism. As we shall see later, the spirit of Falstaff haunts *Henry V* in the form of a self-consciousness of artifice that — to this almost absurd and overreaching degree — is found nowhere else in Shakespeare's canon.

David Bergeron asserts that Shakespeare is able to make "history out of the archives that he inherited, out of his own literary production, and out of ahistorical imagination" (244). Falstaff is the literary creation of Shakespeare who functions as the focal point for these histories, an elusive (almost postmodern) character who can break down the barriers between texts and historical events. If a metahistorical character (or characters) can falsify or side-step history and bring a self-awareness and self-consciousness to the text that merges the narrative history and narrative fiction and presents that merger as historical text, then such characters and possibilities exist not only in Shakespeare's *oeuvre* but, I will argue, in the works of those who would read and appropriate Shakespeare's historicity.

The complete televised and filmed works of Monty Python include some forty-five television episodes, four feature films, several benefit films, and two compilation films made for German television.[12] Of the *Flying Circus* television episodes (1969–1974), there are literally hundreds of characters, sketches, and even entire episodes devoted to historical subjects, including Mozart, Queen Victoria, Queen Elizabeth, Sir Francis Drake, Attila the Hun, Shakespeare, etc. For Python, history is a plum ripe for picking. Of the feature films, two were based on quasi-historical subjects outright, *Holy Grail* (1974) and *Life of Brian* (1979), while *The Meaning of Life* (1983) featured episodes concerning England's colonialism in the Zulu wars and a World War I section. While the Brian character (played by Graham Chapman) in *Life of Brian* might seem to come closer to the Falstaff character — being an ahistorical character amongst many historical figures— Brian only briefly encounters Pontius Pilate, and never meets or interacts with his supposed alter ego, Christ. He is also surrounded by multiple characters who are creations of the filmed text — among them his mother, his girlfriend, the members of the radical Peoples Front of Judea, and Pontius Pilate's friend from Rome, Biggus Dickus. It is Arthur (also played by Chapman) and his Knights of the Round Table (Cleese, Idle, Jones, and Palin) who act the Falstaffian role and make their own history as they seek the Grail.

It is perhaps a happy coincidence that, as she describes the final moments of John Falstaff's life in *Henry V*, the Hostess assures Pistol, Nim, and Bardolph that Falstaff did not go to hell: "He's in Arthur's bosom, if ever man went to Arthur's bosom" (2.3.9–10). *The Riverside Shakespeare* glosses "Arthur's bosom" thusly: "The Hostess confuses Arthur and Abraham" (945n). This is certainly within Shakespeare's characters' reach, as Dogberry will attest in *Much Ado*, but this seems more than simply malapropistic. Whether Shakespeare's Hostess meant "Abraham" for "Arthur" or "Arthur" for "Abraham" is a point beyond reasonable argument, for as Graham Holderness writes: "The ... critical problems of authorship and of intentionality render impossible any straightforward definition of what 'the author' 'meant'" (*History* 16). The author isn't here to tell us. "Abraham" fits, however, in that Shakespeare was able to do away with this pesky character in a way that was very much out-of-character. To die off stage, and without any fighting, cursing, drinking, or general carousing— and then to rest in heaven's bliss— might have been the ultimate insult to Falstaff. But that Arthur— the king of English lore — awaited fallen Englishmen certainly supports the nationalistic fervor that could have been generated by a play like *Henry V*. Replacing an Old Testament prophet — and a foreigner — with an English deity-figure of mythic proportions would have been a very clever social commentary by Shakespeare, a comment that might have drawn cheers from the gathered groundlings.

At another level, though, this could have been Shakespeare's almost backhanded attempt at a compliment, and a fond goodbye to his most troublesome and popular character. The line can be read with the stress on the strange possibility of Falstaff actually going to Arthur in death, and not Abraham. This may be a stretch, considering Shakespeare's feelings toward the character, but it seems an engaging possibility. That Shakespeare meant to identify Falstaff— his ahistorical character — with Arthur, whose actuality as an historical figure is still in question, is yet another reading. Where better to retire a metahistorical character than to coexistence with another mythical, even eponymous figure? Arthur's existence in history may be in question, but his influence, from Malory to Monty

Python, is not. It is no surprise, then, that when the members of Monty Python sat down to hash out ideas for a feature film, they settled on the well-known tale of Arthur's quest for the Holy Grail. As Shakespeare made history out of the archives that were available to him, including the likes of Hall and Holinshed, Python appropriated the fabled history of the man who brought England (as it was anciently) under one rule.[13] Shakespeare adapted the Wars of the Roses; Python the search for the cup of Christ. A close reading of segments of the film, as well as pertinent segments from the *Flying Circus* episodes, will demonstrate that beyond plumbing a national history for dramatic material, Python often quoted themselves, drawing on their own existing literary production. This self-reference dissolves the boundaries between texts, heralding the artifice of the medium and of the production. Finally, we will examine how the ghost of Falstaff haunts the Monty Python texts, as metahistorical characters like Arthur, his knights, and others are given "elusive, ahistorical qualities." These "fictions," to use David Bergeron's terms, intrude upon and within the historical text — acting somewhat tyrannically — and threaten the very "making of history."

Are Python's ventures into history in *Flying Circus* episodes and feature films like *Holy Grail*, then, comic history? More than any other show of its kind, Monty Python seemed to rely on historical characters and events as a wellspring of their humor, a never-ending source of known and accepted names, dates, places and events ripe for comic reappraisal.[14] Like generic conventions which can only be subverted or sent up when they have become codified and accepted as defining a certain generic corpus, it took the accomplishment of history for Python and Shakespeare to be able to appropriate that history in the service of the drama. Graham Holderness describes the comic history as

> a mixed mode, without the stylistic consistency of the chronicle
> play. It is fantastic and Utopian rather than realistic and historically
> accurate. It is a popular form, which makes free use of the conven-
> tions of drama, and thereby provides a space of freedom from
> event, from the necessity of a complete history; thus a historical
> character can be liberated from his historical destiny, can play roles
> not dictated to him by the written authority of history. It is festive
> and saturnalian in character — the mighty are put down from their
> seats, and those of low degree exalted. The plays are written and
> performed as popular entertainment: they make much use of song,
> dance, popular pastime and holiday custom. They are a contradic-
> tory fusion of chronicle and carnival [*Recycled* 19].

As will be shown, though Holderness was specifically referring to *Henry IV* and other of Shakespeare's generically mixed plays, he might as well have been describing the mixture of history and comedic license that Python concocts as their own version of historiographical interrogation (and sending up) is presented. And as Holderness sets out in *Shakespeare Recycled* to prove that in spite of what many critics have written and continue to propound, Shakespeare's history plays offer "a form of historiography *analogous* to the new science, in that it perceives human problems and experiences to be located within a definable historical form, a [feudal] society visibly different in fundamental ways from the society of the late sixteenth century" (14). Other critics tied to the notion of "the rudimentary character of Renaissance historiography" will, according to Holderness,

> consider it very unlikely that a thoughtful Elizabethan would have been able to draw any firm historical distinction between the kingship of Edward III and that of Elizabeth; between the punctilious pride of a Renaissance noble and the 'honour' of a feudal knight; between the crusades and the war against Catholicism, the Turk and the Spaniard; between the bloodfeud and the duel [14].

Holderness hopes to prove that the plays can stand alone as historical drama both set in and about the periods each represent, and that, finally, "there is no question of the plays' confusing the present with the past" (14). It is just such a confusion, a conflation, really, which Monty Python achieves as histories are plundered and made in the service of historical comedy. This mixing also leads to confusion in regard to Arthur's status as king; and because his subjects aren't made aware that, historically, they are his subjects, his journeys among the people lead to a confusion which eventually ends the narrative. Arthur doesn't need to become the king in disguise (like Henry V) to find out the true character of his people — because of the uncertain histories forwarded by the text the people are more than willing to tell him face to face.

The principle of historical conflation is evident throughout *Holy Grail* as the legendary King Arthur moves through Britain in search of knights to join his court at Camelot. He is introduced to commoners and supposed noblemen alike, consorting with his subjects (whether they know he is their king or not) much as those kings and lords depicted in certain Renaissance history plays did centuries before. Holderness identifies the genre of the Renaissance history play as "considerably more elastic and flexible than the deterministic medium of these [Marlowe's *Edward II* and Shakespeare's *Richard II* and *Henry VI*] literary tragedies" (15). These history plays mixed references and sources as the structure of the drama would allow. The chronicles were used, but not slavishly, "actions and situations" were invented, and popular forms of oral history were included (15). In *James IV* and *Edward I* the historical characters mix with and interact among fictional, mythical characters like Robin Hood, just as is evident in Shakespeare's plays featuring Falstaff, and Python's television shows and movies. In Python's episode 40, "The Golden Age of Ballooning," the historically real Montgolfier brothers (c. 1783) are placed into Python's history with one Mr. Bartlett, a Glaswegian who poses as France's Louis XIV. When one of the brothers announces that Louis XIV died in 1717, Bartlett changes himself to Louis XV, and then Louis XVI when that becomes necessary. Bartlett continues to be a factor throughout the episode, attempting to steal the Montgolfier's balloon plans for Scotland (Chapman, et al. 2.40.243–58).

In Dekker's *Shoemaker's Holiday* (covered more in depth in Chapter 4), Henry is a king out among his subjects, and the leveling of king and commoner serves as "an inversion of social roles characteristic of carnival and festive, saturnalian comedy" (Holderness, *Recycled* 16).[15] This fraternization "resolves conflict and promotes harmony" in the plays where it is employed, according to Holderness, and as a generic convention of sorts, is thus ripe for parody. In *Holy Grail*, Arthur's attempts to fraternize are constantly met with rebukes and disappointment. Anne Barton in "The King Disguised: Shakespeare's *Henry V* and the Comical History" identifies the power of a disguised king, the power of freedom from the normal constraints of history and tradition, essentially. The king disguised can mingle with his people, searching out their true feelings, as King Edward does in Greene's *George a Greene, the Pinner of Wakefield* (c. 1590). Peele's *Edward I* (c. 1591) features Edward consorting with Robin Hood and Lluellen, the Prince of Wales, leading to a better understanding of honor for the wayward Prince. Kings can disguise for love, as in *Fair Em* (c. 1590) and *The True Chronicles History of King Leir* (c. 1590). And in *The First Part of King Edward IV* by Heywood (c. 1599), Edward first attempts to woo Mistress Shore incognito, then, in meeting John Hobs, tries to find out if his subjects love him or the imprisoned Henry VI.[16] Ballads of the period featured romantic wanderings by kings looking for the unusual and intriguing, but "it was in the drama proper that the idea of the king's personal engagement with his subjects and their problems flowered and was most fully exploited" (Barton 98). Couple this with the appearance of Henry VI in Dekker's *The Shoemaker's Holiday*, undisguised and still able to "mingle freely with his subjects and dispense justice without resorting to disguise," and the place of Arthur in *Holy Grail* becomes particularly interesting. Maurice Keen cements the position of king in relation to his subjects in *The Outlaws of Medieval Legend*:

> They only knew that the King was the ultimate repository of a law
> whose justice they acknowledged, and they saw treason against him
> as a betrayal of their allegiance to God himself. If they could only
> get past his corrupt officers, whose abuse of the trust reposed in
> them amounted to treason in itself, and bring their case before the
> King, they believed that right would be done. Their unshakeable
> faith in the King's own justice was the most tragic of the miscon-
> ceptions of the medieval peasantry, and the ballad-makers and their
> audiences shared it to the full [156].

This axiomatic belief, then, would seem ripe for the upsetting that Python
enacted in their version of English history, and, more specifically, King
Arthur's stature and place in that history.

In *Holy Grail*, Arthur is not in disguise. In fact, he is dressed very
much like a warrior king might or should be dressed. He wears a sun
emblem on his chest and a gold crown on his head, and carries Excalibur,
the magical sword. A servant follows him, as well, carrying all of the king's
necessaries. The iconography is in place, identifying Arthur as at least
kingly, if not king. Arthur not only dresses and carries himself as sovereign, but makes sure everyone he meets knows just who he is: "I am Arthur,
son of Uther Pendragon. King of the Britons, defeater of the Saxons, sovereign of all England!" He is most often greeted with stares and disbelief.
The goal of the disguised Edward and others was to achieve something
their regalia wouldn't normally allow: honesty from the peasantry without the complications of inherent class differences. Arthur, on the other
hand, looks to use his kingly bearing and uniform to recruit to his (soon
to be) divine purpose. Python, treating the king as representing the state,
turns the "king in disguise" convention on its ear and allows the commoners to meet the king at or above his level, where they almost never
recognize his providential authority. Some go so far as to openly deny such
an authority exists in Nature, and can only arise from the will of the people.

As in Renaissance comic history, a certain rapprochement is achieved
between king and commoner, but it is not, as Holderness describes it, the
classic "comic misunderstanding" which complicates the plot; rather it is
the comic *understanding* (and maybe even, at times a willful misunderstanding), the acknowledgment of class differences or, often, the disapproval or complete disavowal of those differences. More often, though,
Arthur's kingship isn't presupposed at all, except to others of his class: the
knights he recruits for his quest. With these knights (Launcelot, Gawain,
etc.) he is preaching to the choir; with the peasantry he is really only separable by his appearance. This appearance is questioned, as well, by Den-

nis (Palin), a peasant who (as illustrated in the previous chapter) takes umbrage at Arthur's announcement of kingship. Dennis's wife (Jones) asks Arthur how he became king without a popular vote:

> DENNIS: Supreme executive power derives from a mandate from the masses not from some farcical aquatic ceremony.
> ARTHUR: Be quiet!
> DENNIS: You can't expect to wield supreme executive power just 'cause some watery tart threw a sword at you!
> ARTHUR: Shut up! [Scene 3].

Announcement of the right to leadership by divine providence, then, is tantamount to declaring one's own insanity. This is a direct assault on the medieval conception of their king's divinity and fair-mindedness, as Keen points out, for as the peasant faces his king, he embodies the hundreds of subsequent years of political advancement and civil rights crafted in both monarchical and non-monarchical societies. The peasant, then, is as much an aberration in 10th-century England as the bewildered king (who obviously subscribes to the medieval tradition). As Arthur passes through a filthy hamlet, one man asks another who these strangers are. The second man responds: "I dunno. Must be a king." The first asks how he can tell. "He hasn't got shit all over him," is the answer. Cleanliness means status in this world, it's an identifiable iconographic symbol, but it doesn't affect the way Arthur is treated. And he's not "the" king, he's just "a" king, as if kings are commonplace and pass through the village on a regular basis. If the Tudor policy involved the cultivation of so-called "positivistic historiography," then Python actively seeks to undercut any notion of this monolithic paradigm as it exists and is propagated in the late 1960s and early 1970s in England (Holderness 18). Holderness agrees with Barton, noting that the curious "motif of the disguised king" does arise from balladeers and commoners agreeing as to the king's essential goodness (when he can be reached through his corrupt officials), and also identifies the reasons why Python can use the motif so effectively as a comedic weapon:

> ... the image of a king humanized, crossing barriers of hierarchy and class to mingle freely with his subjects in mutual affection and concord, seems almost endemic to the ideology of monarchy itself: it has its modern counterpart in that popular curiosity about the lives of the royal family, which mingles a gratified welcome at their revealed humanity with a malicious and cynical contempt at their descending to the level of their own "subjects" [Recycled 17].

Python even names Launcelot's servant/horse "Concord," and Concord's reward for his service to his king is an arrow in the chest and abandonment by Launcelot. Concord is still able, later, to carry the wounded Prince Herbert back into his father's castle, undermining the father's plans for a more politically, socially and financially favorable union between Princess Lucky and Launcelot. On two occasions it is Concord — the servant, the would-be horse — who has to help Launcelot when Launcelot's vocabulary fails him, and tries to save his master from disgrace in a pathetic escape from Swamp Castle. The barriers are nonexistent for the "peasants" Arthur encounters, and it is the monarchy (and state) which suffers when compared to people in general.

As Arthur tries to recruit the lord of the first castle he finds on his quest, he is rebuffed by first one and then two guards who not only remain above him during their inane conversation, but never recognize Arthur as king, peer, or as even remotely intelligent. As he tries to approach a peasant couple working in a bog and convince them that he is their king, he is turned back by these supposed illiterates who spout leftist political doctrines and call into question the divine right of kingship. The French soldiers who occupy a castle in Arthur's England are similarly disrespectful, refusing to acknowledge Arthur's kingship or leave the castle. They eventually kill one of Arthur's train with a catapulted cow. An old woman refuses to reveal the location of a certain shrubbery, even when faced with threats of torture and reprisal ("Do your worst!" she fires back). The enchanter Tim laughs at the assembled knights as they are attacked by a ferocious rabbit; the Knights Who Say "Ni" will not allow their forest to be crossed without a sacrifice (or two); and Camelot, Arthur's home and the supposed birthplace of the quest, "is a silly place" and holds no welcome or respite for Arthur. Lastly, the Black Knight, who guards a very small bridge on a dry stream bed, stands his ground before Arthur, blocking the way to anyone who cannot best him. Arthur orders him to move, in his own name as king of all England, but the Black Knight remains unmoved and seemingly unimpressed. Even after the battle is engaged and the Black Knight eventually loses both arms and legs, he will only concede to a draw. Despite Arthur's status in legend as king, and his own claims to the throne with Excalibur to back him up, he is given virtually no benefit of historical doubt. Python even gives Arthur the backing of God — albeit a cartoon figure in cartoon clouds — but not even Divine Providence can save this king from ignominy.

The "ruling idea of providence" would allow that Arthur — divinely inspired and chosen to rule — rule as a part of the natural order as laid out by Tillyard in his readings of Holinshed and Hall, "the historical narratives of Daniel and *The Mirror for Magistrates*" (Holderness, *Recycled* 26). If, then, in a Morality play it is the state ("Respublica") which can take the position of central figure or even hero, as Tillyard notes, and this "theme of England" is transferred to Renaissance-era histories and drama, then "this providential pattern implicit in the development of a historical process" can be appropriated by Tillyard to find order, and Python to lampoon the state in the figure of Arthur (26). Arthur does represent authority, the mythic "divine right" of kingship, a class structure, and, perhaps most importantly, Holderness asserts that "the indispensable key to political 'order' is the sovereign" (27). What better way, then, to upset that accepted, ingrained political order than to depose, as it were, the king? If the assassination of Richard II set off the inevitable recriminations when the "natural order" was disrupted, as Tillyard details, then poking fun at (and making essentially politically impotent) the representation of authority in Britain might best serve Python's satirical ends. The "king disguised" takes on a new meaning as his kingship isn't recognized even when it is in full display; or perhaps, as Python practices the convention, it can be termed the "king denied," as the power and authority of the state in the late 1960s and early 1970s Great Britain is undermined, sent up, and ultimately denied.

The *Flying Circus* episode 26, "The Queen Will Be Watching," looks at order and the drama in Monty Python's terms. The audience is told, soberly and politely, that the Queen is scheduled to tune into the program at any time, and all are asked to stand when that moment occurs. So a television show built on mayhem and narrative anarchy now appeals for order, and the show proceeds with a regal bearing. Once, during "The Insurance Sketch," it is announced that the Queen has tuned in, and everyone — actors, technicians, and audience — responds by standing respectfully (2.26.36–37). The action then cuts to the actual 'News at Ten' set, where the newsreader stands as the National Anthem begins, and continues reading his news at full attention. This sort of prescribed, forced order is noteworthy in that if the Queen were to actually tune in, she would see not the show as it is normally played, but the show as played for Her Majesty's sensibilities, or Python's version of what the Queen sees as order in her kingdom. Is this the (Monty Python version of the) Saxe-Coburg version of Tudor order? It is an order which is as artificial as it is acknowledged, though its absence sends the episode into a tailspin. Cutting back to the Python set, the level of decorum goes rapidly down from this point, with sketches featuring exploding classical musicians, cannibalism on a lifeboat, and an undertaker's sketch where it's decided to cook and eat a recently deceased woman (2.26.38–44). The audience has been hissing throughout this final sketch, and finally erupts onto the set *en masse*. General confusion reigns for a few moments as we see cameras, technicians, and audience members moving about, when suddenly the National Anthem is heard again. We can assume that the Queen has again tuned in. Everyone comes to attention as the credits roll, and a reverent air brings the show to its conclusion. There is certainly a myth of order here, since it seems clear that when the Queen is not watching mayhem reigns supreme, as when a teacher leaves a classroom. The "providential pattern" noted above by Holderness is here appropriated by Python to actually support the fact that there is a ruling order, this being most evident in the episode's ending, which is not undercut or subverted. This order, it seems, can be skewered and lampooned at times, but Python does not negate its existence by comic deflation. The credits end and there is a fade out, with no further silliness — strikingly anomalous in the Python *oeuvre*. The nod to at least the appearance — for the Queen's sake — of order in all things keeps the Python troupe members as identifiable British subjects, and as such subject to the order either imposed or expected by the state. And as in Elizabeth I's later years, there existed some uneasiness in England throughout the turbulent 1960s as culture, society, and even the government began to change.

Politically, a funny thing seemed to happen in England on the way from a generation of Conservative rule to Labour in the middle of the 1960s. According to Grace Wyndham Goldie, the BBC had just recently begun televising political figures and events more actively, including elections, party political broadcasts and candid (some might say dogged) interviews with candidates (Goldie 262–3). This more focused foray into politics naturally called into question the notion of fairness, and of equal time for both the party in power and the opposition. Without mentioning *Flying Circus* or any of the other well known comedy shows, Goldie notes, however, that the BBC was given a broader latitude in programming — specifically along political or news-type lines — and this newfound freedom eventually paved the way for programs emerging from the Talks Department (and, later, Light Entertainment) like *That Was The Week That Was* (262–4). "TWTWTW might never have got on the air in a different BBC climate," Goldie writes, as political change led to personnel change at the BBC and political satire — based on the continuing success of the Oxbridge revues and West End shows — came into broad popularity (220; Wilmut 1–9). It was designed to be both politically aware and socially conscious, and with just enough careful structuring so that it looked spontaneous (Goldie 222). The show was an immediate success, though it was also immediately labeled as a dangerous leftist, even "Socialist," platform by members of the Conservative Party (225). A search for parity continued, especially as Polling Day 1963 approached (when Sir Alec Douglas-Home would succeed Mr. Macmillan as PM), and the BBC did not want to be seen as simply a party affiliate (265). This broadening of the BBC's programming needs did result in what might be called "fringe" programs like *Flying Circus* being not only considered for airing but actually becoming funded television shows.[17]

In "Filth, Sedition and Blasphemy: The Rise and Fall of Television Satire," Andrew Crisell describes the two general areas of writing that characterized *TWTWTW* in its year-long run:

> [the] "contemporary scene," politics in the broadest sense — the three main parties (but especially the Conservative Government) and individual politicians of all hues; Britain's lingering pretensions to be a world power, whether through nuclear weapons, colonial endeavours or the "special relationship" with America; the church; the judiciary; the class system; and so on. The second common theme, and one which has become an increasing preoccupation of popular satire, was what might be termed "media culture"— parodies of various aspects of newspapers, film, advertising, and notably television itself [152].

Add to this olio a significant obsession with English history and tightly controlled narrative anarchy — and *Flying Circus* comes into focus. Python would eventually mock and send up the conventions of not only the "contemporary scene" and "media culture" (especially television), but would also attack the very conventions of *TWTWTW* and its offspring. By 1969, television history, which by then included David Frost and *TWTWTW*, could be treated as history by Python — treated with the same irreverence as any historical depths they chose to plumb.

Python would go on to raid history in television and film work, and make the necessary historiographical decisions regarding what to use and what to ignore. Arthur finally suffers a rather ignominious defeat as he and his remaining knights are hustled into police vans as they attempt to storm the castle wherein the Holy Grail (supposedly) is kept. The constables are, of course, just the anachronistic touch needed to bring the pretext of historical verisimilitude crashing down as the film ends. Also, the audience is further jolted out of the period by the image of the film strip itself, the plastic nature of the medium exposed — after a constable has put his hand over the camera lens— slipping out of the film gate in the projector. This explicit acknowledgement of the artifice is the impression left on the viewer as the narrative ends. It places the viewer not as an active participant or even unwitting subject, but as just one of many voyeurs sitting in an acknowledged theater watching an acknowledged film. One history (the modern constables) invades another history (Arthur and his siege), and a "kind of history" is made.

But *Monty Python and the Holy Grail* begins, as well, by immediately calling attention to itself as a construction, an artifice; in one moment promulgating a certain history, and at the same time undercutting that history with another. The opening credits begin auspiciously enough, with an appropriately mysterious orchestral score setting the stage, as it were, for the coming performance. These credits have no connection to the historical nature of the film, and might be completely disorienting to an audience not familiar with the convention. Similarly, scene cards may have been used to set the stage for the opening of a performance of *Henry V* (if you believe Laurence Olivier's version of Tudor history), and an Elizabethan viewer would have recognized the card as the introduction that it was intended to be. When the Chorus took to the stage to welcome all and introduce the play, characters, and opening scene, nothing would seem amiss, even as he addressed the audience directly, acknowledging them. This same direct address is borrowed by Python. The integrity of the opening credits (and remember, as accomplished cinema viewers we have been desensitized to such artificial displays as rolling credits accompanying a "realistic" film) is undermined almost immediately as a running sub-title appears, in fractured Swedish, offering a completely unrelated story of "loveli lakes" and various moose. The credits are stopped, and restarted, stopped again, and restarted, and all the while intertitles address the viewer directly. The producers of the film (via intertitles) continually apologize for the difficulties with the credits, and report that the problem is being dealt with. This may seem overtly self-conscious, but remember that in *Henry V*, the Chorus identifies the stage for what it is, and that actors await to tread the "unworthy scaffold" that can't possibly pass for the "vasty fields of France" (3–12). He even reminds the groundlings— who probably need no reminding on this point — that they stand in the "cockpit," and not Agincourt (11–14). Suspension of disbelief was just as important to Elizabethans as it is for the modern film viewer. But it is just this willing suspension that is so often undercut by Shakespeare and Python, as if the audience needs to be poked every so often, and reminded that what they are watching is a construction.

With the credits passed, the title "A.D. 932" appears, and the mood is set again for a historical text. There is a fade up to a gray, cold English morning, and the sound of wind and an approaching horse. A desiccated body lays atop a high pole, and the legendary barbarism of the dark ages is suddenly realized. The horse gets closer, and closer, still hidden behind a low hill. A knight rides into view, with crown and regalia, and the picture is complete. We are transported to this historical place, and it becomes real. The moment is just as abruptly undercut as we see that instead of riding a horse, the knight is trotting on his own two legs, and being followed by a manservant who bangs two halves of a coconut together. The knight is even pretending to ride a horse. I mentioned that the ghost of Falstaff haunts *Henry V*, and his legacy can be seen in Monty Python. Here as Arthur pretends to ride, the voice of the Chorus can almost be heard: "Think, when we talk of horses, that you see them, / Printing their proud hoofs i'th' receiving earth" (26–27). Shakespeare doesn't resort to banging coconuts together, but the call for illusion is essential. This is not real. The coconuts don't belong, in a geographic or historic sense, and attention is drawn to the film as a constructed, comedic representation. Similarly, the Chorus asks the audience to imagine horses, great armies, and towering castles where there are none, and the artifice of the stage is acknowledged. This kind of visual and verbal incongruity is central to Python's historical episodes. In *Life of Brian*, which is set in the time of Christ, a spaceship carrying aliens accidentally picks up Brian for a while, and the narrative is put on hold until the ship crashes. In the *Flying Circus* episode entitled "Whither Canada?" a mannequin meant to look like Admiral Horatio Nelson (1758–1805) "leaps" from a high window in a modern office tower, yelling "Kiss me, Hardy!" (Chapman, et al. 1.1.1). Nelson, of course, died at the Battle of Trafalgar in 1805, not in 1969 London. This celebrity death is a part of the television program *It's Wolfgang Amadeus Mozart*, hosted by the eighteenth-century composer (discussed in Chapter 2). These visual incongruities (the latter being an anachronism, as well) tend to violate the unity of dramatic space and time, wrenching the viewer out of the past, forcing the viewer to be aware of the artificiality of the text. Later the quest is temporarily halted as Arthur and the two castle guards (mentioned above) argue about coconuts, Mercia, climatic zones, and swallows. This entire conversation, by its very nature, doesn't belong in a tale of Arthur searching for the Holy Grail. It doesn't belong, which is precisely why it is there. This is a disruption that, as I mentioned above, serves to keep the narrative running smoothly—or in an expected manner—for the viewer who is aware of history as Monty Python creates it. Though often not visual, this undercutting or self-awareness can be found in Shakespeare's work, as well. There are many references, for instance, to acting and actors, including Buckingham's speech in *Richard III*:

> Tut, I can counterfeit the deep tragedian,
> Tremble and start at wagging of a straw,
> Speak, and look back, and pry on every side,
> Intending deep suspicion; ghastly looks
> Are at my service, like enforced smiles,

> And both are ready in their offices
> At any time to grace my stratagems [3.5.5–11].

No coconuts or aliens here, but certainly a self-reflexive moment that the audience would share, reminding them that the people who prowled the stage before them were, in fact, actors.

In *The Writing of History* Michel de Certeau argues that the mere act of writing itself produces history (Bergeron 215). Certeau "suggests that writing is an archive that makes possible the creation of a stable history" (215). If this is the case, then both Shakespeare and Python threaten their histories as they undercut, whether aurally or visually, the illusion of a seamless narrative. For Shakespeare, this can be dangerous, as his purpose of creating a stable history for a moral lesson is jeopardized. Falstaff was one such threat, and he was done away with. Python, on the other hand, seeks to create no stable history, but to set up and then shoot down various histories, like ducks in a gallery. Python may have created, however, a cultural history—or a history that is tainted and informed by Pythonisms. For different purposes Shakespeare did the same thing. They both created histories: Shakespeare, it seems, for the purposes of entertainment and perhaps national identity; Python, certainly, to disrupt any notion of monolithic power structure, but, strangely enough, creating a certain nationalism in that the Python members were famous, they were admired, and they were Englishmen. Michael Palin describes

> England as a middle-aged country relying on postwar respectability
> and the conventional, conformist way of looking at things. The
> power of the army, church and major institutions was unchal-
> lenged, but they became unsure of themselves in this period [the
> 1950s and '60s], and these breakthroughs started the ball rolling.
> Satire's always been at its healthiest when there's a Conservative
> government, because they rely on stuffy, pedantic and pompous
> establishment targets to tilt at [Rubenstein 6].

So Python was not attempting to shore up what it saw as an unstable government, relying instead on humor to poke at the humorless. The Pythons laid bare the artifice of their medium as they pointed out the foibles of national government in historical terms. To remind an audience that they are watching a play sounds modern and Brechtian, but is evident in many of Shakespeare's works, as well. That he let Falstaff run around so long as an ahistorical construct testifies both to the power of the character and the confidence Shakespeare had in his ability as a writer to overcome any disruption.

Monty Python felt this same confidence, and even depended upon the disruption to keep the narrative together, albeit in an oxymoronic sort of way. Shakespeare depended upon his own literary history for cohesion in both history and characterization. The "Gad's Hill robbery" conversation mentioned above between Prince Hal and Falstaff was not one based in national history, but relied on the viewer's knowledge of Shakespeare's previous plays, specifically *1 Henry IV*. This allusion might have been lost on the viewer who missed the previous play, as it operates as something of an "insider's allusion." The viewer who remembered would have nodded as he or she cast back to complete the allusion. Bergeron writes that "Shakespeare joins the links between history and fiction by reproducing his fictionalized versions of national history from earlier dramas. History therefore, and explicitly here [in the Gad's Hill reference], contains a fiction" (237). Bergeron calls these insider allusions "intertextual constructs" (237), which can be found operating in *Holy Grail*, as well.

As Sir Bedivere (Jones) uses science to determine whether an unfortunate young woman (Connie Booth) is a witch, she and a duck are weighed simultaneously. For a moment she outweighs the duck (meaning she is not a witch), but then the scales return to an equilibrium, and she is pronounced a witch. At that moment we are given a close up of the young woman, and she speaks directly to the camera: "That's a fair cop." As mentioned above, this phrase is a quote from a number of *Flying Circus* episodes (and drawn from the vernacular of British culture), including episode 29, "The Money Programme" (2.29.80). The indication here is that since this text is set in the Middle Ages, the intertextual construct connects the television episode, which was created chronologically earlier, to the film version, as if the phrase had its beginnings in A.D. 932.[18]

Similarly, Monty Python's presentation of history is consistent with their previous television work — including anachronisms and visual and verbal incongruities — and they use that history to support and create these new histories. Their historical episodes, whether in the feature films or television shows, always undercut at some point the history that is being presented. Attila the Hun "sweeps mercilessly across Central Europe," then stars in his own sitcom (1.20.264); Dennis Moore rides through the land robbing travelers not of their money, but of their lupins (2.37.195); Cardinal Richelieu appears, flowing robes and all, as a character witness in traffic court (1.3.29); Beethoven argues with a mynah bird (1.21.289), and on and on. There is a point where the Monty Python writers are obviously aware of the history they are making — full of gaps and breaks, anachronisms and incongruities — for in episode 11 a distinguished history professor (Chapman) attempts to narrate a serious film about the Black Death. His narration about the history of the plague is constantly interrupted by undertakers, he warns the camera (the tyrannical narrative, actually) to behave and stay focused on him, and when it doesn't he finally gets up to leave in a huff. The camera lens begins to zoom after him, to follow. As he goes, though, he tells the documentary team behind the camera: "And don't zoom in on me, no I'm off, I'm off" (1.11.137). In that brief moment the artifice of the camera has been acknowledged, the action of the camera (to zoom) has been predicted and denied, the audience made self-aware, and the relating of a history has been abrogated by disruption. The film is then finished by the undertakers, who create their own version of history. This fictionalized history is consistent from television show to television show, and then from television show to film.

This last motif— the learned professor cut off— even appears in *Holy Grail*. A subtitled "a Famous Historian" lectures to a fixed camera/audience (us) about Arthur and his knights on their perilous quest. The historian can be likened to the Chorus in *Henry V* as he fills in the dramatic or historic gaps, and comments upon the unfolding of history in a narrative form. Bergeron writes that "constructing history underscores its fictional quality" (232). Nowhere is this underscoring more evident than in this scene. The Famous Historian, commenting on what we have just seen within the narrative, is only allowed to speak for a few moments before a knight on horseback (it could be anyone) rides through the scene and with sword hacks the historian down. It is as if Monty Python is denying the staid facts and dates of traditional history and, by actually killing the historian, lays to rest any preconceived notions the audience may have regarding historical verisimilitude. In *Henry V* Shakespeare denies the tyranny of history by having the Archbishop of Canterbury assert that David II of Scotland was not only captured by the English, but taken to France as prisoner (1.2.160–62). Evans points out that though David II was captured by the English he was never taken to France (939n). The added insult was intended by Shakespeare as a furtherance of the anti–French sentiment necessary to the plot of *Henry V*.

In the Famous Historian instance here we have an intrusion of a different time (the modern professor) into what we had thought were the Middle Ages, but might now actually just be a re-creation. Another intrusion occurs as the knight is somehow able to cross the span of time between the past and present, across history, and kill the historian. It is unclear at this point whether the historian is trespassing in the knight's narrative, or vice versa. Yet another distinct intrusion in this scene is the presence of an actual horse, since up to this point and even after, to the end of the film, Arthur and his knights are horseless. There seems to be a contradiction here, a clash between worlds. The historian would be narrating, ideally, an Arthurian saga complete with actual horses, not coconut-clapping servants, so it is as if his own historical re-creation has ridden across the screen to destroy him. Just as the historian is separated from the world of the narrated film by implied time and space, the horsed knight is also anomalous, and is as separate from the world of the film as it is being enacted as is the historian who attempts to narrate that action. The historian's attempts are overrun by representations of the very historical verisimilitude he is offering. History will now proceed, or be created, by those who have been participating; or more precisely, those who have been narrated. The rogue knight here is much like Bergeron's description of the character Falstaff in that he seems "impossible to pin down and possessing elusive, ahistorical qualities: a fiction that threatens the making of history" (241). He was certainly a threat to the Famous Historian.

The film began as a historical tale, and was interrupted by the school film narration provided by the historian; in essence, there existed a tension between authors of that history, and the fictional characters took over. The question also remains as to which is the tale being told. Have we been watching a self-sufficient movie about Arthur and his quest, or have we been watching a film as created and controlled by the Famous Historian, and we are only now being made aware of this exerted influence? And once the Famous Historian is dead, whose narration are we seeing? The policemen who arrive to investigate the historian's death are able to cross between filmed worlds—from the educational film to the events being narrated in that film — eventually bringing all narrative sequences to an abrupt halt. If this is Arthur's narrative, however, then his forces have violently repelled a narrative intrusion; if this is the Famous Historian's narrative, then his creation has attempted to shrug off his narrative influence and make the narrative their own.

The opening scenes of *2 Henry IV* exhibit this struggle between competing histories, as Lord Bardolph brings "certain news" of the death of Prince Harry at Shrewsbury (1.1.12). This news is history until it is displaced by another, more reliable history not dependent upon hearsay. Louis Mink writes that "historical narratives are capable of displacing each other"— this fact is clear in *2 Henry IV* as narratives compete for acceptability, and in Python's work where the competing narratives are so forceful that they almost seem to take on lives of their own. One history is offered, then displaced by another, and another, and another until the text's position within history is constantly in question. Graham Holderness writes of the difference between Shakespeare as "the author" and "'Shakespeare,' the inferred author; a volatile, flexible, changing construction, engendered, and constantly reborn and rewritten, by the plays"

(*Recycled* 16). Falstaff walked the line between narrative history and narrative fiction; in the Famous Historian scene of *Holy Grail*, history itself is rewritten by the players.

With the players having some agency in the making of history, Falstaff's influence on *Henry V*—the play in which he is only discussed—can be broached. Bergeron defines Falstaff as "ahistorical," a fictional character in an attempt at historical verisimilitude who threatens the making of Shakespeare's history by his mere presence. Falstaff is dead by the writing of *Henry V*, and Shakespeare may have thought he was rid of this character who blurred the line between narrative history and narrative fiction. But as Shakespeare was fond of meddling or prophetic ghosts wandering through his plays, *Henry V* is steeped in the spirit of Falstaff. For reasons unexplained by Shakespeare, the Chorus takes the stage to set the stage, but does so in an unusual manner. He asks pardon for the unworthiness of the stage and performance, he reminds the audience that they are watching a play, he apologizes for staging battle scenes with only a few men (which are never staged anyway), and for telescoping time. For these things—bits of dramatic action that he has been performing for years prior to *Henry V*—he now apologizes, and asks that they be overlooked as necessary limitations of the stage. The playwright Shakespeare's lamentations through the Chorus continue: "Linger your patience on…" (2.0.31); and, "the scene / Is now transported, gentles…" (2.0.34–35); "We'll not offend one stomach with our play…" (2.0.40); "Suppose that you have seen…" (3.0.3); "Play with your fancies…" (3.0.7); "Grapple your minds to…" (3.0.18); "Work, work your thoughts…" (3.0.25); and, finally: "Still be kind, / And eke out our performance with your mind" (3.0.34–35). In *Henry V*, Shakespeare (through the Chorus) supposes a willing suspension of disbelief on the audience's part during the somewhat crude presentation of this history:

> Thus far with rough and all-unable pen
> Our bending author hath pursued the story,
> In little room confining mighty men,
> Mangling by starts the full course of their glory [Epilogue 1–4].

It seems apparent that the specter of Falstaff—the character out of history who drew attention to the artifice of the production of history—made Shakespeare extremely self-conscious of the limitations of the stage in recreating or reproducing historical episodes. The "full course of their glory" is the vast history that surrounded Henry and his countrymen, a history mangled, truly, as Shakespeare constantly reminded the audience of its shortcomings. That which he had taken for granted in past productions—

suspension of disbelief, imagination, illusion — he was now apologizing for. So as he strove to create a more believable history by giving all sorts of stage direction and setting details to the Chorus— in other words, fore-grounding the narrative history — he was simultaneously undermining the narrative fiction by consistently bringing its fictional nature, its artifice, to the audience. In attempting to make a truer history by shuffling off Fal-staff, Shakespeare threatened the history he was trying to make; this was a noble English history that might remind the people of London of their heritage, and smooth the way for a clear succession. What remains a strange turn of events in Shakespeare's work, however, became Monty Python's *metier*.

The whisper-thin veil between the past, present and future in Monty Python allows for a fluidity of narrative unhindered by normally pre-scribed boundaries. This freedom allows elements from times past or still to come to invade a Python sketch, often without any remark from the sketch's characters. In episode 28, just following the "fish-slapping" sketch, a Chinese fish — which has just swallowed a British fish which has just swallowed a Nazi fish — takes a bite from the bottom of a luxury liner, and the ship begins to sink in a great storm. As it sinks, the captain addresses the passengers, reciting the well-known "women and children first" maxim, just as he and some of his crew are dressing up as women and chil-dren. Other members of the crew enter the bridge dressed variously as "red indians," "spacemen," and a Flemish merchant, since the women and children disguises are all gone. The captain (Jones) must update his list as they appear, of course.

> CAPT: All right! All right! (*into the PA*) this is your captain speaking... Do not rush for the lifeboats ... women, children, Red Indians, spacemen (*stock film of long shot of sinking vessel, the voice over fading*) and a sort of idealized version of complete Renaissance Men first! [Chapman, et al. 2.28.70–71].

What is apparent from this short section are the transgressions of time and space Python employs as authority is lampooned, time-honored tra-ditions ("women and children first!") are sent-up, and an ever-present is created as characters from various historical eras appear on the stage, are acknowledged, and interact. In *Shakespeare Recycled* Holderness notes that "Tillyard, Wilson Knight and Dover Wilson all found in Shakespeare's his-tory plays a ruling ideology of order *because that is what they wanted to find*" (22; emphasis added). These scholars' view of the need for order in their own England became realized in their ordering of Shakespeare's his-tory plays. As Michael Palin points out, the very orderliness of the Conservative government of Monty Python's time seemed the ideal windmill at which to tilt, and Python's historiography reflects their attempt at disorderliness. Python found in Shakespeare and British history the chinks of disorder they wanted to find. In *Monty Python's Meaning of Life*, while hundreds of British soldiers are being massacred in the Zulu wars, the officer class worries about sleep disturbed by mosquitoes and the uncleanliness brought on by the war around them. The veneer of order, however, remains intact as the officers never fully admit that there is a war, much less a war they are losing badly. It even takes the officers a good deal of time and convincing that one of their own has lost a leg, though his leg is obviously missing. These kinds of aberrations, the chinks in the myth of Tudor order (and, by association, all British governmental rule) allow for the orderly conventions of a generic history to be parodied.

One final, marvelous example of Monty Python's skill at straddling the line between narrative fiction and narrative history is the "Tudor Job Agency" sketch from episode 36. One characteristic of Python writing (for their television series, especially) is the use of leitmotifs that run throughout the episode, undergoing changes occasionally, but always resurfacing in a later sketch. The "Spanish Inquisition" segments of episode 15, for instance, reappear within that episode anytime anyone says "I didn't expect a kind of Spanish Inquisition" (1.15.192). But the intertwining of narratives, both history and fiction, and the competition between these narratives—as Bergeron illustrated to some extent in his reading of *2 Henry IV*—become meticulous and readily apparent in Python's "The Tudor Job Agency" sketch.

In episode 36 a customer (Chapman) enters the Tudor Job Agency, which is decorated in Tudor style, and the man inside (Jones) is dressed in Tudor dress. Since the demarcation between the past and present can be so tenuous in Monty Python texts, the question of time must be constantly addressed. The outside of the shop is relatively modern, but the inside is Tudor: have we crossed time as the customer crossed the threshold? Or is this an elaborate façade with its true purpose waiting to be discovered? At first the man at the desk insists they are hiring for Tudor jobs only ("traders," "vittlers," "master joiners"), but then admits that they haven't placed anyone since 1625 (2.36.180). Now it appears that the job agency might merely be a front, and that the assistant has been reciting memorized lines as cover. But the assistant doesn't fall out of character; he is still a Tudor, but no one either has or wants Tudor jobs. If the façade were going to be put aside, then this seems the natural place for it—a moment of deflation of the Tudor story. As they continue, though, we will see that the cover isn't nearly as easy an explanation as it first appears:

ASST: Then came James the First and the bottom fell out of Tudor jobs. 1603 — 800 vacancies filled, 1604 — 40, 1605 — none, 1606 — none. The rest of the Stuart period nothing. Hanoverians nothing. Victorians nothing. Saxe-Coburgs nothing. Windsors ... what did you want?

CUST: Dirty books, please.

ASST: Right. (*Produces selection of mags from under the counter*) Sorry about the Tudor bit, but you can't be too careful, you know [2.36.180].

The invisible line between past and present has been reaffirmed as the job agency's true nature is revealed. Again, this would be a very clean explanation if the writers had left well enough alone. But after the customer asks for material which is more graphic, the assistant calls out to "My Lord Warwick" and asks for the drawbridge to be raised that Gloucester's troops might enter (2.36.181). The wall of the Tudor shop slides open to reveal a "dirty bookshop" back room, where several trench-coated customers browse. The second assistant is also clad in Tudor dress. A man (Palin) enters the back room dressed in Tudor gear:

GASK: All right. This is a raid. My name is Superintendent Gaskell and this is Sergeant Maddox.

2ND ASST: Ah! Sir Philip Sidney. 'Tis good to see thee on these shores again.

GASK: Shut up.

2ND ASST: Your suit is fair and goodly cut. Was't from Antwerp? [2.36.181].

Here we are drawn back into the Tudor timeline, with the second assistant picking up where the first left off. Gaskell, however, is in Tudor dress, and no one will believe that he is not Sir Philip Sidney. Sidney is, of course, a historical figure conversing here with literary characters, just as Prince Harry interacted with Falstaff, another literary creation. Whether Gaskell is actually Sidney isn't important — for the remainder of the episode he *is* Sir Philip Sidney. He is either acting the part, which is quite possible, or we have crossed the fringes of time again and are back in Tudor times. As he leaves the back room he is suddenly in a lush countryside — a Tudor countryside, as it turns out. He has left whatever vestiges of time he thought he knew and is actually Sir Philip Sidney. But even this immersion in the late sixteenth century is undercut, as Sidney fights the Spanish not for their gold, but to impound their dirty books:

VOICE OVER: The battle raged long and hard, but as night fell Sidney overcame the Spaniards. 6,000 copies of "Tits and Bums" and 4,000 copies of "Shower Sheila" were seized that day. The tide of Spanish porn was stemmed. Sir Philip Sidney returned to London in triumph [2.36.182].

Again, the making of history is difficult when a character like Falstaff is present; a character who doesn't have to conform to the rules of historical veracity. In Monty Python's work, this notion of the Falstaffian element can be extended to the constant subversions of history, and the completely unreliable line between the past and present, or between narrative fiction and narrative history. Historically, Sir Philip Sidney did fight the Spanish, and he was also a Tudor gentleman, scholar, poet, and courtier.[19] Python shaped a new history for and with Sidney, and that history was displaced by another, and another later in the episode.

Both Shakespeare and Monty Python made history out of the archives they inherited. Shakespeare may have been attempting a national history, or a history that would both point out significant events of the past and apply those events as lessons for the present and future. He freely adapted these histories, shaping them to suit his own dramatic purposes. And as Jonathan Hart indicates, just when other writers of Shakespeare's time (Camden, Stow, and Bacon) are "shifting away from rhetoric and myth toward scientific inquiry," Shakespeare is reinforcing his control and mastery of "history":

> Although Shakespeare's history plays are not scientific, they use
> their medium to represent history with great effect. The plays make
> an innovative use of sources, give a complex shape to history other
> than a simple linear chronological structure, focus on what are seen
> as primary problems while avoiding verbiage and extraneous detail,
> and help create a dramatic form that increases popular interest in
> history. Shakespeare brings to history a powerful historical imagi-
> nation [211].

Python accessed history, as well, but as Michael Palin mentions: "...it [history] was a terrific liberation to go back to the past. We wanted to put across the comedy in the re-creation of an interesting historic period" (Rubenstein 7). Python took history and shaped it to their comedic purposes, creating yet another literary history. Palin admits that they relied on the rigidly conservative government for much of their humor; instead of calling for a calming or a smooth royal succession, as Shakespeare had, they tilted at the "conventional, conformist" way of English life (6).

Both Shakespeare and Monty Python culled their own archives— quoted themselves— as they created histories. Shakespeare created a literary history, then cited that history in subsequent plays, further validating it as history. Python used their own history to connect characters and events which may have spanned time, often violating time. Both were able to create for the stage out of "ahistorical imagination," or use the Falstaff character and influence as a way to overcome the rigid confinement of history, and as a way ⸰f bringing narrative history and narrative fiction together. Even after his death, the Falstaff character continued to influence the sense of artifice and self-awareness of *Henry V*, while laying the groundwork for almost all of Python's "displacing" humor. It seems that Shakespeare and Monty Python used, not abused, history to create history. Python read the National Poet Shakespeare, adopting and adapting his creative historicity. Bergeron notes that "the dramatist dismembers history in order to *re*-member it" (233). And whether the subject is the elusive Falstaff or Sir Philip Sidney, Police Inspector, the histories that are made become memorable.

Notes

1. See the tavern scene, just after the robbers have been robbed, in *1 Henry IV* 2.5.233–34 of *The Oxford Shakespeare* (or 2.4.229–230 in *The Riverside Shakespeare*). For perhaps obvious reasons, both texts will be used to illustrate commonalities and differences throughout.

2. Rollins and Baker note Warner's *Albion's England* as well as *Piers Gaveston, Cromwell, Mortimeriados* and *Heroical Epistles* by Drayton and Daniel's *Complaint of Rosamond* and *Civil Wars* as just a few of the many Tudor quasi-historical works that would have been available to Shakespeare and his contemporaries.

3. It should be noted that by 1612 Drayton's slavish attention to Tudor historicity was the essential end of such practices, and following historians would turn a more penetrating eye on the bricolage of these quasi-historical compilations. See Rollins and Baker.

4. The possibility of Shakespeare's history plays noticeably emerging with the post–Armada nationalism is given support by Felicia Londre in her article "Elizabethan Views of the 'Other': French, Spanish, and Russians in *Love's Labor's Lost*." She dates the play from 1578, and the sympathetic treatments of Braggart must, she argues, survive from the earliest version. Braggart's name change (to, appropriately enough, Armado) and his "more ridiculous attributes ... may well have been added after the 1588 defeat of the Armada, at which time his name would have been changed from Braggart to Armado" (10). Londre's dating of the play seems suspect, at best, but doesn't conflict with the possibilities of adaptation and post–Armada fervor. NB: Londre's accompanying view that Shake-speare is actually Edward De Vere, 17th Earl of Oxford *isn't* appropriated or promulgated in my study. See Felicia Londre's "Elizabethan Views of the 'Other'" in *The Elizabethan Review* 3.1 (1995): 3–20.

5. Quoted from comments received by the author from William Proctor Williams, 1 April 2000.

6. For a much-expanded treatment of Sir John Oldcastle see Ellison's *Oldcastle: The Man and the Legend* found on the Internet at Exeter University's web page, http://www.ex.ac.uk/~PEllison/revels/oldc/contents.html. This page allows for access to the complete text of *The Oldcastle Controversy* (including plays, appendices, etc.). Al o, see W.T. Waugh's "Sir John Oldcastle" in *English Historical Review* 20 (1905): 434–456, 637–658.

7. In working on a separate chapter I found it necessary to access another electronic version of Shakespeare's works, this time at www.litrix.com, a so-called "quiet reader's library" of Shakespeare. In *Hamlet* (2.2.168–219) at this site I was somewhat amazed to find no less than forty-eight textual differences between this electronic edition and the printed *Riverside* edition. The common changes—commas, apostrophes, etc.—were there, of course, but "good kissing carrion" became "god kissing carrion" in the electronic text; "but as your daughter may conceive" somehow became "but *not* as your daughter may conceive" (emphasis added); and "any thing that I will *not* more willingly part" is electronically rendered as "any thing that I will more willingly part" (emphasis added). Hamlet's entrance is also moved from before the Queen's final line in the scene to after she and the King exit. The source for this electronic edition of *Hamlet* is unknown by the site's webmaster, but it is almost certainly Q1.

Electronic versions of and links to Shakespeare's works can be found at these websites: http://www.ludweb.com/poetry/sonnets/links.html (an MIT page) and http://wiretap.spies.com:80/ftp.items/Library/Classic/Shakespeare/ (the Moby site), among many other (linked) sites. The Internet is teeming with such sites and links, with, perhaps, the same textual "norms" being carried over from site to site. The MIT page featured more than one spelling error ("television"), which seems to be the bane of even the most respected sites. Copy editing may be low on the list of electronic media priorities.

8. See Stanley Wells' and Gary Taylor's *The Complete Oxford Shakespeare* (Oxford: Oxford UP, 1987). For more complete accounts of the conditions of all extant Shakespeare manuscripts see the notes in Evans' *Riverside* and Wells' and Taylor's *Oxford*.

9. There are many texts which list those historical plays contemporary with Shakespeare, but Marie Axton's *The Queen's Two Bodies* (London: Royal Historical Society, 1977) is particularly interesting in that she focuses on the Inns of Court entertainments prior to and during Elizabeth's rule.

10. See Anne Barton's *Shakespeare and the Idea of the Play*, as well as Chapter 3 of this study, for more on Shakespeare's use of theatricality.

11. It is important to note here that Falstaff is the only major ahistorical character in all of Shakespeare's history plays, and that he was originally based on the Protestant martyr Sir John Oldcastle. Complaints from Lord Cobham (for several months Elizabeth's Lord Chamberlain), a direct descendant of Oldcastle, probably prompted the change from Oldcastle to Falstaff. Wells and Taylor note that even after the change in 1596, the name "Oldcastle" may have been used, occasionally, on stage. See Wells and Taylor, 261. In my own opinion, the change from Falstaff to Oldcastle is an unfortunate caprice based on little more than Wells' and Taylor's admission: "Our edition restores Sir John's original surname for the first time in printed texts…" (Wells and Taylor 263). The key words may be "our edition," which function proprietarily to not only prove ownership of this redeemed text (and Shakespeare, by implication) but to put the stamp of originality on the edition. If nothing else, they may have created a collector's item.

12. For a complete listing of Python films and television appearances, see Wilmut. Python also released books, songbooks, record albums, etc.

13. Though far from absolute, it is generally assumed that the historical Arthur was born *c.* A.D. 465, and may have gained fame with military victories over Germans. Histories today continue to offer conflicting interpretations of

extant historical records, some giving credence to Arthur as military leader, others dismissing him completely. The Arthurian timeline at www.britannica.com is most helpful.

14. The Pythons have cited *The Goon Show* (both on radio and later television (1948 and beyond)) as their major influence, along with other British comedy shows like *The Last Laugh* (1959) and *Beyond the Fringe* (1960), the constructed artificiality of *That Was The Week That Was* (1962–65), satiric journals like *Private Eye* (1962), and the overall work of men like Spike Milligan, Alan Bennett, Peter Sellers, Peter Cook and Dudley Moore, and even David Frost. The various university revues (at Oxford and Cambridge) also played large roles in paving the way for Monty Python. None of these shows, however, relied so heavily and consistently on history (including *Fringe*, which took on Shakespeare and the Second World War, for instance), and especially British and English history. A show modeled after the success of Python and created in America in 1975, *Saturday Night Live*, also only dabbled in history, and almost never in American history. For a more complete review of the (televised) subject see Roger Wilmut's *From Fringe to Flying Circus* (London: Methuen, 1987). See "Pass Notes No. 1616" in *The Guardian* (17 April 2000) for a thumbnail sketch of the history of the journal *Private Eye*, which is still being published fortnightly as of April 2000.

15. Historically this king would have been Henry VI, though, as Rabkin points out, the king as a mingler amongst the common folk was probably modeled more on Henry V. See Fraser and Rabkin, 483n.

16. Anne Barton discusses these plays and their place in Renaissance drama in interesting detail and more completely in "The King Disguised: Shakespeare's *Henry V* and the Comical History" found in *The Triple Bond: Plays, Mainly Shakespearean, in Performance*, edited by Joseph G. Price (University Park and London: Pennsylvania State UP, 1975): 92–117.

17. Python would later satirize party political broadcasts in episodes 32 and 38. In episode 32, the Conservative party representative dances as he recites his party's recent successes, and in episode 38, the party political broadcast is actually a children's bedtime story about rabbits. See Chapman, et al. 2.32.128 and 2.38.211.

18. The *OED* indicates the phrase "It's a fair cop" first appeared in print in 1891. See the 2nd edition, 1989.

19. Sidney was also, interestingly, more than a little taken with the physical attributes of his fancy, Penelope Rich, so much so that some recent criticism of his *Astrophil and Stella* sonnet sequence purports to reveal a man corporeally obsessed. Paul Allen Miller argues that rather than the announced Petrarchan tradition of chaste love from afar, Sidney just as often embraces the Ovidian fascination with body parts and sexuality (see Miller's "Sidney, Petrarch and Ovid, or Imitation as Subversion"). This attraction to the body is a noteworthy element as the specter of Python's Sidney as a fighter *against* pornography — or the objectification of the female body — is presented in the Python sketch. Miller sees Sidney's approach as descriptive of Bakhtin's later "phenomenon of 'grotesque degradation,'" or the "bringing down" of both the object of affection/obsession and the objectifier. So is Python appropriating Sidney the respected public figure, the gentleman who lives up to his station and waxes Petrarchan in writing? This Sidney would naturally, rightfully, be against the practice. Or is this the more licentious, Ovidian Sidney who lusts where he cannot love and describes in what must have

been considered at least mildly pornographic detail ("her belly," her "Cupid's hill," her "spotless mine," and "her thighs") the object of his unfulfilled carnal desire for a married woman? For the well-read Pythons, the more "earthy" Sidney must have been at least unconsciously appreciated, and the irony of Sidney the porn fighter then becomes possible.

Chapter 4

"I Pray You Lend Me Your Dwarf": Structures of Humor

This epigraph is found in Ben Jonson's biting satirical play *Volpone*, and is uttered in the context of Lady Politic's attempts to discover her husband's infidelities with a certain "cunning courtesan of Venice" (3.2.185). The moment is ridiculous enough as the schemer Volpone's manservant (his "parasite") Mosca sends Lady Politic out with the "quick fiction" after her philandering husband, her own perfidies convincing her that her husband must be untrue, as well. With all of the betrayals, subterfuges, plotting and conniving detailed by Jonson and affixed to these foolish, eminently gullible characters, the casual remark regarding the lending of a dwarf is almost lost in a sea of humors. But it remains a terrific visual. One of the cardinal problems that must be faced when confronting works of humor is the very breadth and depth of the various terms used to define humor — a sort of "missing the forest for the trees" situation which is well illustrated by Jonson in *Volpone* and *BF*, among others, and is ultimately apparent in Monty Python's farrago of converging comedies centuries later. Saul Steinberg writes that "trying to define humor is one of the definitions of humor" (Gutwirth 1). And since Monty Python — unlike Shakespeare, Marlowe, Jonson, et al. — cannot be approached but for the troupe's comedic take on life, working definitions of the structures of humor become essential.

There exist literally hundreds of theorists and texts with an equal number of theories that explain, delimit, categorize, codify, and finally define — or attempt to define — for example, satire, parody, the parodic satire, the mock epic and mock heroic, the lampoon, and the myriad derivations thereof. Scott Blanchard cites Pierre Pithou, who once satirized those who would attempt to "vainly" categorize satire — in this case, Menippean satire — saying that Pithou criticized "the human compulsion to impose well-defined boundaries upon our aesthetic experiences" (11). One of the principal joys, though, of dealing with humor is that the forms are so varied and malleable that categorizing becomes a target shoot where the target is free to move at will. Classify the comic ineptitude of Dogberry in Shakespeare's *Much Ado About Nothing*, the loquacious lawyer in Webster's *The White Devil*, the ribald wordplay of Doll, Face, and Subtle in Jonson's *The Alchemist*, or a discussion about customs regulations and restrictions with a lizard, duck, and cat in a *Flying Circus* episode. The comedy debt that Monty Python owes to Shakespeare, Jonson, Marlowe, Dekker and others of the English Renaissance stage is, however, very real and identifiable.

As has been treated previously, Shakespeare's disregard of the unities, his rather creative use of history, and his reliance on historical anachronisms and use of the character of Falstaff as a metahistorical figure are anomalies which can be found in variant forms in Python's television and feature film plays. Ben Jonson's scathing attacks on religion and the corrupt and corruptible, his treatment of fair-goers in *BF*, and his precise and often scatological or grotesque wordplay are echoed in Python's work, as well. Even the general silliness but effectiveness of a Dogberry or an inanely-accented Francischina or Katherine all stand as examples of the humor that eventually found its way to the twentieth-century (television) stage and Monty Python. The utilization of the professional troupe, with characters written-to-type for particular actors, as found with Shakespeare and the King's Men has also been broached. A healthy chunk of work remains in regard to the fascinating use of men to play female parts, as well as the treatment of females and female characters and the specter of effeminization and homosexuality in both Shakespeare and Python. These will be addressed in detail in Chapter 5.

In this chapter we will explore specific comedic structures in several examples of English Renaissance drama and as they are later manifested in Monty Python's television shows and feature films. The emphasis of the work will be on Thomas Dekker's *Shoemaker's Holiday* and Python, with support and examples from pertinent Elizabethan drama brought in when applicable. Specifically, the Monty Python troupe's utilization of satire and parody, the grotesque and carnival, and minute derivations of and constant overlappings within these areas will comprise the work. The theatrical or presentational aspects of humor have been approached in Chapter 2, and will be expanded below. But, first, a set of useful definitions.

M. H. Abrams provides some serviceable direction, broadly calling satire "the literary art of diminishing a subject by making it ridiculous and evoking towards it attitudes of amusement, contempt, indignation, or scorn" (167). He identifies formal or direct satire, including the works of Horace and Juvenal, and indirect satire, which includes the Menippean tradition as well as many other works and writers, from Ben Jonson and *The Alchemist* to T. S. Eliot and *The Waste Land* (168–69). The "satiric voice speaks out in first person" to the reader or to one in the text known as the "adversarius" in formal satire. (168). Pope exemplifies these traits in his *Moral Essay* and "Epistle to Dr. Arbuthnot," respectively (168). In *Arbuthnot* Pope sets his sights on those publishers and critics who have been particularly nettlesome: "Many will know their own Pictures in it, there being not a Circumstance but what is true; but I have, for the most part spar'd their Names, and they may escape being laugh'd at, if they please" (Butt 597). Horatian satire is a so-called formal satire which offers "polished and artful" satire from a speaker who is often "a stern moralist" but possessing "a gentle humor" and a "mobility of tone and nuance" (Griffin 8–9). Juvenalian satire is more serious and lofty, where the "modes of vice" are decried and "unillusioned sadness at the aberrations of men" reign (169). Dr. Johnson practiced this style in *The Vanity of Human Wishes* and, most pointedly, *London*:

> For who would leave, unbrib'd, Hibernia's Land,
> Or change the Rocks of Scotland for the Strand?
> There none are swept by sudden Fate away,
> But all whom Hunger spares, with Age decay:
> Here Malice, Rapine, Accident, conspire,
> And now a Rabble Rages, now a Fire;
> Their Ambush here relentless Ruffians lay,
> And here the fell Attorney prowls for Prey;
> Here falling Houses thunder on your Head,
> And here a female Atheist talks you dead [*London* 9–18].

It is the note of sadness found in this type of satire which is missing from Python's work, unless it is a sadness effectively masked by a comic veneer. Monty Python certainly diminishes subjects, though, from the Inquisition to the English legal system and the crown; and from effeminate bobbies to stereotypically-affected gay judges. A group of antlered Masons hopping about on a busy street wearing their trousers about their ankles is ridiculous, to be sure, as is the image of a member of the government stripping down to his underwear and stripper tassels as he recites English monetarist policy. Authority figures are lampooned at every turn, including Python's employers at the BBC, but so are commoners, all foreigners

(but especially the French), and even the Pythons themselves. Their Englishness is both a high ground from which to lob comedic missiles, as well
as the perfect target for their humor of self-deprecation. It is difficult to
justify permanently affixing Monty Python with either appellation — Horatian or Juvenalian — since the loftiness and indignation of the Juvenalian
is just the type of target Python often chooses. The reflexivity and self-
deprecation found in Horace, along with the more "relaxed and informal"
nature of the Horatian speaker might be more suitable. The Python attacks
often seem scornful, but that supposed scorn is quickly deflated by a following segment, which is itself undercut by another segment, and so on.
Elements of other forms, specifically the carnival and the grotesque, which
will be discussed below, must also be considered. Abrams notes that "any
narrative or other literary vehicle can be adapted to the purposes of indirect satire" (169). Indirect satire includes the Menippean tradition
wherein — formal considerations aside — "both the heroic values associated with more elite forms of literature and of the hierarchical organization of both classical aesthetics and the social order that classical aesthetic
categories mirror" are objects of ridicule (Blanchard 26–27). In short,
Menippean satire as practiced by the Greek Cynic Menippas, the Roman
Varro, and later Burton in *Anatomy of Melancholy* (1621) contained often
excruciatingly long passages of

> extended dialogues and debates ... in which a group of immensely
> loquacious eccentrics, pedants, literary people, and representatives
> of various professions or philosophical points of view serve to
> make ludicrous the intellectual attitudes they typify by the argu-
> ments they urge in their support. (Abrams 169)

Jonson pokes fun at Puritans often, and just as often allows his Puritans
to talk themselves into other characters' disdain, as Zeal-of-the-Land-
Busy does so well in *Bartholomew Fair*:

> *Busy*. Hinder me not, woman.
>   *He speaks to the* Widow.
> I was moved in spirit to be here this day in this Fair, this wicked and foul
>   Fair (and fitter may it be a called a foul, than a Fair) to protest against
>   the abuses of it, the foul abuses of it, in regard of the afflicted saints,
>   that are troubled, very much troubled, exceedingly troubled, with the
>   opening of the merchandise of Babylon again, and the peeping of pop-
>   ery upon the stalls, here, here in the high places. See you not Goldy-
>   locks, the purple strumpet, there, in her yellow gown and green sleeves?
>   The profane pipes, the tinkling timbrels? A shop of relics [3.6.90–100].

As Busy rails against gingerbread figures and all things idolatrous, his righteous indignation would be more respected if we had not already heard from Jordan Knockem of Busy's own drunken, gluttonous debauchery earlier at the fair (3.6.48–53). His convoluted reasonings as to why pig can and should be eaten within the confines of the fair betray his Janus-like abilities, and give ample reason for Jonson's scorn:

> Pure. O brother Busy! your help here to edify, and raise us up in a scruple. My daughter Win-the-fight is visited with a natural disease of women called "A longing to eat pig."
>
> Lit. Ay sir, a Barthol'mew pig, and in the Fair.
>
> Pure. And I would be satisfied from you, religiously-wise, whether a widow of the sanctified assembly, or a widow's daughter may commit the act, without offense to the weaker sisters.
>
> Busy. Verily, for the disease of longing, it is a disease, a carnal disease, or appetite, incident to women; and as it is carnal, and incident, it is natural, very natural. Now pig, it is a meat, and a meat that is nourishing, and may be longed for, and so consequently eaten; it may be eaten; very, exceeding well eaten; but in the Fair, and as a Barthol'mew-pig, it cannot be eaten, for the very calling it a Barthol'mew-pig, and to eat it so, is a spice of idolatry, and you make the Fair no better than one of the high places. This, I take it, is the state of the question. A high place.
>
> Lit. Ay, but in state of necessity, place should give place, Master Busy. (I have a conceit left, yet.)
>
> Pure. Good brother Zeal-of-the-Land, think to make it as lawful as you can.
>
> Lit. Yes, sir, and as soon as you can; for it must be sir; you see the danger my little wife is in, sir.
>
> Pure. Truly, I do love my child dearly, and I would not have her miscarry, or hazard her first fruits, if it might be otherwise.
>
> Busy. Surely, it may be otherwise, but it is subject to construction, subject, and hath a face of offense, with the weak, a great face, a foul face, but that face may have a veil put over it, and be shadowed, as it were. It may be eaten, and in the Fair, I take it, in a booth, the tents of the wicked. The place is not much, not very much; we may be religious in midst of the profane, so it be eaten with a reformed mouth, with sobriety, and humbleness; not gorged in with gluttony, or greediness. There's the fear; for, should she go there, as taking pride in the place, or delight in the unclean dressing, to feed the vanity of the eye or the lust of the palate, it were not well, it were not fit, it were abominable, and not good.
>
> Lit. Nay, I knew that afore, and told her on't; but courage, Win, we'll be humble enough; we'll seek out the homeliest booth i' the Fair, that's certain; rather than fail, we'll eat it o' the ground.
>
> Pure. Ay, and I'll go with you myself, Win-the-Fight, and my brother, Zeal-of-the-Land, shall go with us too, for our better consolation.
>
> Win. Uh, uh.
>
> Lit. Ay, and Solomon too, Win; the more the merrier, Win; [Aside to Win] we'll leave Rabbi Busy in a booth.—Solomon, my cloak.
>
> Sol. Here, sir [1.6.42–96].

But even though Busy's been painted a Rabbi (for his stand against pig), he isn't about to be left out of the feasting, and even manages to make a clever rationalization for his participation:

> *Busy.* In the way of comfort to the weak, I will go, and eat. I will eat exceedingly, and prophesy. There may be a good use made of it, too, now I think on't: by the public eating of swine's flesh, to profess our hate and loathing of Judaism, whereof the brethren stand taxed. I will therefore eat; yea, I will eat exceedingly.
> *Lit.* Good, i' faith, I will eat heartily too, because I will be no Jew; I could never away with that stiffenecked generation. And truly, I hope my little one will be like me, that cries for pig so, i' the mother's belly.
> *Busy.* Very likely, exceeding likely, very exceeding likely [1.6.42–109].

Busy's high-handed temple scourging comes off then as laughable and hypocritical, not reverential. So it is the Puritans' often self-righteous image which puts off others, and not necessarily who they are, how they worship, or even their actions. Anyone familiar at all with the works of Python will recognize the Menippean aspect of their satire, including the incredibly self-absorbed Tourist who complains incessantly about others just like him, creating a sort of prototypical "Ugly Englishman" character:

> TOURIST: [...] and complaining about the food, "Oh! It's so greasy isn't it?" and then you get cornered by some drunken greengrocer from Luton with an Instamatic and Dr. Scholl sandals and Tuesday's "Daily Express" and he drones on and on and on about how Mr. Smith should be running this country and how many languages Enoch Powell can speak and then he throws up all over the Cuba Libres [...] [2.31.117].

This stream of insensitive British consciousness flows on for much longer, until and after the police are called. These kinds of self-reflexive and socially revealing arguments are put into the mouths of many Python characters, but most often the likes of City Gents, Investment Bankers, and various public figures. Whatever their ilk, they certainly "make ludicrous" their lofty positions and ideals. City Gents are often given the most inane things to say, and their bowlered, buttoned-down, umbrella-carrying seriousness is always played against their singularly vitriolic sound bites. In episode 24 they voice their opinions about life in the city:

> FIRST CITY GENT: (Palin) Well, I've been in the city for over forty years and I think the importance of looking after poor people cannot be understressed.
> SECOND CITY GENT: (Chapman) Well I've been in the city for twenty years and I must admit — I'm lost.
> AN OLD GRAMOPHONE: (Cleese) Well, I've been in the city all my life and I'm as alert and active as I've ever been.

FOURTH CITY GENT: (Cleese) Well I've been in the city for thirty years and I've never once regretted being a nasty, greedy, cold-hearted, avaricious, money-grubber ... *Conservative* [2.24.9].

These City Gents appear often in the "vox pops" sections of the episodes, and they usually come down on the side of the conservative government — or, at least, a lampooned version of that conservatism. In episode 5 a Pepperpot (Idle) thinks that customs agents ought to be able to shoot on sight anyone caught with more than 200 cigarettes, and she later confides that satire is actually the best weapon of attack, though admits that others should be making up her mind for her. Typical of the lethal nature of much of the satire is heard from a City Gent-type in episode 5:

STOCKBROKER: (Cleese) Well I think they should attack the lower classes, er, first with bombs, and rockets destroying their homes, and then when they run helpless into the streets, er, mowing them down with machine guns. Er, and then of course releasing the vultures. I know these views aren't popular, but I have never courted popularity [1.5.62].

Aside from the noted elements of Menippean and indirect satire, instances of direct satire can be just as easily recognized. A look at the mixing of comedic modes in another popular play from the English Renaissance will serve to prepare the way for a close reading of Monty Python's comedic structures; a reading that will bring together — in satiric parlance — characters such as Dekker's Simon the Shoemaker, and Python's Roger the Shrubber.

In Thomas Dekker's *The Shoemaker's Holiday* (*SH*) (1599) the boundary between classes is made ambiguous, and the common shoemakers rise to the point where they consort with the King, and the King with them. This creates humor via the incongruous — the spectacle of a king as mythologized as Henry[1] meeting his subjects face to face and without the benefit of disguise. Anne Barton mentions that in medieval ballads, kings and commoners often met, only to "discover unanimity of opinion and mutual respect" (97). Maurice Keen identifies this "misconception" as arising from country folk and their fantasies, specifically because they were further separated from the person of the king — further meaning both in distance and in numbers of officials blocking their pathway to the king (156). Keen notes, however, that even in London the tradition endured through and beyond Shakespeare and Dekker's times. One would be hard-pressed to classify *SH* as a satire, though the noblemen — the King excepted — are occasionally made to look ridiculous, as Lincoln must eventually give in to both the King's request regarding his nephew's love for a commoner and his forgiveness as a traitor. And he must do so publicly. This is, in fact, an acknowledgment of his social status relative to the King: he may be a nobleman, someone "of name," but he isn't royalty. In *SH*, however, Dekker employs a very mild satire in an overall comic structure that can be called — according to Margaret Rose — a "sophisticated parody," a more complicated mock-epic that would treat a Simon Eyre like a sort of king (2–18). Simon Eyre, a shoemaker who "served the mayor and his household with shoes," from the beginning lauds his craft and apprentices and all shoemakers as more than just craftsmen. As Rafe — one of Eyre's journeyman apprentices — is being conscripted to fight in France, Eyre lavishes him with praise before the military officers:

> Take him, brave men! Hector of Troy was an hackney to him, Hercules and Termagant scoundrels. Prince Arthur's Round Table, by the Lord of Ludgate, ne'er fed such a tall, such a dapper swordsman; by the life of the pharaoh, a brave, resolute swordsman! [1.1.173–78].

Thanks to Eyre's enthusiastic recommendation, Rafe is promised protection (by Askew, cousin to the noble Lacy) in his foreign service, and that his new wife will certainly be with him again:

> *Ask.* I am glad, good Master Eyre, it is my hap
> To meet so resolute a soldier.
> Trust me, for your report and love to him
> *A common slight regard shall not respect him* [1.1.182–85; emphasis added].

This last line is key here as Askew — a man of high birth — promises Rafe protection and care beyond that which Rafe's low social status, his "slight regard," would normally merit. Rafe has been elevated, lifted up from above, to a higher social standing. It is for this very reason — the upward social mobility — that J. A. Faber calls *SH* not only unrealistic, but "utterly fantastic, a wished-for world into which to escape" (359). Wished-for, certainly, but as Keen has indicated, this is a shared cultural wish for escape, shared by those who established the myth in the agrarian communities, and those who continued to breathe life into it on the London stages. Eyre concludes this scene by inviting more to this "wished-for world" as he sends Rafe off with a flourish:

> Hold thee Rafe: here's five sixpences for thee. Fight for the honor of the gentle craft, for the gentlemen shoemakers, the courageous cordwainers, the flower of Saint Martin's, the mad knaves of Bedlam, Fleet Street, Tower Street, and Whitechapel. Crack me the

crowns of the French knaves, a pox on them! Crack them! Fight, by
the Lord of Ludgate. Fight, my boy [1.1.223–34].

Eyre himself has nearly knighted Rafe and put him at the head of an army
of courageous shoemakers and assorted London laborers and lunatics, all
rising as they embrace Eyre's vision of honor: "Am I not Simon Eyre? Are
not these my brave men? Brave shoemakers, all gentlemen of the craft.
Prince am I none, yet am I nobly born, as being the sole son of a shoemaker" (2.3.49–54). Even though no worldly degrees of social advancement have yet been rendered upon these men, the elevation has come down
to a simple case of "Simon Says." Simon sees himself as at least equal to
the acknowledged nobility, and it seems then only natural that he himself
should eventually ascend to the Lord Mayorship. The text proves that
Simon's word, no matter how outlandish or seemingly beyond the pale,
becomes reality. Rafe becomes a shoemaker/warrior, and is even wounded
as he is elevated above his social status (though, to Simon, as a shoemaker
Rafe is already a true warrior and noble man).

   Mirroring the ascendancy of Rafe is the "descendancy" of Lacy, a
nobleman, nephew to Lincoln (Sir Hugh Lacy), who, after being assigned
to lead the King's troops in France and promising "to add glory to the
Lacys' name" (1.1.89), remains instead in London, disguising himself, iron-
ically, as a humble shoemaker. The circle is thus complete: the common
shoemaker Rafe becomes an ennobled warrior, and is recognized as such
by the nobility, while the would-be warrior-nobleman Lacy becomes a
common shoemaker, and will be recognized as such (though assuming a
Dutch persona). This turnabout is not as simple as it appears, though,
since in the eyes and proclamations of Simon — whose words, as we've
seen, often ring prophetic — the common shoemaker Hans/Lacy is a
princely noble. The paradigm of the lower class being elevated to a higher
standing, at least textually, would appear to be sound as it is played out in
SH. Faber writes of the fantastic nature of Dekker's created social London,
positing that, for the shoemakers, the "realms of work and play are rec-
onciled; class distinctions — real enough in Dekker's day — all but vanish,
so that even the King has a proletarian air about him…" (359).

   The case can be made, then, that instead of just an elevation from
lower class to higher, there is a general leveling of the classes, creating a
common ground where a king can be and act proletarian, while the shoemakers revel in their self-aggrandizement. Anne Barton calls this kind of
king "a benevolent *deus ex machina*," an anomalous leader who would put
aside the trappings of state to confront his subject on an even level (*Shakespeare and the Idea of the Play* 98). The minstrels who had sung of these

kinds of kings were thus proven right, in Dekker's work, at least: "Anni-hilating objections based upon wealth or class, he acts from principles of perfect equity as soon as he examines the case himself, just as the medieval minstrels had always believed he would" (98). Simon himself, upon learn-ing of his new position, wastes no time in assuming his king-like duties and proffers his hand to those around him, beginning with his good wife: "See here, my Maggy. A chain, a gold chain for Simon Eyre. I shall make thee a lady" (3.2.160–61). Simon can now bestow this two-fold appellation of honor: she is to be more refined and better-dressed, but also a titled member of the elite, as he calls her "a lady." Not only assuming the power of naming (a sort of Adam-like power given to very few), Simon actually says he will "make" her a lady, denoting a godlike, creationary power reserved for fewer still. This is a rather complicated parodic structure, then, as humor and goodwill (rather than the derision and open ridicule of some satire) are used to level the class hierarchy. The King is subtly shaped more proletarian, while Simon and his retinue are fashioned more nobly. In the context of the parody, Margaret Rose writes, the "target text may not only be satirised but also 'refunctioned'"—the refunctioning here being the textual acceptance and promotion of this new social order (28–29). The fantastic nature of this world is confirmed as there arises no outcry against the new peerage; the King cannot wait to meet this "gal-lant," and the former Lord Mayor, himself a grocer by trade, accepts this cobbler nobility, and even welcomes Simon in: "Now, by my troth, I'll tell thee, Master Eyre, / It does me good and all my brethren / That such a mad-cap fellow as thyself / Is entered into our society" (3.3.8–11). "Our soci-ety" is the world of the monied and titled, a society where former grocers and gentle tradesmen can mingle with the elite. This society also happens to be the world of the text. Simon continues speaking to his wife and employees, his generosity and his text-given (and borne out by continu-ance of the medieval tradition) ability and right to grant boons assured:

> Here's a French hood for thee — on with it, on with it! Dress thy brows with this flap of a shoulder of mutton to make thee look lovely. Where be my fine men? Roger, I'll make over my shop and tools to thee. Firke, thou shalt be the foreman. Hans, thou shalt have an hundred for twenty. Be as mad knaves as your master Sim Eyre hath been, and you shall live to be Sheriffs of London. How dost thou like me Margery? Prince am I none, yet am I princely born [161–69].

And, in this world where those of the gentle craft are peers, there seems little doubt that Simon can be taken at his word. One of those words in his oft-repeated epigram can also be taken more than one way. "Prince am I none, yet am I princely *born*" would not be a statement read by an audience (at least initially), but heard by that audience. In that case it could very well be understood, by that same listening audience, that Simon is saying "borne," and not "born." It creates a play on words which connotes a doubling of the term's possibilities. He may not have been *born* a prince, but he *bears* himself like a prince, or he carries himself in a princely fashion. He also strives to lift others up with him. This would alert the audience that acting like a member of the elite brings a sort of social denotation of nobility. Remember that Subtle tells Dol Common, a prostitute, to "bear" herself in a stately manner — a manner which will make possible their intended subterfuge (*The Alchemist* 2.4.6). Appearances, then, and even self-esteem, seem to affect the assumption of noble characteristics, a sort of acting endeavor which elevates the actor to a higher social status. Simon respects his heritage enough to mention it often, as it qualifies him, along with the "princely" bearing he assumes, for consideration as an equal in the company of anyone — even the king. Simon assumes some of the characteristics of the ruling class, as he counsels Rose, the daughter of the former Lord Mayor, to marry within her class: "Had I a son or daughter should marry out of the generation and blood of shoemakers, he should pack" (3.4.49–51).

Faber writes that Dekker's world of the play is a place where the normal rules of social mores don't necessarily apply, that "[i]nstead of anxiety about what a person's proper place is, *SH* is suffused with an impudent confidence which makes the question of decorum or propriety irrelevant" (360). This "decorum" and "propriety" includes those things which should or shouldn't be done or said between and even within classes, as well as levels of awareness, enlightenment, or intelligence that the higher class should, by definition, possess and use in abundance. It is Simon, however, who carries the secret of life, as he tells the King to "let care vanish" and become "young like Apollo" (5.5.35–37), and it is only after the King's encounter with Simon that the King can dismiss Lincoln's misgivings about Lacy and allow an interclass marriage: "Lincoln, no more; / Dost thou not know that love respects no blood, / Cares not for the difference of birth or state?" (5.5.108–10). This turnabout-is-fair-play motif appears elsewhere in Elizabethan and early Jacobean drama, and with similar results. John Webster's debt to Shakespeare and Jonson is well-known; in fact Russell Fraser amusingly labels these two predecessors as "quarries" for Webster rather than "sources" (431). Webster's plays are most often about real events and, more precisely, recent real events. Vittoria, as she stands accused in Webster's *The White Devil* (1610–12), is a fiery, unrepentant female character who verbally challenges her prolix prosecutor: "Surely, my lords, this lawyer here hath swallowed / Some pothecaries' bills, or proclamations; / And now the hard and undigestible words / Come up, like stones…" (3.2.36–40). She proves both intellectually and verbally that she is more than a match for the proceedings, and especially this smarmy lawyer. As the lawyer attempts to regain his customary highbrow scorn, he challenges Vittoria with the language of an impending duel: "Well, then, have at you!"[2] (3.2.24). She picks up the gauntlet and responds with a withering challenge of her own, from which he never recovers: "I am at the mark, sir. I'll give aim to you, / And tell you how near you shoot" (3.2.25–26). Beatrice, in Shakespeare's *Much Ado About Nothing*, gives as good as she gets, and better, and is even able to command Benedick to commit to a duel with his best friend on her behalf. Portia disguises herself as a young lawyer in *The Merchant of Venice*, sneaking into the realm of male dominance and patriarchal values, and manages to overcome Shylock. She also, like Beatrice, is wittily able to catalogue the shortcomings of the male species: "I pray thee over-name them, and as thou namest them, I will describe them; and according to my description level at my affection" (1.2.36–38). She then names, describes, and renders unfit for husbandly consideration each man her waiting-gentlewoman mentions, beginning with the Neapolitan prince:

> *Por.* Ay, that's a colt indeed, for he doth nothing but talk of his horse, and he makes it a great appropriation to his own good parts that he can shoe him himself. I am much afeard my lady his mother play'd false with a smith.
> *Ner.* Then is there the County Palentine.
> *Por.* He doth nothing but frown, as who should say, "And you will not have me, choose." He hears merry tales and smiles not. I fear he will prove the weeping philosopher when he grows old, being so full of unmannerly sadness in his youth. I had rather be married to a death's-head with a bone in his mouth than to either of these. God defend me from these two!
> *Ner.* How say you by the French lord, Monsieur Le [Bon]?
> *Por.* God made him, and therefore let him pass for a man. In truth, I know it is a sin to be a mocker, but he! why, he hath a horse better than the Neapolitan's, a better bad habit of frowning than the Count Palentine; he is every man in no man. If a throstle sing, he falls straight a-cap'ring. He will fence with his own shadow. If I should marry him, I should marry twenty husbands. If he would despise me, I would forgive him, for if he love me to madness, I shall never requite him.
> *Ner.* What say you then to Falconbridge, the young baron of England?
> *Por.* You know I say nothing to him, for he understands not me, nor I him. He hath neither Latin, French, nor Italian, and you will come into the court and swear that I have a poor pennyworth in the English. He is a proper man's picture, but alas, who can converse with a dumb-show?

> How oddly he is suited! I think he bought his doublet in Italy, his round
> hose in France, his bonnet in Germany, and his behavior every where.
> *Ner.* What think you of the Scottish lord, his neighbor?
> *Por.* That he hath a neighborly charity in him, for he borrow'd a box of the
> ear of the Englishman, and swore he would pay him again when he was
> able. I think the Frenchman became his surety and seal'd under for
> another.
> *Ner.* How like you the young German, the Duke of Saxony's nephew?
> *Por.* Very vildly in the morning, when he is sober, and most vildly in the
> afternoon, when he is drunk. When he is best, he is a little worse than a
> man, and when he is worst, he is little better than a beast. And the worst
> fall that ever fell, I hope I shall make shift to go without him [1.2.40–91].

It turns out that only the Venetian Bassanio holds any place in her heart
(Portia can, in fact, actually name him without Nerissa's help); while the
others she prays will just go away. The fact that Vittoria, Portia and Beatrice are women makes the elevation into man's domain all the more
remarkable, and the leveling here is both political and cultural. These questions of decorum and propriety and the anarchic dismantling of societal
constraints become consistent motifs in Monty Python's work, as well.
Though often taken to the most absurd degree and delivered in a postmodern frenzy of juxtapositions and self-conscious non-linearity, there
exists in the Python corpus, as Faber wrote of Dekker's world in *SH*, "little
spatial or temporal perspective, but instead a striking simultaneity of awareness" (359). Once again we encounter the ever-present, previously discussed
in Chapter 3 in relation to Falstaff and Python's *Holy Grail*. This, coupled
with the raising/lowering/leveling of the classes, creates many Pythonesque conflations of cobbler and king, characteristics which lead us to the
important category of the clown as displayed in Shakespeare and Python.

Oscar James Campbell in *Shakespeare's Satire* identifies the clown as
descending from the Vice of earlier morality plays (4). The clown is an
impudent, trick-playing, joke-making upstart who pokes fun at the upper
classes and attacks with satire. Erasmus describes the reasons why "[the
clown] is so effective an instrument of satire":

> A fool speaketh like a fool (videlicet) plainly — of fools oft times,
> not only true tales but even open rebukes are with pleasure
> declared. That what word coming out of a wise man's mouth were
> an hanging matter, the same yet spoken by a fool shall much delight
> even him that is touched therewith [Campbell 4].

The clown, then, is allowed the leeway of speech and attack which might
be reserved for those of so-called diminished capacity — he is a fool, so he
is not to be taken seriously. Campbell calls him an "innocent 'natural,'" a
sort of idiot savant with a talent for silliness and social satire (4). Camp-

bell further describes the attributes of his clowning, including obvious visual silliness (what we might call slapstick today), and his penchant for malapropisms and imitative mono- or duologue (5). Campbell points out that Launce in *The Two Gentlemen of Verona* plays this role (as probably played first by Will Kemp), but these characteristics can also be seen in abundance in the person of Dogberry in *Much Ado*.[3] Dogberry, in his attempts to imitate the speech and bearing of the men of name around him, delivers malapropisms with consistent ease as he attempts to live up to his calling as peacekeeper. He seems to recognize that he is the social inferior to men like Antonio and Leonato (the latter being governor of Messina) as he addresses them politely and respectfully, but he also seems to rise to their level (or bring them down to his) as he addresses them on a co-equal basis, and his malapropisms deny every compliment he may be trying to pay. And Leonato's responses to Dogberry are — as Keen has mentioned being indicative of the clown's presence — exhibiting the "much delight" that can only arise when harsh but sugared words come from fools. Leonato calls Dogberry and Verges "honest" neighbors (3.4.1) and "good friends" (3.4.8), and also "tedious" (3.4.18), though the fools, of course, take the word as a treasured compliment, promising all their tediousness back to Leonato. When the truth has been made known and Dogberry's charges are shown as the culprits, Leonato is truly thankful to the clown for the clearing of his daughter's good name: "I thank thee for thy care and honest pains" (5.1.314). Perhaps Shakespeare has injected this view, that it takes a fool to see what others may miss, as a more indirect form of satire. Indirect, as no one in the play mentions or makes note of just who solved the case, as it were, and who would have continued on in their duped ignorance without this proffered solution. This clowning can be mimicked on stage, as Hamlet undertakes when he "feigns madness," and can be used to forward the plot in a direction favorable to Hamlet's plans for the "outing" of his stepfather and even his mother:

> *Queen.* But, look, where sadly the poor wretch
>   comes reading.
> *Pol.* Away, I do beseech you, both away.
> I'll board him presently.   *Exeunt King and Queen.*
>   O, give me leave,
> How does my good Lord Hamlet?
> *Ham.* Well, God-a-mercy.
> *Pol.* Do you know me, my lord?
> *Ham.* Excellent well, you are a fishmonger.
> *Pol.* Not I, my lord.
> *Ham.* Then I would you were so honest a man.
> *Pol.* Honest, my lord?

Ham. Ay, sir, to be honest, as this world goes, is to be one man picked out
of ten thousand.

Pol. That's very true, my lord.

Ham. For if the sun breed maggots in a dead dog, being a god kissing carrion — Have you a daughter?

Pol. I have, my lord.

Ham. Let her not walk i' the sun. Conception is a blessing, but as your
daughter may conceive, friend, look to't.

Pol. [*Aside.*] How say you by that? still harping on my daughter. yet he
knew me not at first, 'a said I was a fishmonger. 'A is far gone. And
truly in my youth I suff'red much extremity for love — very near this.
I'll speak to him again. — What do you read, my lord?

Ham. Words, words, words.

Pol. What is the matter, my lord?

Ham. Between who?

Pol. I mean, the matter that you read, my lord.

Ham. Slanders, sir; for the satirical rogue says here that old men have grey
beards, that their faces are wrinkled, their eyes purging thick amber and
plum-tree gum, and that they have a plentiful lack of wit, together with
most weak hams; all which, sir, though I most powerfully and potently
believe, yet I hold it not honesty to have it thus set down, for yourself,
sir, shall grow old as I am, if like a crab you could go backward.

Pol. [*Aside.*] Though this be madness, yet there is method in 't. — Will you
walk out of the air, my lord?

Ham. Into my grave.

Pol. Indeed, that's out of the air. [*Aside*] How pregnant sometimes his
replies are! a happiness that often madness hits on, which reason and
[sanity] could not so prosperously be deliver'd of. I will leave him, [and
suddenly contrive the means of meeting between him] and my daughter. — My lord, I will take my leave of you.

Ham. You cannot take from me any thing that I will not more willingly
part withal — except my life, except my life, except my life.

Pol. Fare you well, my lord.

Ham. These tedious old fools! [2.2.168–219].

Hamlet's "madness" fades, of course, when his friends Rosencrantz and
Guildenstern appear, and the theatrical nature of his clowning, his fool-
ery for the benefit of Polonius (and by association, his mother, the King,
Laertes and Ophelia) is made clear. He plays the madman, and his veiled
barbs and accusations upset and disturb but bring him no retribution, nor
does his hand show to the murderer Claudius. He is thus able to bide his
time behind the cloak of the tragic clown. His madness is also unsettling
to those around him, as there is a general confusion as to what to do with
him. Hamlet of course fuels this fire by appearing "mad" in different ways
to different people. He is almost nonsensical but abusive with Polonius;
he is accusatory and blameful with Ophelia. She is, he tells her, the cause
of his madness after all:

Ham. I have heard of your paintings, well enough. God hath given you one
face, and you make yourselves another. You jig and you amble, and you
[lisp,] you nickname God's creatures and make your wantonness [your]
ignorance. Go to, I'll no more on't, it hath made me mad.

....

Oph. O, what a noble mind is here o'erthrown! [3.1.142–150].

His "sweet bells jangled out of time," Hamlet can proceed with his plans
for retribution, already having promised to kill — "Those that are married
already (all but one) shall live…"[4] — without much direct interference from
his stepfather. Hamlet is even able to expand this madness, and thus the
righteousness of his planned retribution, to the kindling wrath of deity:
"Heaven's face does glow / O'er this solidity and compound mass / With
heated visage, as against the doom; / *Is thought-sick at the act*" (3.4.48–51;
emphasis added). Though most often not comedic in *Hamlet*, Hamlet's
role as a sort of mad clown in this tragedy creates the same freedom of
expression and opinion that the comic clown enjoys in comedy, a freedom
which eventually allows him to "triumph" in a roundabout way. He is the
"clown shall make those laugh whose lungs are [tickle] a' the' sere"— in
other words, few will find the tragedy very funny (2.2.323–24). This also
could be a reference, as Evans mentions in the notes to his edition, that
the situation Hamlet is preparing will be so highly charged and easily set
off that there is the great chance the clown will affect everyone (Evans
1135–40). This clownish influence — a freedom of expression and opinion
not available to a conventional character or person in everyday life, for that
matter — is finally realized more fully, more omnisciently, in the works of
Python. The influence of the clown leads to an almost carnival atmosphere as Hamlet sparks the play's climax, and Python strikes into the
grotesque.

In *Monty Python and the Holy Grail*, the Arthurian legends serve as
the setting for several of these "striking" moments of altered perspectives
and simultaneous awareness. *Holy Grail* is at least a hybrid comic form. It
is a comic parody of English history, specifically the Arthur legends, and
of classic films (as Ellen Bishop notes) like Bergman's *The Seventh Seal*,
and it also pokes fun at previous attempts at the cinematization of the
Arthurian legend. According to Kevin Harty, this element of the film raises
it above other farces:

There is, however, more to the Python film than slapstick. What is
being lampooned is not the legend of Arthur but earlier treatments,
cinematic and otherwise, of that legend. Against carefully chosen
authentic backdrops of castles and their ruins, the film presents
what may at first only appear to be the broad satire and farce that

became the Python trademark: holy hand grenades, killer rabbits,
fear-inducing shrubbery, a castle of maidens begging for X-rated
punishment for the sin of lighting a Grail-shaped beacon in the
tower, and so on, but there is clearly method to the madness here.
The film abounds in conventions from and threads of the Arthurian
legend, as well as takeoffs on Hollywoodesque swashbuckling
adventures, spectacles, and fights to the death... ["Lights!" 23].

Even acknowledging its parodic nature, the film's satiric elements cannot
be overlooked, as intellectualism is skewered (often literally). A white-
haired professor — subtitled "A Famous Historian" — who has been narrating the film as a sort of historical reenactment, is slashed in mid-sentence
by a knight from the film story, becoming the very image of intellectual-
ism/-izing that is under assault in *Holy Grail*. Though this is a parody, it
has its roots in Menippean satire. The conflation of satire and parody are
apparent her : from the outset, but there is more at work. Ellen Bishop (in
one of the few existing "serious" articles on Monty Python) connects this
film's comic form to Bakhtin's notions of the carnival, calling it "The New
Grotesque" (49). Bakhtin wrote of a type of comedy that was "particular
to the Middle Ages," and faded during the Renaissance, a form he called
carnival (Bishop 49). Performed in the marketplace, carnival was a
seething, bustling form characterized by raucous crowds, hawkers and
vendors, and a performance somehow rising up out of the melee. Bakhtin
writes that carnival is ambivalent (both "gay" and "mocking"), grotesque
(imagine a "pregnant, senile old hag"), and universal, or "directed at all
and everyone, including the carnival's participants" (Bishop 49–50).
Bishop writes that "what took its place were 'reduced' forms of comedy
that Bakhtin labels variously as parody, satire, humor, sarcasm, and irony"
(49). The list of subsequent scholars who have taken Bakhtin to task for
his reductive argument — especially those who tend to favor parody, satire,
humor, sarcasm, and irony — includes Margaret Rose and Terry Blanchard,
both quoted above. Yet Blanchard, citing Bakhtin, addresses the grotesque,
calling it "the literary anarchist's *ars poetica*, it is both profound and silly"
(24). This may describe much of Python's work perfectly. And Bakhtin's
own description of the carnival-type laughter echoes responses to Jonson's
and Python's crudities and patter: "This laughter is ambivalent: it is gay,
triumphant, and at the same time mocking, deriding. It asserts and denies,
buries and revives" (11–12).

Hamlet's sardonic swipes at Ophelia, his mother and Polonius, his
self-congratulations intermixed with self-incriminations create a pervasive gloom that eventually encompasses just about everyone within Hamlet's influence. Philip Thomson offers the grotesque as "a gratuitous mixing

together of incompatible elements" (Blanchard 25). It seems, though, that elements which are truly incompatible could not be mixed together — see oil and water — so a compromise description must be found. Blanchard, writing in support of Menippean satire, sees the formal "violation of generic boundaries" that he ascribes to the Menippean tradition as complementary to the grotesque: "The more complicated nature of the Menippean form, as well as its more anti-intellectual cast, makes it possible in my mind for the categories to overlap" (25). The Pythonesque categories then are satire, parody, carnival, and grotesque, at least. And overlap they do in *Holy Grail*.

King Arthur (Graham Chapman) and his valet/mock-horse, Patsy (Terry Gilliam) are searching for knights to join Arthur at Camelot. As they "gallop" across the countryside — with Patsy clopping coconuts together in lieu of a real horse — they come across the ruins of a castle, and encounter a filthy peasant pulling a handcart. Arthur calls after the peasant, mistaking the man for an old woman. When the peasant tells him that he is a man, he is not old, and that he has a name —"Dennis"[5]— Arthur apologizes, but the peasant isn't satisfied:

> ARTHUR: But I didn't know you were called Dennis.
> DENNIS: Well you didn't bother to find out, did you?
> ARTHUR: Well I did say sorry about the "old woman," but from behind you looked —
> DENNIS: What I object to is automatically being treated like an inferior[6] [Scene 3].

If the audience hasn't caught on already, this retort from a lowly peasant to a very regal-looking king-figure signals that there is something amiss in the social order of this world. Instead of bowing and scraping and mumbling poorly-formed apologies, "Dennis" has made it clear that he is at least on the same intellectual and cultural level with Arthur. Remove the tart tongue and the obvious disrespect, and he is Simon Eyre conversing with his peer/king. The Menippean tradition — again, matters of form aside — can be seen here. Blanchard writes of Lucian's satirical work:

> The shattering of social stratification through a technique of comic role-reversals (such as Alexander the Great working as a cobbler in Hades) and the debasement of both elite social groups and dignified literary forms in Lucian's satires serve to destabilize the classical hierarchy of styles, stripping the more privileged forms of their dignified dress [17].

In this scene, both the elite social group represented by Arthur and the dignified literary form of the historical epic are subverted, undercut and sent-up as Dennis refuses to recognize his appointed class and reaches beyond the boundaries of the text for motivation and dialogue. Arthur maintains his bearing and assumed status as the conversation continues, attempting to set right the unbalanced power base:

ARTHUR: Well I am king.
DENNIS: Oh, king, eh? Very nice. And how'd you get that, eh? By exploiting the workers. By hanging onto outdated, imperialist dogma, which only perpetuates the economic and social differences in our society. If there's ever going to be any progress—[Scene 3].

Bishop notes this section of the film, writing that "the Pythons thus challenge the origins of the aristocracy's claim to power, while pointing to the bureaucratic absurdities of an overly self-conscious Marxist obsession with the division of power" (57). So as in satire, there is an attack on an institution, with the peasant here acting as a sort of adversarius, or a guide for the satiric speaker. These are elements of direct satire. But there is also an attack on the adversarius and his Marxist proclivities, elements of indirect satire, where the characters make themselves ridiculous by their own utterings. The clownish influence is pervasive, creating satiric targets at every turn and leaving no one person, thing or institution untouched. Everything is fair game for attack, and then the satiric attackers are attacked. This Menippean ridicule is evenly distributed between Arthur, the symbol of aristocratic authority, and Dennis, the peasant who will not conform to his designated class strictures. In a very convoluted way Dennis describes the political structure they employ, calling it an "anarcho-syndicalist commune":

DENNIS: We take it in turns to act as a sort of executive officer for the week. But all the decisions of that officer have to be ratified at a special bi-weekly meeting, by a simple majority in the case of purely internal affairs, but by a two-thirds majority in the case of [...] [Scene 3].

Arthur tries to interrupt impatiently, finally ordering Dennis to "shut up." When Dennis's good lady asks who Arthur thinks he is ordering people about, it is Arthur's turn to look and sound ridiculous. The soundtrack assists this satire, as a lovely swell of strings accompanies Arthur's proclamation:

ARTHUR: The Lady of the Lake, her arm clad in the purest shimmering samite, held aloft Excalibur from the bosom of the water, signifying by divine providence that I, Arthur, should be your king. That is why I am your king! [Scene 3].

Dennis then proceeds to ridicule Arthur's "tarts lying about in ponds distributing swords" rule of political and royal ascendancy. The segment ends with a frustrated Arthur grappling with Dennis, who cries out that he's being repressed. There is a meeting here of the mythological and legendary right to rule and the proletarian power of the masses, neither of which end up untainted by the satire.

What Bishop dances around but never truly addresses regarding this scene is that the social leveling Dekker offered in *SH* has reappeared, that in this fantastic world a peasant can stand toe-to-toe with a king, debate political systems and, eventually, deny the king's seemingly inalienable right to govern. The Pythons do, textually, "knowingly [trample] over all so-called civilized restraints" in the rush to comedy (Gutwirth 140). This can be called an "intellectual/verbal" leveling or subversion. Just as Simon is able to use his mirth and wit to elevate himself and his gentle tradesmen, and Vittoria and Beatrice joust verbally (and, of course, intellectually) with benefactors and detractors, Dennis the peasant — one among many other Python characters — is able to raise himself to the level of a king, while the king is forced to step down and accept a parity based on an intellectual and/or verbal challenge. In the "swallow" example from earlier in the film, Arthur and Patsy have "ridden" away from another castle after the guards on the walls wouldn't allow for the direct questioning Arthur desired and expected as king. Instead of answering Arthur's questions regarding their lord and master, the guards grilled him. In this scene there is even a visual separation between classes created by camera and character positioning. Arthur and Patsy stand on the ground, while the two guards lean over the castle wall far above. Arthur must then always be craning upward to look at his subjects, creating a visual representation of Arthur's lack of authority over his inferiors. Dennis (and his wife) also overcome Arthur by reaching beyond Arthur's knowledge, accessing and using as offensive weapons political and cultural cudgels with which Arthur — often because he is forced to remain within the confines of his prescribed role as the real Arthur — has no familiarity. Dennis' wife appears, crawling on all fours through the mud:

> WOMAN: King of the who?
> ARTHUR: The Britons.
> WOMAN: Who are the Britons?
> ARTHUR: Well we all are, we are all Britons. And I am your king.
> WOMAN: I didn't know we had a king. I thought we were an autonomous collective.
> DENNIS: You're fooling yourself! We're living in a dictatorship! A society in which the working class [...] [Scene 3].

In this scene the concepts of authority, political enfranchisement, class struggle, and political/economic power are thrown out as clay pigeons to be blasted. Nineteenth- and twentieth-century political discourse filters into the confrontation without a hiccup in the rhythm, as the temporal perspective of the so-called history play is challenged. Again, Arthur is at a disadvantage, since he isn't allowed knowledge beyond his role. He can't respond to Dennis' explanations regarding the "anarcho-syndicalist commune" since it is beyond his character. Dennis, the filthy peasant, is as ready as Firke and Hodge were to throw down the challenging gauntlet before the symbol of authority (in their case, Simon, and here, an alleged king): Dennis is ready to defend his beliefs and his political self-awareness. Similarly, when the knights of Camelot are later searching for the Grail, they encounter the Knights Who Say "Ni," and are forced to find a shrubbery before they can proceed. They then happen upon Roger the Shrubber, who scolds them for intimidating an old woman in their search for a shrubbery. He can scold this king figure because he, like Dennis, does not recognize Arthur's kingship. Roger the Shrubber, like Simon the Shoemaker, has been elevated to a place of great importance in the narrative world, far above — assumedly — the level to which most medieval shrubbers could have hoped to rise. In this case, the simple shrubber is so important that the film story cannot continue without his help (for without a shrubbery offering, Arthur and his knights cannot pass the Knights of Ni), and he is elevated to the level of a king, who has, conversely, been remarkably proletarian in his working quest for the Holy Grail.

Other significant examples of this intellectual/verbal elevation can be found in many of the *Flying Circus* television episodes. The comic is, as Alexander Bain wrote, "the occasion of the Ludicrous ... the Degradation of a person or interest possessing dignity, in circumstances that excite no other emotion" (Gutwirth 68). Marcel Gutwirth sees Hobbes and his superiority theory as the inevitable flip side to Bain's conclusion. For Hobbes, the "sudden glory arising from some sudden conception of some eminency in ourselves, by comparison with the infirmity of others, or with our own formerly," is the comic (59–60). In other words, the ridicule of an authority figure — a ridicule which does not lend itself to anger or hatred — is placed opposite, by Gutwirth, the rising effect felt by those watching others' struggles. Remembering that Thomson above claimed a "gratuitous mixing together" of incompatibles accounted for the grotesque, these elements— of Bakhtin's "degradation" and Hobbes' "elevation"— shouldn't appear together to create the comic. But Python has managed to allow both to exist, often hand in hand, in these scenes where characters and classes are elevated, lowered, or leveled. Neil Rhodes has identified the framework of the satirical grotesque as it was practiced in the Elizabethan era, and the description (citing Montaigne, among others) may resonate with the images from both Dekker and Python we've already discussed:

> ... it is illogical and colloquial ... "a shapeless, ruleless way of speaking, a common patter and a way of proceeding without definitions, partitions or conclusions" ... it is a bundling together, as of kindling wood.... It is all-embracing ... "No subject so trivial but it finds a place in this concoction" [19].

The place of cobblers in Dekker's London may have seemed trivial, but they are the heroes of his text. In *Holy Grail*, an old woman banging the dust out of a cat, or the power of the sacred word "it" to overcome the Knights Who Formerly Said "Ni" are both illogical faggots of wood that, when bundled, become Monty Python comedy. Rhodes quotes Montaigne further, who writes that the grotesque can only be truly present and represented when "[e]verything connects with everything else by some kind of similarity" (19). Found more readily in Elizabethan pamphlets and essays than stage plays (though Rhodes cites Dekker as practicing elements of the grotesque in connection to food and sexual imagery in *SH*), this associative practice provides the foundation for most of the *Flying Circus* episodes, and can even be found in the more conventional — though by no means monothematic — feature films. In episode 17, the Gumbys[7] introduce "The Architect Sketch," then intrude upon the beginning of that sketch; the sketch turns away from architecture and into Freemasonry, then back to architecture, and then architects who are freemasons. There is a transition from the architects who are freemasons to the identification of masons in public, and the Gumbys then return to announce "The Insurance Sketch," wherein a bishop is denied coverage. Once that bishop leaves, crying, another bishop breaks in, and captions introduce him as the star of *The Bishop*, a television drama starring a crime-solving clergyman. After a series of chases, the bishop bursts through a door, only to be back in the insurance office, and *The Bishop* credits begin again. The bishop reappears later, and the BBC interrupts to apologize for the unwarranted repetition in the show   twice. The show is closed by the Gumbys, who have appeared in each of the segments in some ostensibly introductory (chorus-like) way (Chapman, et al. 1.17.220–234). This associative aspect of the grotesque, again, is common throughout Python, breaking down the barriers between segments, sketches, and even historical time periods within the texts.

Rhodes sees as one of the important ways that the grotesque satire functions in comedy "the formulation of conflicts in which abuse and vilification are raised to extravagant levels of artistry" (68). The ultimately lethal abuse heaped upon an entire class in "Upperclass Twit of the Year" springs to mind here, as does the attack on party politics and the British viewing public's taste for sordid television fare in episode 45, "Party Political Broadcast." What this episode becomes, as well, is a scathing attack on the modern British family, both as portrayed on television and, by the end of the sketch, the families who might be watching such television. The scene is a filthy, tastelessly decorated flat with equally filthy and tasteless occupants strewn about. Mr. Garibaldi (Jones) is eating various laxatives, Kevin (Gilliam) is lying on the couch spooning beans onto his chest and flatulating, Ralph (Palin) is eating at the table and breaking everything he happens to touch, Mrs. Garibaldi (Idle) irons small appliances one by one, and Valerie (Chapman) is dressed in a bright red miniskirt, plastered beehive, and is putting on yet another layer of makeup (2.45.327). In this scene, the topics range from bowel movements to gluttony to British foreign policy in Africa to parliamentary prostitution, all exhibiting Python's penchant for "extravagant" levels of "abuse and vilification" (2.45.327–329). The British family is certainly under assault, from anally-obsessed patriarchs to either clumsy or gluttonous and flatulent sons to ignorance about one of Britain's own former colonies, Rhodesia. Valerie's garish makeup and her accompanying transsexual or hermaphroditic language ("my sodding wick") either identify her as just a slut, or, perhaps more, becomes a reflexive allusion to the cross-dressing employed in this scene. Chapman does, after all, have the anatomical features to use such a curse, but does Valerie? Mrs. Garibaldi is actually as destructive as Ralph, ironing flat everything within her reach. The Liberal Party candidate is also mocked, as elsewhere in the *Flying Circus* episodes. No one can answer Ralph's Rhodesia question (about how it got its name), either, a motif that will reappear later in the same sketch, though Valerie at least has an opinion on the subject. Valerie, in her miniskirt and face paint, is actually the elected representative of Britain's legislative body as offered in this episode. She is able to mention, at least, the pressing issues before the august body (the need for housing, for example), though her father sees it all as merely a grope-fest in his hallway. The "snogging" partner is a Chairman of the Housing sub-committee, which paints the entire process with the same broad brush stroke of parliamentary slap-and-tickle. No one challenges Valerie on the "Member of Parliament" claim; in fact, it's her mother who identifies her as an MP. This kind of wild incongruity isn't noticed or commented upon in this grotesquerie, and isn't even the most unusual mixing of incompatibles that we are to see. Ralph is still unable to get an answer to his "Rhodesia" question, and won't, since neither his mother or father probably know that it was named after the area's first white colonizer, Cecil Rhodes. The prominent mentioning of a troubled British colony like Rhodesia adds a political level to this seemingly unstructured grossness.

Neil Rhodes mentions that the Elizabethan satirical grotesque featured the "illogical and the colloquial," a fitting description for this scene that seems to be all over the place but is actually aiming at recognizable targets and drawing on known quantities. In fact, it is absolutely necessary that the viewer understand a certain vernacular if the scene is to be completely appreciated — a vernacular probably lost on today's audiences. In 1974 (the year episode 45 was written and broadcast) Rhodesia was struggling under economic sanctions brought about by the British and even the United Nations. Ian Smith's picture hangs in a shrine-like setting on the Garibaldi's wall, an explicit evocation (for those, of course, who would recognize the photo) of Smith's secession with Rhodesia from the commonwealth in 1965 — hence the sanctions. But without the script version of *Flying Circus*, there is no mention of who the man is or what he represents. It is only an understanding of the vernacular — the cultural lexicon of 1974 London and including British foreign affairs — that allows an explanation of this significant cultural and political reference. Smith and his party were flying in the face of years of British colonial policy as they attempted to create an independent country.[8] So Valerie's hysterical description of the ravaged Rhodesia, oddly enough, may actually fall in line with the Conservative stand on the former colony's political situation. The fascists she rails against would be those Smith supporters (and Smith himself) who called for the termination of British colonial status in Rhodesia. This would also fit in nicely with her general teenager attitude that her parents and family know nothing, and that she — as both a teenager and a Member of Parliament — truly understands the situation. So yet another incongruity is created here — the specter of an over-the-top teen as an MP *and* a supporter of Conservative causes.

Near the end of the sketch the mother takes a phone call which is obviously about some pending movie deal in Hollywood, perhaps based on the Garibaldis' notoriety as one of Britain's most awful families. It seems that the implication of families across the Atlantic is made, as well, since once again this movie deal is treated as if it were an everyday event, as if the Garibaldis would fit right in to a southern California neighborhood (or at least a Hollywood version of that neighborhood). With the sound of the gong all the characters stop acting, and the scene changes to yet another attack — this time on the standards of British television, where it's discovered that there are even worse families than the Garibaldis, some even higher on the social ladder, namely the "Fanshaw-Chumleighs of Berkshire." So not only are the Garibaldis a middle class nightmare, but the Fanshaw-Chumleighs are actually worse, though there isn't a hint of squalor. It becomes a measure of inbred priggishness, perhaps, which elevates the rich family above the middle-class family, and Python attacks the haves and the have-nots with almost equal gusto. Interesting, though, that whereas the middle-class "Most Awfuls" (the Garibaldis) are at least given some personality, some characterization (no matter how gross), and thus some humanity, the upper-class folk here are treated like the "Twits" – they almost don't deserve to live. Add to this the ultimate implication of the viewer — not only the Pepperpot household, who are as grotesque and dysfunctional as we've seen and would give the Jodrells a run for their money, but all viewers in general — and the scope of Monty Python's scourging becomes apparent. The levels of "watching" or voyeurism are also forwarded, as first the Garibaldis are shown to be a watched show, then the judges and presenters, then the Pepperpots, and finally the original Python studio audience, home viewers and us. But instead of pushing the viewer away from implication, this multivalent voyeurism indicts all viewers. The carnival atmosphere is more complete, then, as everyone is brought into play, and like those disparate individuals in Jonson's *BF*, there is a certain guilt by association offered by Monty Python. In the "fair" environment everyone brushes up against everyone else. We are all part of a dysfunctional family. The humor in this extended scene is purposely vulgar, it is lavatorial and scatological, it is sexual and deviant, it is biting political satire, and it depicts both television families and "real" families as interchangeably bad. There is certainly a conflation of seemingly incompatible elements, of slutty girls as MPs and cats being ironed and used as doorbells. In Python, these conflicts often arise between history and fact, between historical verisimilitude and incongruity, and, as we've seen, between the intellectual and verbal talents of the classes.

The direct, personal satiric assault is a rare occurrence in Monty Python, just as it was for either Shakespeare or Jonson, but for different reasons. Libel laws existed, of course, in the London of Monty Python, laws which protected both people and institutions from specious verbal or printed attack. The troupe even fell afoul of these laws when many religious conservatives reacted strongly to the "blasphemies" of *Life of Brian*. But these weren't direct, personal attacks on individuals. We've seen how Shakespeare responded to complaints about his use of the historical personage Oldcastle —changing the name to Falstaff— as the possibilities of fines, jail sentences and even torture for slander and libel were very real during the Elizabethan era. Jonson, of course, was nearly executed for killing a man in a duel, spent time in prison on a number of occasions for his writing and performance missteps. Elizabeth was so angered by the outright impertinence exhibited on the London stages (i.e., *The Isle of Dogs*) that in July 1597 she even ordered all playing to cease and all performance spaces to be eradicated (Miles 32). The latter didn't happen, of course, but there was a cessation of public performance for a time and the row eventually cost the Earl of Pembroke's Men their livelihood. According to Miles, the Swan never did fully recover from Elizabeth's "Tudor capacity for animosity," and by Privy Council's order licenses were granted to only two companies, the Lord Chamberlain's company at the Curtain and the Admiral's Men at the Rose Theatre (32–33). Perhaps this stands as one reason Jonson never settled with a single company, as Shakespeare did, writing instead for various companies and, eventually, the Stuart court. This doesn't mean, of course, that Shakespeare and Jonson avoided topicality — they most assuredly did not — but they were forced to write under the protection of "history," foreign settings, and broad satire to avoid prosecution. And while the chances of landing in jail and being subjected to torture were fading by the late 1960s, Monty Python did ruffle establishment feathers with their pointed satire.

Occasionally a personal, actual name is tossed into the mix of the rapid-fire comedy, like "Margaret Drabble" (Chapman, et al. 1.5.60) or "Robin Day" (1.1.5), but it is almost always just that — a tossed-off line before cutting to another subject.[9] But there is at least one example of this kind of directed satire, and like Jonson before them, the Pythons attack both friend and foe alike, as exhibited by the dead-on send-up of the Python's former "boss" and writing mate, David Frost in the "Timmy Williams Interview" sketch (1.19.255–259). Jonson had blasted both Dekker and Marston in *The Poetaster* (1600–1), and was himself attacked later as a vain stuffed shirt in *Satiromastix* (1601). The rift was eventually sutured and they later collaborated, but the intervening acerbity is well worth the strained relations. Just so with Python and David Frost. The script for the sketch even acknowledges the satiric target: "Timmy Williams comes in. He has just the faintest passing resemblance to David Frost" (1.19.255). Actually he looks, sounds and acts very much like David Frost. The studio audience responds enthusiastically to Timmy's appearance, obviously recognizing the impersonation. What follows is a series of interruptions by reporters, staff members, writers, etc., all fawning over, photographing and writing about the unctuous Timmy. A desperate acquaintance's personal problems get entered into Timmy's public record, and we eventually see that the entire conversation is being filmed for German television. The clapper board for the show reads "The Wonderful Mr. Williams," and Timmy stays just long enough to finish this "scene" and ruin the desperate friend's life:

TIMMY: Sorry, I was on the phone to America. It's been super having this lovely little chat. We must do this again more often. Er ... will you get the coffees? I'm afraid I must dash, I'm an hour late for the Israeli Embassy. *(there is a shot; Nigel slumps over the table, gun in his hand)* Er ... did you get that shot all right, sound? [1.19.257].

The "Timmy Williams" sketch then ends with extra large "Timmy Williams" production credits and unreadably fast credits for everyone else. For those who had watched the BBC over the previous ten years or so, this glibly malevolent attack on David Frost would be instantly recognizable. Without resorting to outright insults or hysterical caricatures, Python is able to skewer Frost via Timmy with simple satire. The power of derision is acknowledged early in Monty Python's work as the crime world's Piranha brothers— Doug and Dinsdale — are profiled in episode 14. The Piranhas are described as incredibly violent, with a particular penchant for nailing body parts, as Vince (Chapman), a "small-time operator" explains:

> ... and Dinsdale said "I hear you've been a naughty boy Clement"
> and he splits me nostrils open and saws me leg off and pulls me
> liver out, and I said my name's not Clement, and then he loses his
> temper, and nails my head to the floor [1.14.187].

But just as this violence can't seem to get any worse or more threatening, the real terror is mentioned in relation to the other brother, Doug. Dino Vercotti (Palin), who we've seen as a gangster threatening army bases in episode 8, describes his encounter with the more feared of the Piranha brothers after his extortion check has bounced:

> INTERVIEWER (Jones): What did he do?
> VERCOTTI: He used sarcasm. He knew all the tricks, dramatic irony,
>   metaphor, bathos, puns, parody, litotes and satire.
> PRESENTER (Cleese): *(voice over)* By a combination of violence and sarcasm
>   the Piranha brothers, by February 1966, controlled London and the
>   South East [1.14.189–90].

Derision and ridicule, the making ridiculous of authority figures, and the overall comedy of deflation fueled not only Python's writing and subject matter, but served as a *modus operandi* for their characters' most effective narrative elements. Commenting on the making of *Life of Brian*, Michael Palin notes the power the unempowered can actually wield over those in positions of authority. During the filming of Pilate's speech to the assembled mob, local extras were to laugh uncontrollably at both Pilate (Palin) and his Roman friend, Biggus Dickus (Chapman), for their speech impediments:

> I suddenly realized, "God, ridicule is such a strong weapon in the hands of a really determined crowd." I think much more [so] than hatred. You know, hatred sort of breeds hatred; comedy just breeds more comedy! It's all about people's fears about comedy. That's why people in positions of power don't like comedy, because it's essentially subversive... [Morgan, *Speaks* 237].

And the other text-given power of the normally disenfranchised or socially restrained in Monty Python? Ridicule, yes, but also knowledge. Knowledge often beyond other, more "deserving" characters (the rich, the cultured elite) and even beyond the text, as exhibited by the peasant Dennis in *Holy Grail*. Episode 28 of *Flying Circus*—wherein a ship is sinking and different costumes are donned—discussed above in reference to its incongruous visual humor, is also important when character knowledge is broached. As we've seen (and will see again) it is often the minor character in Monty Python who is the holder of knowledge. Roger the Shrubber assumes terrific significance to the narrative's successful completion, as do shoemakers in Dekker's work. As the ship sinks in episode 28 an argument erupts over the proper dress codes for a "Renaissance courtier artist" connected to the Medicis or Borgias (2.28.71). Some feel the attire is more Flemish than Italian, and of a later time period, noting details like "tassels," "hand-embroidered chevrons" and "fitted doublets going down into the full hose" (2.28.71). It is a point argued intelligently by the junior officers as the Captain just waits for them to come to an agreement. In fact, the Captain (the authority figure present) never chimes in with his own opinion, a deflation of authority which is even more apparent in an earlier episode. In episode 26 of *Flying Circus*, entitled "The Queen Will Be Watching," the announcer (Cleese) has already told us that it is possible the Queen will tune in to the *Flying Circus* at any time, but that she is currently watching *The Virginian* (an American television western which aired 1962–71). This possible royal audience has cast a sedate but nervous pall over the presentation of the show, including more sensible music and regal, austere credits. The Queen has already been lowered a peg closer to the commoner as it is admitted she actually watches TV, and perhaps even lower when the particular show she's chosen is an American western drama. The scene is set in a Welsh coal mine, and we see several miners digging with pick-axes. Two miners, played by Graham Chapman and Terry Jones, have been talking when they suddenly go face to face, then begin to pummel each other. The foreman, Eric Idle, steps in to break up the fight, only to find that they've been arguing about the proper dating for the Treaty of Utrecht, the Thirty Years War, and even which historian said what about the subjects, and on what page:

FOREMAN: He's right, Jenkins. It was ratified September 1713. The whole bloody pit knows that. Look in Trevelyan, page 468.

THIRD MINER (Palin): He's thinking of the Treaty of bloody Westphalia.

SECOND MINER: Are you saying I don't know the difference between the War of bloody Spanish Succession and the Thirty bloody Years War? [2.30.31].

Here another fight develops, only to be broken up by the foreman, who reminds them that the last time they fought it was over the "bloody binomial theorem." A fourth miner (Ian Davidson) then runs in with a question about "triglyphs in the frieze section" in Greek Doric temples. Another fight breaks out. A Management Man arrives carried in a sedan chair by two black flunkies. He wears a colonial governor's helmet and a large sign reading "Frightfully Important." All the miners prostrate themselves on the floor.

FOREMAN: Oh, most magnificent and merciful majesty, master of the universe, protector of the meek, whose nose we are not worthy to pick and whose very faeces are an untrammelled delight ... we beseech thee, tell thy humble servants the name of the section between the triglyphs in the frieze section of a classical Doric entablature.

MANAGEMENT MAN: (Cleese) No idea. Sorry [2.30.31].

With that the miners throw down their picks and go on strike, and a newsreader tells us that the miners will not return to work until management defines a metope. Once again it is the common man, the working man, who carries the knowledge of culture and history, creating an incongruity between their slovenly demeanors and their obvious intelligence. The foppish upper class have no ideas, literally and, moreover, don't seem to care. This is, as Ellen Bishop pointed out earlier, a two-fold attack. The empty-headed aristocracy who has access to education but is not educated is lampooned, but so is the verbose and pedantically intellectual lower class. The treatment of the aristocracy in this short scene comes close to what M.H. Abrams sees as the main difference between satire and the comic: derision. The man in the sedan isn't allowed anything beyond a few vapid words and an absolutely blank stare, as he is lampooned for his entire class. There is also scathing derision cutting across many institutions as Python satirizes what they consider to be traits of awful families.

The Pepperpots and female characters in general will be discussed in much greater detail in Chapter 5, but their significance as carriers of knowledge despite their deliberately frumpy appearance is worth mentioning here. In episode 4 ("Owl Stretching Time") we are introduced to two such women, Janet (Cleese) and Marge (Chapman) as they tour an art gallery. Also very apparent in this scene is the satirization of these ladies' mothering skills, which seem to include little beyond verbal abuse and arbitrary corporal punishment. They greet each other, then Janet asks about Marge's unseen child, Ralph, and Marge says that he's been a handful since they arrived, even eating some of the exhibits:

> JANET: Yes take my word for it, Marge. Kevin's eaten most of the early nineteenth-century British landscape artists, and I've learnt not to worry. As a matter of fact, I feel a bit peckish myself. *(she breaks a bit off of the Turner)* Yes…
> MARGE: I never used to like Turner.
> JANET: *(swallowing)* No … I don't know much about art, but I know what I like [1.4.42–43].

Janet and Marge both do seem to know about art, in fact, being at least familiar with the titles, artists and movements featured at this particular gallery. And their knowledge of the subject matter ranges across continents and across the centuries of art history — not bad for two shabby-looking women who tend to slap their children too much. There is even the hint of a nurturing presence — perhaps hard to discern between the slaps — as it is Janet who hints that not only do they attend these exhibitions at least semi-regularly, but will continue to do so in the future (as long as the children behave). It is a knowledge delivered without fanfare or pretense, as well. Neither woman draws attention to the fact that she is well-versed in art history, and no one else in the narrative mentions this incongruity, either. The fact that the scene dissolves into another absurdism — the eating of paintings— precludes any time spent on such considerations. They are who they are — abusive mothers, *idiots savants*? — and the narrative moves on. Interesting that their intelligence in this area is offset by the shallowness of their mothering skills and their doughty looks. It's as if the brightest flashes of light often come from the smallest candles. The Pepperpots and Dogberry and the Gumby Surgeons all possess certain gifts, but they also fail to meet at least the minimum standard of what we might consider "normal" folk to be like.

If there is an example of Python's use of satire as a weapon of seemingly unredeemed derision, then it might be the *Flying Circus* episode 12 which contains the "Upperclass Twit of the Year Show" (1.12.155–58). In this segment, shot on film and narrated in voiceover (Cleese), several over-the-top upperclass twits take part in a contest of their intellectual abilities. They are dressed similarly (and, like the Gumbys, behave similarly) in nicely cut suits and matching hats. With names like Vivian Smith-Smythe-Smith, Simon-Zinc-Trumpet-Harris, "who is married to a very attractive table lamp," and Gervaise Brook-Hampster, and the fact that each of the twits has a receding jaw and buck teeth, the twits are mocked for their cultural, social, familial, and even genetic predilections. At the starting line none of them respond to the starter's pistol, and the judge must explain the concept to them. The gun is refired, and they move off in different directions. Their first obstacles or tests include walking a straight line (where most of them fall over), leaping over a stack of three matchboxes, and an event called "Kicking a Beggar." They seem to be able to kick the beggar fairly well, with the exception of Oliver St. John Mollusc, Harrow and the Guards, who was "thought to be this year's outstanding twit" but has "a little trouble with his old brain injury" (1.12.156). The commentator describes him as having no "sort of sensory apparatus" (1.12.157). They must then with a car run over a photograph of an old woman, insult a waiter (while Oliver runs himself over and is called a "great twit!"), walk under a bar of wood suspended above them, and shoot a rabbit that's been staked to the ground. Each manages to shoot everything but the immobile rabbit. The commentator offers that they are, after all, shooting from a range "of at least one foot" (1.12.158). After attempting to remove a bra from a shop window mannequin, they all approach the final obstacle, a table with five revolvers on it, with the eventual winner being the twit who can most effectively shoot himself. The last image we are shown is a shot of three coffins draped with medals on the victory stand.

This satire seems to not only deride and scorn, but to even offer a solution for the insufferable class in question: death. The unspoken competition between members of the upper class in everyday social life is parodied, as well. Neil Rhodes notes that the "common principle" of the satirical grotesque is "the reductive physicality which involves the dehumanising or dismembering of the object of scorn" (68). Here the "abuse and vilification" of the upperclass twits has been raised to "extravagant levels of artistry," reducing the accepted nobility in this paradoxical ascension. And while the attack is unrelenting, and the upperclass twits are made to look as ridiculous as possible, the following skit once again redeems Python from any charge of favoritism in their satiric or parodic assaults. In her essay "How to Handle a Woman, or Morgan at the Movies," Maureen Fries addresses this favoritism issue in regard to the gender of the object of satire, as well: "Pythonic satire is at least nonsexist since chivalry, the Holy Grail, and romance staples like heroic action and marvelous beasts come under its unsparing gaze as well" (72). In fact, the link from this scene to the next begins to tip the scales back toward parity. A letter appears, and a voiceover (Jones) reads the letter:

READER: Dear Sir, how splendid it is to see the flower of British manhood wiping itself out with such pluck and tenacity. Britain need have no fear with leaders of this calibre. If only a few of the so-called working classes would destroy themselves so sportingly. Yours etc., Brigadier Mainwaring Smith Smith Smith etc. Deceased etc. PS etc. Come on other ranks, show your stuff [1.12.158].

Nowhere is Rhodes' notion of "dismembering" more apparent than in Terry Gilliam's linking animations, which were created using bits of artwork cut from myriad sources, colored, and xerographed into animated links.[10] Terry Gilliam would later describe his animation technique as based on dis-membering and re-membering:

I'd have the ground, and I'd have different skies, and I could build a background very quickly after a certain point, and then I just started, totally a magpie approach, things that I liked I use and chop up. If it was photos I needed, I'd send the books to the photographic place and blow them up to the sizes I want and start cutting them out..." [Morgan, *Speaks* 58].

A soldier coughs until he's fallen to pieces, literally; the heads of heads of state (Heath, MacMillan, the Queen, etc.) are animated into scenes, given dialogue, leering eyes, and hinged jaws; Michelangelo's "David" wears a fig leaf or boxer shorts and swats hands away from his "naughty bits." In episode 19 a particularly visceral evocation of dismemberment depicts an animated woman plucking off a man's head, and then using the oozing, bloody stump as a lipstick applicator (1.19.255). Episode 26 features numerous animated scenes of cannibalism, including a woman scooping a man's brains out like ice cream, and others being eaten like pieces of candy (2.26.42). Many of these images offer known people, objects and works of art as parts of Gilliam's Frankenstein-creature animation — a leg here, a torso there — effectively dismembering and dehumanizing the figures in question. A well-known image of Queen Victoria — three-quarters profile, unsmiling, looking regal — says with a spinsterish voice: "We are not amused" (1.21.283). A projectile then shoots through her head, leaving a perfectly round and ridiculous-looking entry hole. A sober Cardinal Richelieu can suddenly pull up his robes to reveal female legs and a bicycle, and he then rides off. The images aren't to be trusted, as it turns out, as they are constantly and consistently changing, adapting, mutating, and behaving in incongruous ways. This incongruity, this ever-refreshing transmogrification, then, becomes the norm, the expected, and formerly held expectations must be amended. This is why the actual appearance of real women in *Flying Circus* can be so startling, as will be discussed in the next chapter.

The collapsing police officer animation is followed by the "Ken Shabby" sketch. Shabby (Michael Palin), a commoner, is described as "a ghastly thing: a grubby, smelly, brown mackintoshed shambles, unshaven with a continuous hacking cough, and an obscene leer" (1.12.159). Shabby turns out to be as filthy and disgusting as he appears, and is seeking the hand — and whatever else he can grope — of a fine young woman. He also announces that all he's interested in is the young girl's sexual parts, that he cleans public bathrooms without a brush, and that as a married couple they'll be living in an attic where his grandmother used to train polecats (1.12.159–160). Once again the humor involves multiple bodily functions and the authority figure — a position assumed here by Rosamund's father — seems to not notice Ken's filthy demeanor and off-putting habits, and proceeds to schedule the church wedding.

If it was apparent on the Elizabethan stage that a young woman character was actually a boy, or that a disguise showed the disguised unquestionably, or that a soldier in the fourth act was obviously a page in the first act, the suspension of disbelief — the acceptance of the modes of contemporary theatricality — covered over the these glaring spots and allowed the drama to continue. With Python the generic convention becomes often character opacity or sheer blindness (or a cessation of all sensual functioning), since a creature like Ken Shabby must have at least had a smell to him that the father could notice. But he doesn't, and the scene continues. A man cannot be a watch smuggler since the customs inspector thinks he doesn't look like one (1.5.58–59); the fact that a naked man is being served as an entree isn't noticed by customers or employees at an upscale restaurant (1.13.164–166); and a vendor can hawk dead albatross successfully (1.13.167). Part of the structured comedy in Python is this very banality in the face of absurdity or incongruity, the simple "not-noticing" of things which could never be missed in real life. In *Meaning of Life*, for example, the British officers in the Zulu wars are more concerned about difficult tonsorial moments (broken mirrors, interrupted shaves) than legs that have been amputated or their horrific losses in general. Also in this feature film, while a woman's husband has his liver torn from his body and blood splatters everywhere to his horrifying screams, she breezily chats with another technician. She blames the whole messy affair on her husband, missing entirely the fact that his life is bleeding out on the dining room table before her. She is so inured to the specter of imminent death — or so uncertain as to the "meaning of life" — that she eventually volunteers herself as a live organ donor to the blood-spattered technicians.

This type of parodic satire employed by Python, as defined by Margaret Rose, relies heavily on both imitation and incongruity. There is an

imitation of the monolithic and perhaps overzealous English public health
and both public and private education systems in *Meaning of Life*, mingled with the incongruous elements of live organ donations and live sexual education demonstrations in school. *Holy Grail* parodies revered
Arthurian legends, the epic medieval film genre, including period costumes and settings, and forwards the incongruity of horseless knights and
arresting constables. The careful, believable imitation of a Welsh coal mine
is made incongruous by the elevated intellectualism of the miners' ban-
ter; while imitation of an Olympic-type competition is rendered humorous by the incongruous contestants and the silly, anti-heroic and ultimately
lethal events. Python's most ambitious parodies, though, are found in their
feature films *Life of Brian* (1979) and *The Meaning of Life* (1983). The satire
in *Life of Brian* was so fierce, to some, that the film was variously pick-
eted, banned, and railed against by many religious groups and citizens'
organizations around the world.[11] What is satirized in the film, though,
isn't necessarily religion or religious belief, but unthinking conformity, as
John Cleese was to explain later: "...I don't know in what way we're a
heresy. What we are is quite clearly making fun of the way people follow
religion but not of religion itself" (Morgan, *Speaks* 247). In the film Brian
is a character who is mistaken for a messiah — the Three Wise Men accidentally come to his manger before realizing their mistake and moving on
to Christ's— and who must try and live his ordinary life as people flock to
him as a savior and the Romans hunt him as a seditious element. Christ
actually only figures into the film momentarily, and isn't attacked or satirized in the least. Like Brian's followers, Christ's followers tend to fight
amongst themselves over his misunderstood words ("Blessed are the
cheesemakers," and some certain "Greek" will be inheriting the earth).
Jones is careful to point out that heresy wasn't foremost on their minds as
the project was conceived:

> Well, it's not blasphemous because it accepts the Christian story; in
> fact, the film doesn't make sense unless you take the Christian
> story, but it's heretical in terms of [being] very critical of the
> Church, and I think that's what the joke of it is, really [247].

So using an accepted set of situations and terms— some of which have
come to be perceived by many as holy and sanctified — Python employs
satire to reveal human frailties in organized religion. Not unlike Ben Jonson, who satirized Puritans and their duplicitous zealotry, or even, perhaps, Shakespeare, as he offers the Archbishop of Canterbury and Bishop
of Ely as ecclesiastical rubber stamps for interpretation of the "law Salique"
vis à vis the French throne. It's interesting that here, perhaps more than

anyone else, Python truly approaches what Dr. Johnson accomplished in *Vanity* and *London*: the more serious and lofty Juvenalian satire. This film is by far the least self-conscious of itself as a constructed artifice of all Python's work. *Holy Grail* consistently called attention to its filmed-ness, from direct address to anachronistic elements; *Meaning of Life* features direct address, a "middle of the film" section, and even closing comments to the audience; and *Flying Circus* is for and about television, and recognizes its medium's constructedness each episode. *Life of Brian* is a bit different, as it does have an air of righteous superiority that the others do not, which may have caused viewers all the more aggravation. Is there present the "unillusioned sadness" on the part of the speaker in regard to the foibles of the men he portrays? Certainly not to the level that Johnson reached, but similar moments are present, and are, as usual, eventually undercut or alleviated by a sight gag or pratfall or funny sound. If not narratively fueled by sobering event after sobering event, the entire project seems at least draped with a Juvenalian gossamer. Again, it is perhaps this loftiness, this association with anti-religiosity (deserved or not), which laid Python open to charges of blasphemy—a more self-conscious film might have escaped similar scrutiny. When Brian is running from Centurions, he accidentally takes the place of one of a row of prophesiers on a city street, and as he tries to blend in, he mimics both those around him and Christ, whom he's heard earlier. Like the film itself, Brian tries to look, act, and sound like these existing and accepted representations. Brian's preaching, though, will come much closer to Christ's than any of those he tries to mimic, relying on a softer voice and less boisterous presentation, probably to avoid attracting the roaming Centurions' attentions. It is just this furtiveness, though, which ultimately draws his hearers in, and attracts the craning sycophants, who can't stand the fact that he's trailed off as the centurions move away:

> BRIAN: ...and to them only shall be given—to them only ... shall ... be given...
> ELSIE: What?
> BRIAN: Hmm?
> ELSIE: Shall be given what?
> BRIAN: Oh, nothing [Scene 16].

The people are certain that he's holding back the secret of eternal life. Brian's evasiveness isn't purposeful—he just wants to slink away now that the Centurions have gone. He probably had nothing more to say, since his piecemeal memories of Christ's parables are more than likely exhausted. He's obviously heard Christ on more than one occasion, as well, and as exhibited by his eagerness to listen to Christ in scene 2, has absorbed at least a portion of the teachings. This is a connection to Christ and the sacred that none of the Pythons have commented on, nor do they seem to appreciate the importance of such a relationship, especially as the cries of "blasphemer" erupted with the film's opening. Brian is actually trying to hide by using his memorialized version of Christ's words, to preach in a Christ-like, messianic way, which to many of today's viewers might be tantamount to actual blasphemy, or even the appropriation of God's will and authority. Brian's own attempts at faux-preaching include Christ's words regarding judgment (Luke 6:37; Matthew 7:1; John 7:24), "lilies" and clothing (Matthew 6:28; Luke 12:27), "birds" as cared for by God (Matthew 10:29, 31 and Luke 12:6–7), and the somewhat mangled parable of the talents (Matthew 25). The crowd's reactions, at first, to Brian's teachings are as skeptical and accusatory as the nature of the film's satire. But the skepticism stops when Brian stops. He eventually trails off with a fractured version of something he may have heard at the Sermon on the Mount, and stops before finishing his sentence. But the crowd won't allow him to slip away, following him even as he tells them he's no prophet or seer. The gourd he's been carrying — which has been the subject of such animated (and lengthy) haggling — is suddenly noticed by the crowd:

> GIRL: It is His gourd! We will carry it for you, Master! Master?
> YOUTH: He's gone! He's been taken up!
> GIRL: Hhhh!
> FOLLOWERS: For He's been taken up!
> DENNIS: Eighteen!
> ARTHUR: No, there He is. Over there.
>   (Followers chase Brian) [Scene 16].

The gourd becomes a sacred relic, an item of this messiah's power and earthly divinity, and the crowd carries it before them as they chase Brian through the streets and out of the city proper. These farcical moments seem to be the central objects of satire in the film, as willy-nilly followers chase an unwilling savior, looking for any kind of guidance he might offer. This worship reaches a fevered pitch just moments later as the religious efficacy of the gourd versus Brian's lost sandal is debated:

> SHOE FOLLOWER: No, no, no. The shoe is...
> YOUTH: No.
> SHOE FOLLOWER: ...a sign that we must gather shoes together in abundance.
> GIRL: Cast off the shoes! Follow the Gourd!
> SHOE FOLLOWER: No! Let us gather shoes together! [Scene 17]

There are those who then race off to follow the shoes, and those who follow the gourd, and those who look to be cured (of blindness, lameness, baldness) by Brian, but he turns them away. The crowd isn't daunted, though, by his unassuming behavior, instead taking it as a sign that he is the true redeemer:

> BRIAN: I'm not the Messiah! Will you please listen? I am not the Messiah, do you understand?! Honestly!
> GIRL: Only the true Messiah denies His divinity.
> BRIAN: What?! Well, what sort of chance does that give me? All right! I am the Messiah!
> FOLLOWERS: He is! He is the Messiah! [Scene 18]

This parodic satire obviously hit too close to home for many, leading to the difficulties experienced by the film and Python in the months following its release. This is also a mock-epic, as previous movies "about" the Savior — including *Ben Hur* (1959) and *The Greatest Story Ever Told* (1965) — are parodied by *Life of Brian* in their scope and design. That *Life of Brian* looks so much like these other, more serious films is, of course, part of the problem and a big part of the reason the satire is so effective. Python's attacks on this type of hysterical following fuel the rest of the film, as Brian is pursued, by ever-increasing crowds, until his arrest and crucifixion.

It seems appropriate to look at Abrams' useful definition of general satire here — "the literary art of diminishing a subject by making it ridiculous and evoking towards it attitudes of amusement, contempt, indignation, or scorn"—and note that Python seems to have done just that in satirizing sycophantic behavior. Being able to laugh at a man who knows a savior when he sees one because he's "followed a few" might be difficult, though, for those who see themselves as true followers of a true Savior. *Life of Brian* is a case where the subject almost invariably gets in the way of successful satire, the subject being something as amorphous as "the Church," and when those satirized do in fact see themselves in the satire and aren't amused. Contempt, indignation and scorn were evoked, certainly, but were directed at the Pythons themselves, and not the intended subjects of ridicule. Couple this with the accompanying moments of coarse language, nudity, and the general accoutrements of an "R-rated" film (a "15" in the UK rating system), and the stage is set for backlash. This kind of reaction wasn't unprecedented, of course. Jonson was himself imprisoned in 1597 for his participation in the scurrilous satire *The Isle of the Dogs*, a production, now lost, which was seen as both seditious and slanderous (Miles 31–32). Jonson and his cohorts spent time in jail for their satiric exploits, and Monty Python very nearly did, as well, though cooler heads eventually prevailed (Hewison 8).

This same type of parodic satire often targeted the medium of television, from deadly game shows to sporting events featuring incontinent athletes to the ubiquitous interview show. As early as episode 2 the Pythons turned their gaze on their own medium, satirizing television documentary exposés, in "The Mouse Problem" sketch. In this sketch, a host (Palin) for the *Panorama*-like show *The World Around Us* introduces the rising problem of men dressing as mice, attending mouse parties, etc., and he is followed by furtive interviews with admitted mouse fetishists, hidden camera footage of mouse parties, and commentary from medical specialists. What sets this sketch apart from much of Python's satire is its sustained nature—the sketch and theme are allowed to play out without the usual interruptions or digressions, and the mock-serious scenario is supported throughout. According to Cleese, the sketch was based on an idea hatched while he and Chapman wrote material for Peter Sellers' *The Magic Christian* film, but which Sellers rejected.[12] The sketch was then rewritten for *Flying Circus*. The very generic elements of a show like *Panorama* are spoofed as the sketch unfolds—the concerned, hushed-voice interviewer, the key lighting in a darkened studio, hand-held 16mm camera "guerilla" footage of the illicit activities, even a representative of the medical community whose role it is to explain and contextualize these "perverts"—are part of the tightly-conceived and quite flawlessly executed parody. The differences, of course, lie in the object of scrutiny—mouse "tendencies"—rather than homosexuality, masturbation, the emergence of the "I'm OK, You're OK" social/sexual scenario, or the Profumo scandal, all of which this documentary alludes to in obvious ways.[13] Also, instead of warning against such behavior, the psychiatrist (Chapman) actually promotes the lifestyle. Pope wrote in an epic fashion about a lock of cut hair; Python somberly exposes the seedy, unseemly world of men who dress and act like mice.

After the *Flying Circus* years and for their final movie, *The Meaning of Life* (1983), Monty Python veered away from the Biblical era and television and into more familiar, episodic structures of skit comedy. The film begins with a "short feature presentation," a small film (directed by Terry Gilliam) separate from the balance of the main feature, and entitled *The Crimson Permanent Assurance*. In this short feature—a sustained parodic satire—historical, political, and cultural texts are referenced in a mock-epic form: a pirate movie.

The title visual offers us the title in crimson, actually, against a backdrop of fluttering canvas, and the swashbuckling image is created. As we see rows of old men laboriously and methodically pulling the handles of adding machines, the narrator tells us that the setting is the "bleak days" of 1983 England, when the country "languished in the doldrums of a ruinous monetarist policy."[14] "The Very Big Corporation of America" has taken over the Crimson Permanent Assurance, and the old and new aren't mixing well. Handsome, suit-clad young American men patrol the aisles, watching the old men; they take notes, time their workers, and register general disapproval in their performance: "Terrible, just terrible." There is a matched jump cut transition to a slave galley ship, where the same old men now pull laboriously and methodically on the oars before them, the young men now slave keepers with stinging whips. This striking visual metaphor/juxtaposition, coupled with the fact that the corporation that has caused and seems to be benefiting from these doldrums is foreign (specifically one of the former colonies) create a setting of sociopolitical satire — a satire directed at American venture capitalists, the Reagan administration, Margaret Thatcher and the Conservatives, by association, and the financial world in general. These targets, unlike the church-related ones chosen for *Life of Brian*, don't seem to lend themselves to much controversy. Another match cut wipe takes us back to the "now," and the labor continues unabated. The satire takes on a parodic structure when, after one of the workers has been "sacked," the old men begin an uprising. The young corporate types are jumped, beaten, and herded into a large wall safe, while one is tied up with adding-machine and ticker-tape paper and made to walk the plank. The "captain" of the ship — who looks remarkably like an older Douglas Fairbanks, Jr.— gives the orders to mount the rigging, man the weapons, and — addressing the only woman of the crew — put the kettle on. He also gives the order to raise anchor. The crew fashion weapons from office supplies, including file cabinet cannon and ceiling fan swords. The old men cut loose the construction tarpaulins which cover the "prow" of the old building, creating a sail, and an anchor is pulled from the ground to the surprise of many passersby. The "desperate and reasonably violent men" of the Crimson Permanent Assurance then set sail upon the "high seas of international finance."

Soon they spy "the prize they [seek] ... a financial district swollen with multinationals, conglomerates, and fat, bloated merchant banks." They pull broadside of the glass skyscraper occupied by "The Very Big Corporation of America" and open fire. This is a parody of *Captain Blood* or any number of Hollywood swashbuckler films, complete with grappling hooks and ropes as the "pirates" board the flagship of their "oppressive corporate management." Inside the boardroom, more young executives put up a fight, but are no match for the seasoned marauders. Their raid is successful, and as the Crimson Permanent Assurance sails on to new targets, the narrator continues to revitalize and reinforce the parodic structure: "The outstanding returns on their bold venture became apparent. The once proud financial giants lay in ruins; their assets stripped, their policies in tatters." Not afraid to borrow from any genre, in true musical form they break out in unmotivated song: "It's fun to charter an accountant, / And sail the wide accountancy / To find, explore, the funds offshore, / And skirt the shoals of bankruptcy...." The vignette then ends in typical Python fashion, as the ship sails off the edge of the earth.

The elevation motif discussed above is apparent here, as well. The slaves of the corporation are able to rise up and overcome their masters, their betters. As we've seen in *Shoemakers Holiday* and *Holy Grail*, there is an inability on the part of the so-called "upper class" to adequately defend themselves against what the text sees as inevitable: a change in status. The world of the text allows for such happenings, creating, certainly, as Faber noted, an "utterly fantastic, wished-for world." There is a leveling, as well, since the "once proud, family firm" that had been taken over becomes a corporate takeover entity itself. As seen in *Flying Circus* and the other feature films, there is general distrust of any authority figure, be it a king, a mine manager, or a multinational conglomerate. Margaret Rose writes that

> [i]n parody the comic incongruity created in the parody may contrast the original text with its new form or context by the comic means of contrasting the serious with the absurd as well as the "high" with the "low," or the ancient with the modern, the pious with the impious, and so on [33].

The original text here is the perceived world of high finance in contemporary England, while the new form is a full color cinematic representation of English family business acumen battling the hostile forces of American venture capitalism. It's the cottage industry versus the Industrial Revolution all over again, though no amount of tossed sabots can keep the little ship/family firm from being destroyed in the end. The "serious" conglomerate is overwhelmed by the "absurd" little assurance firm, though, at least for a short while. Again, as with the "Upperclass Twit" segment, there is the temptation to put too much stock in Python's direct satire, their scorn for the crass "Other"; the fact that the building/ship sails off into nothingness reinforces the quid pro quo nature of much of Python's comedy. The absurd is therefore reinforced by further absurdities. A strict Marxist reading is even possible. Speculative capitalism and conglomerates create needy have-nots who can then rise up against the owners of wealth, of production. But this reading is undercut, as well, by the ending. As the ship is lost, the message becomes one of anti-capitalism, that even the smaller players will eventually be lost, as well. This is a heteroglossic text that references countless other texts and cultural/historical/social venues, and is truly a rich parodic satire.

Elements of satire, both direct and indirect, parody, the mock-epic and mock-heroic, carnival, and the grotesque are well represented in Monty Python's collected works. This chapter attempted to address just some of these structures, laying bare momentarily the inner workings of what Gutwirth calls "the comedy of outrageousness" (140). One conclusion that can be drawn (without being terribly reductive) is that no single comic structure holds the stage for very long in any of Python's creations. Indirect satire may give way to parody and mock-heroic, but are themselves displaced by Menippean satire, then carnival, grotesque, and perhaps back to indirect satire. The lack of "spatial or temporal perspective," and the presence of a "striking simultaneity of awareness" that Faber found in Dekker's *SH*, has been revitalized for the popular culture of twentieth-century London, allowing Python to access the styles and structures of humor freely and associatively. It is a protean form that Monty Python practices, violating boundaries wherever they can be found. Many of Python's best-known affects/effects can be traced back to playwrights of the English Renaissance, and the fact that much of Python's work was done on a stage (a television sound stage) and in front of a live audience creates interesting parallels in production, staging, and troupe utilization. Like Shakespeare's work, Python's sketches and scripts are meant to be performed, realized visually, and not read as poetry or literature. If anything, Python attacked the notion of effete intellectualism in favor of experience. The broad knowledge base that seems necessary for a full appreciation of the many texts referenced in even a single episode of *Flying Circus* speaks well of the comedy, and of its value in study, and again hearkens back to its roots in the Elizabethan and Jacobean playwrights and theaters.

Notes

1. For the discussion on Henry V being the ideal king who mingles with his subjects (even though, historically, Henry VI would have been in power), see Chapter 3.

2. In an interesting sidebar, these are just the words spoken by the Black Knight in Python's *Holy Grail* before he loses both arms and legs in a duel with Arthur. The lawyer suffers much the same fate at the hands (and intellect and tongue) of Vittoria.

3. See "The Clown" in *Shakespeare's Satire* (London: Oxford, 1943). Campbell spends a good deal of time with the role of Will Kemp in Shakespeare's company, as well.

4. See 3.1.148–49. Later, in 3.4, when Polonius accidentally betrays himself behind the arras, Hamlet's first response (after stabbing the hidden intruder), is to ask if it is the king (3.4.26). He doesn't realize he hasn't triumphed until line 31, and then admits that he mistook Polonius for his "better," the king (3.4.32).

5. Here we have another example of the deflationary use of names and naming in Python — Dennis the Peasant, Roger the Shrubber, Tim the Enchanter, etc. Arthur's horse/valet in *Holy Grail* is named Patsy; there is also Sir Robin the Not-So-Brave-As-Sir-Launcelot; and the women at Castle Anthrax have names such as Zoot (Carol Cleveland), Piglet (Avril Stewart), Winston (Sally Kinghorn), and Dingo (Cleveland). Names usually reserved for more modern folk and even pet names are consistently used to create yet another incongruity in what are already incongruous settings, as well as remind the viewer — via acknowledgement of the comedic artifice — that a staged production is being watched, not a historical event. Jonson often used names to signal characters' roles (much like the practice of the early morality plays)— their vices or shortcomings or habits (Volpone the Fox, Mosca the Parasite); he also simply made fun of Puritan folk in the manner of Zeal-of-the-Land-Busy and Tribulation Wholesome.

6. Again, all quotations from these feature films are taken verbatim from videotape versions, with after-the-fact printed Internet versions used to identify scenes. Screenplays with line numbers are not yet available, and the final shooting version as it is available on videotape is significantly altered from any existing printed version (including Internet sources). See Chapman, et al., *Monty Python and the Holy Grail* (1975).

7. Gumbys are oafish characters who wear handkerchiefs on their heads, clench their fists at their waists, wear rolled-up pants and similar vests, and shout a great deal. They are, according to William Proctor Williams, "modern or urban village idiots."

8. The photo of Ian Smith would have little effect on most viewers, and there would be no connection between Ralph's questions, Rhodesia, and Smith without significant annotations. For more on Rhodesia (now Zimbabwe) go to www.britannica.com, and search under the keyword "Rhodesia."

9. Margaret Drabble (1939–) is the most recent editor of *The Oxford Companion to English Literature*, though in 1969 she was better known as a novelist and biographer. A Cambridge grad, Drabble had published *A Summer Bird-cage* (1962), *The Garrick Year* (1964), and *The Millstone* (1965) by this time. She also understudied Vanessa Redgrave at the RSC, and wrote television reviews for the *Daily Mail* in the 1960s. See article under Drabble, Margaret at www.britannica.com, and a helpful web page found at www.redmood.com/drabble. Robin Day was the Liberal Party candidate for South Hereford.

10. See David Morgan's *Monty Python Speaks* (New York; Avon, 1999): 20, 58.

11. See Hewison's *Monty Python: The Case Against* (London: Metheun, 1981) for a close look at the uproar over the film, including the possibility of jail sentences for the alleged offenders.

12. See Johnson *20 Years*, 50. The unrelenting nature of this particular sketch can perhaps be attached to its previous life as a proposed part of a feature film.

Panorama, incidentally, was a long-running (1953 and on) interview and current affairs show on British television.

13. Satirizing "probing" television documentaries, the writers have fetishized rodents, making dressing like a mouse akin to transvestism, homosexuality, recreational drug use or orgiastic sexual practices— or just about any other practice society might constitute as "deviant." The impetus for this sketch must have been documentaries about illicit drug use, spousal swapping, closeted homosexuals, etc., or, even more likely, a combination of many such documentaries dealing with obsessive-compulsive behaviors and alternative lifestyles of all kinds. Again, it's the unrelenting nature of the narrative that sets this apart from most of Python's other work in *FC*. When the man in question (Mr. Jackson, played by Cleese) admits that he's "more comfortable with mice," the sketch sounds very much like a nod to the then-current Dr. Thomas Harris book *I'm OK You're OK*, released in 1969. These mice-men, in Harris's co-opted "Transactional Analysis" scenario, would be the "not-OK" types who resort to secretive, ritualistic behaviors, including withdrawal and games to avoid the pains of intimacy with "OK" types. Mr. Jackson's comment that he felt more at ease with other mice seems to put us firmly in this new and dynamic world of interpersonal relationships. Harris's work was based on Eric Berne's earlier work (*Games People Play* 1963), which may also have influenced this sketch (in its original iteration).

Also, the mention of perverse man-mouse statistics bring to mind teenage masturbation statistics, possibly from David Reuben's 1969 book *Everything You Always Wanted to Know About Sex but Were Afraid to Ask* (1969), or a similar quote from either Kinsey (*Sexual Behavior in the Human Male* (1948) *and Sexual Behavior in the Human Female* (1953)), or Masters and Johnson (*Human Sexual Response* (1966)). All of these landmark studies would have been prominently in the public view during this period, and could easily have influenced Cleese and Chapman's writing.

This entire satire is also at least partially an allusion to the Profumo scandal. Elizabeth II's Secretary of State of War (1960–63), John Profumo had an *affaire du coeur* with a young prostitute, Christine Keeler, who also happened to be bedding a Soviet naval attaché, Captain Eugene Ivanov. It was feared for years afterward that at the height of the Cold War the Soviets were given access to top secret "pillow talk" regarding the NATO alliance. There arose allegations (many reported in the *New York Post*) that orgies were conducted in various palatial residences in and around London. These orgies included judges and ministers participating in acts of prostitution, sadomasochism and the wearing of masks, according to *John Profumo and Christine Keeler 1963*, by Alfred Thompson Denning (2000). The various young women involved also sold their story to the London tabloids. Profumo lied to the House of Commons about the affair. He resigned, but didn't have to do so ceremoniously, as was the norm. The U.S. FBI gathered 1,500-plus pages of documents as it quietly investigated the scandal that nearly toppled the Macmillan government.

14. All quotations from this movie are taken verbatim from the videotape version. See *The Meaning of Life* (1983).

Chapter 5

(Ad)dressing the Other

"There are lots of *others* in this theater" writes Stephen Orgel in "Nobody's Perfect: Or Why Did the English Stage Take Boys for Women?" (9). And the "others" on the Elizabethan stage to whom he refers are not only many in number, but varied in type. He points out that Elizabethan comedies and pastorals are often set elsewhere (than London), and that tragedies are also either set elsewhere or anciently or both. "The Other, for this theater," he writes, "is as much foreign as female" (9). Othello, then, can be approached as Other, as well as Aaron the Moor, the Dolphin (Dauphin), and many more. But women? Most scholars and even Elizabethan-era critics and diarists acknowledge that of the audiences who regularly attended theatrical productions, many attendees were female. Treating the female characters on stage as Other, it would seem, might alienate the largely female audience, becoming a financial issue affecting every theater. There were abundant female viewers, but no females actually on stage in the English public theaters. It is well known that young boys were an important part of Elizabethan and Jacobean theater troupes; not only did they serve as actors, understudies, stagehands and prop masters, but they donned dresses and wigs and acted the female roles. In Elizabethan England, "fair Beatrice"; "too fair, too wise, wisely too fair" Juliet; and Laertes' "dear sister" Ophelia — no matter how feminine the "chariest maid" of these may have been described — each was played by a boy or young man. Cross-dressing kept the English stage free of innocent young girls and women who would otherwise be compromised.

Cross-dressing for members of the Monty Python troupe — though by no means a convention of the late 1960s, of British television, or of comedy shows in general — allowed for the furtherance of Python's humor by incongruity and visual farce. It also significantly affected the creation of the Other — specifically the female as Other, effectively marginalizing

the female actor. Shakespeare, Jonson, Dekker, Marston, et al., and all producers of plays for public consumption had to comply with the "no women
on stage" rules common to the time; Python chose to adopt this stage
practice. And even with cross-dressing on the Renaissance English stage a
given, Shakespeare's (and others') sexuality and, more directly, his treatment of sexuality within his plays will be mentioned in order to discuss
theatrical aspects of sexuality like cross-dressing, audience titillation,
homoeroticism, the treatment of women (characters and players), and the
unavoidable homosocial and homosexual flavors of both Elizabethan life
and theater and Monty Python. The specter of an Other inevitably sur-
faces here as these categories of "alternative" sexualities (alternative to
both heterosexual attraction and the patriarchal order) are encountered,
and must be addressed, as well. The effects of these practices are the subject of this chapter, from the critical reception (then and now) of men and
boys as women (then cross-dressing as a man or boy, often) to specifically
the ways in which Monty Python wrote and acted female characters, as
well as the place in their world for the odd real woman who appeared with
this all-boy troupe. Overarching the men-as-women practices, foreign settings, and representations of both women and foreigners (and alienated
friends, even) is the specter of the Other that seemed to populate and even
define the Shakespearean stage and the Monty Python (sound)stage. But
first to the Elizabethan playhouses where "sodomitical" perversions—at
least in many contemporary critics' opinions—occupied the "unworthy
scaffold" of the "wooden O."

In "'Bargaines of Incontinencie': Bawdy Behavior in the Playhouses,"
Ann Jennalie Cook cites John Northbrooke, who warns that young women
would undoubtedly be captured by "crocodiles, which devoure the pure
chastitie," eventually teaching them "how to playe the harlottes ... howe
to ravishe, howe to beguyle, howe to betraye, to flatter, lye, sweare, for-
sweare, how to allure to whoredome" (271). Northbrooke continued, arguing that "women (especiallye) shoulde absent themselves from such playes"
(271). Northbrooke here is specifically addressing the women as audience
members being instructed by the corrupt stage, and not necessarily the
women who might dare to venture into the life of an actress; but the broad
brush of his attack smears all women in or around the theaters. Cook also
cites Anthony Munday, who in 1580 warns that the

> comical discourses (al which are taken out of the secret armorie of
> Venus, & practising bawderie) turne al chastitie upside downe, &
> corrupt the good disposition & manners of youth, insomuch that it
> is a miracle, if there be found anie either woman, or maide, which

with these spectacles of strange lust, is not oftentimes inflamed
even unto furie [275–76].

By the 1590s, though, Thomas Nashe welcomes young men into these educational "publike places" where they can interact with "faire women" while
"frequenting the company of Poets" (278). Nashe, a member of the so-
called "University Wits" with Greene, Lodge, Marlowe and Lyly,[1] makes
the further point of congratulating the theatrical companies for not
employing "whores and common Curtizens to playe womens partes" (278).
In short, Nashe, as liberal as he may appear (being a playwright himself),
seems to be saying that even the lowest, most debased of English women
aren't degraded enough to become actresses. That the English stage is for
men and boys seems clear.

Recent scholarship in the area seems to reach the same "promised
land": homoerotica. Young boys dressed as women excited the male audience member in the "wrong" way, according to contemporary anti-theatricalists like the widely-quoted Stephen Gosson. The former
playwright-turned-clergyman, publishing in 1579 and 1582, was afraid
that theater would "effeminate" the mind of the viewer: "The whole prac-
tise of Poets … [is to] vnfold theyr mischiefe, discouer theyr shame …
[they are] effeminate writers, vnprofitable members, and vtter enimies to
vertue" (Gosson 19–20). Orgel notes what appear to be the "fear of a universal effeminization" on the part of not only these anti-theatricalist writers, but men in general during this period (17). Around the same time
Phillip Stubbes echoed Gosson's claims, and announced that wearing
women's clothing would "adulterate" the male gender; this paved the way
for the much later publication of William Prynne's lengthy tract charging
that men who dressed in women's clothing would eventually "degenerate"
into women (Levine 10). This last example of anti-theatricalism which
appeared in 1632, according to Laura Levine, may actually "have hastened
the closing of the theaters" (10). The much-published fear that men might
become women or assume women's attributes (perhaps even physically)
if they dressed as women, especially on the stage, fueled the anti-sodomit-
ical fires but, paradoxically, continued to keep women off of the English
stage during and after Shakespeare's lifetime, as well.

Both Jean Howard and Stephen Orgel argue that the effect of cross-
dressing was, essentially, the "castration of female sexuality" to "produce
a chaste, silent, and obedient female subject" on the stage (Sedinger 65).
Orgel, however, also notes that the women weren't entirely outside the
male circles, identifying that "the men in *Merry Wives* lose hands down to
the women and Emilia on the relationships between the sexes" (9). Portia

in *Merchant* receives an apology and a public affirmation or surety of Bassiano's love (5.1.240–246). Beatrice in *Much Ado* gives as good as she gets to all men, not just her "very dull fool" Benedick. In fact, when it is concluded that both Portia and Bassiano and Benedick and Beatrice have been somewhat duped by the machinations of their friends (who wish to see them coupled), they, of course, deny their feelings. But it is Beatrice who is allowed the last words in their verbal joust before Benedick surrenders. Beatrice agrees to take Benedick, conditionally: "…I yield upon great persuasion, and partly to save your life, for I was told you were in a consumption" (5.4.94–96). "Peace," Benedick pleads, "I will stop your mouth," and the couple is finally created (5.4.97). Benedick's complete surrender to the joys of marriage follows, with Benedick even admitting that he and all men are actually "giddy" things, a trait usually reserved by men to describe women and their fickle natures. This seems an interesting and pointed leveling of the sexes as the play closes, and another argument for the position of women, at least on occasion, as insiders rather than distant Others. Shakespeare's treatment of sexuality runs the gamut from the "celebration of heterosexuality" to kinds of "protofeminism" to "sexual loathing or fear of the female"—the gamut, as can be seen, being of a decidedly heterosexual refinement (Porter 130). Marlowe, on the other hand, has been read as more misogynistic, less protofeminist, more "aggressively sensual" and certainly more interested in the physical pleasures of homosexuality and the theatrical aesthetics of homoeroticism (130). The cross-dressing, then, for Shakespeare and Marlowe, may have served very different purposes and aimed to satisfy different sexual orientations. The anti-theatricalists then may have had more call to fear the cross-dressed actor of a Marlowe play than a Shakespeare production, perhaps, but the broad brush paints a wide swath, and the sodomitical perversions of the stage knew no boundaries. Lisa Jardine writes of the "homoerotic object of desire" inherent in the theatrical conventions of the time; and both Jardine and Levine shrug off the more recent feminist readings which tend to "romanticize the 'real female feeling' of Shakespeare's comedic heroines" (Sedinger 66). In short, much recent scholarship holds as suspect the cross-dressed convention, its intentions, practices, and effects.

But as Stephen Orgel indicates, the fact that the English stage was peopled by men and boys is treated as *a priori* by many scholars and critics, as if "the fact merely constituted a practical arrangement and had no implications beyond its utility in a number of disguise plots" (7). Orgel notes that though most of Europe was of one mind concerning women as actresses, it was the English public theater alone which depended entirely upon male actors in female roles. He mentions Spain, which banished women from the public stage in 1596, but four years later repealed the ban, finding "the spectacle of transvestite boys ... more disturbing than that of theatrical women" (8). In fact, it wouldn't be until at least 1644 that women as actors began to appear, and this only in "private theatrical, provincial dramas," occasional dramas which allowed for some experimentation with casting and scenery and which were outside the public realm.[2] Taking a different tack, Glynne Wickham argues in *Early English Stages* that women may have been excluded from the English stage because they were given little or no oratorical training, but this explanation seems to have been poorly accepted in light of the patriarchal, emblematic aesthetics proffered by most recent scholarship (272).

And it certainly wasn't the case that England had no opportunity to see women on the stage, since Italian companies with female cast members (usually family affairs) would occasionally appear in London, and there is even record of a French company playing at least three performances in 1629 with women players (Orgel 9 and note). So Londoners had the opportunity to see women on the stage, but, as Orgel notes, "what they did not see were *English* women on the stage" (9). Orgel identifies a distinctive "us" versus "them" dichotomy not just with regard to sex, but nationality. In other words, what might be good for foreigners— the ubiquitous "Other"— is not necessarily good for an English(wo)man. This tension between foreigners and Englishmen is apparent in myriad plays of the period; from the tortuous linguistic machinations forced upon Katherine and Macmorris's affected "What ish my nation"in *Henry V* to Franceschina in *The Dutch Courtesan*, for example. Shakespeare even distinguishes between "English" and "British," offering the "whole of the British Isles" into a concerted effort against archenemy (and arch–Other) France in *Henry V* (Bate 220). "Others" include, then, those who are not English (including the British), who have different speech patterns and who are therefore at least somewhat suspect. In *Richard II*, John of Gaunt, offering "inspir'd" prophecy, identifies his homeland as "This royal throne of kings, this sceptred isle, / ... This fortress built by Nature for herself / Against infection ... This blessed plot, this earth, this realm, this England" (2.1.31, 40, 43–44, 50). The "infection" of women actors— and the specter of foreigners setting trends on the home soil— was a contagion best kept far from England's unsullied stage and shore.

It is also useful to remember that otherness can include rather stereotypical categorizing, as in the case of Aaron the Moor in *Titus Andronicus* being evil simply because he is who he is— a Moor; Don John in *Much Ado About Nothing* leans to evil because he is a bastard (as all bastards were in Elizabethan drama); and Richard (Gloucester) is despised as "a lump of foul deformity" by Anne and even his own mother, at least in part, because of his misshapen body (1.2.57). Because he "cannot prove a lover" he determines "to prove a villain," and sets out to achieve his "libels, and dreams" (1.1.28, 30, 33). Anything or anyone that happens to be non–English can fall into this Other category, including Scots, Irish, provincials, and all continentals. Former friends and confidantes can achieve Other status, as well, if they transgress Englishness, as exemplified by almost anyone Richard of Gloucester drew near him, and the legendary Falstaff. First, though, to Falstaff and his fateful journey from Hal's playful "Sir John Paunch" to Henry's rebuked "fool and jester"—and into a doomed Other status.

Whether Shakespeare simply grew tired of Falstaff's unparalleled popularity or not, this larger-than-life character was put aside (and put down, effectively) by Shakespeare and Hal-cum-Henry in *2 Henry IV* and *Henry V*. And even though Falstaff—called "that authentic triumph of the literary imagination"—is a fascinating and likable character, he must be overcome, as G. Blakemore Evans mentions, before Hal can become Henry V and ascend the royal mount (845). Henry IV has died, and Hal is to take his place. Falstaff, however, can feel no wind of change beyond that which might blow him to fortune—which might be Shakespeare's way of both judging his creation and crushing him mightily—and accosts the new King as an old mate: "God save thy Grace, King Hal! My royal Hal!" (*2 Henry IV* 5.5.42). "Hal," of course, is no more, and like the unwanted and pathetic acquaintance who embarrasses more than enriches, Falstaff caroms into his own humiliation without the slightest awareness he's doomed or, more substantially, that anything's even changed following Henry's ascendancy. "Stand here by me, Master Shallow," Falstaff tells his companion as the King approaches, "I will make the King do you grace ... do but mark the countenance that he will give me" (5.5.5–8). The very language of Falstaff's promise—"I will *make* the King..."—rings of an influence over the young Hal which "tutor" Falstaff no longer has over Henry. The myopic Falstaff also promises Pistol a part of the spoils to be had as friend to a friend of the King; and when Falstaff is told by Pistol of the plights of old companions Doll and Helen, his sublimity reaches a new level: "I will deliver her" (5.5.38). Our depiction here is of Falstaff, then, as a Moses or messiah for those who had been Hal's friends. He will either lead the chosen (chosen by their former association with both Falstaff and Hal) to the promised land of the new king's court, or he is the intercessor for the fallen between the "profane" of Hal's past and the "grace" of Henry's kingship. Falstaff is, instead, an Other, as much a foreigner as any, and more loathed because he knows the "Hal" in Henry. The King answers Falstaff's hail, likening Falstaff to an unfortunate nightmare:

> I know thee not, old man, fall to thy prayers.
> How ill white hairs becomes a fool and a jester!
> I have long dreamt of such a kind of man,
> So surfeit-swell'd, so old, and so profane;
> But being awak'd, I do despise my dream [5.5.47–51].

Falstaff has been relegated to Otherness, and this from Henry V, whom many consider to be the most patriotic, chest-thumping king of all Shakespeare's Englishness. Falstaff will die, transformed into an Other, off-stage and ignominiously in *Henry V*, mourned only by the kind of rabble Henry so vehemently detached himself from, the "misleaders" of the king's "former self" (5.5.58, 64).

Prince Henry — prior to his ascension and transformation from rogue to royal — anticipates his own looming change, but announces it to none save himself and the audience. The otherness of his youthful, feral character will be put off, he prophesies, in favor of the royal mantle he must assume. He bids goodnight to his accomplices in the first act of *1 Henry IV*, then waxes contemplative:

> *Prince.* I know you all, and will a while uphold
> The unyok'd humor of your idleness,
> Yet herein will I imitate the sun.
> Who doth permit the base contagious clouds
> To smother up his beauty from the world,
> That when he please again to be himself,
> Being wanted, he may be more wond'red at
> By breaking through the foul and ugly mists
> Of vapors that did seem to strangle him [1.2.195–203].

Young Henry will only keep his present lifestyle and friends for as long as it is textually significant, then he will transform himself. This textual authority (granted by the author) is also evident in the arc of events in *Henry V*, as Lisa Jardine indicates, wherein the French are transformed from both enemies of England and allies of the (conspicuously Other) "coursing snatchers" Scots (1.2.143), to Henry's cousins (by way of royal marriage), with Henry himself called "fair son" by the King of France (5.2.281, 348; Jardine 7). Thus a "marital alliance" transforms Others into mere others, and Shakespeare's text resolves the differences, including the rather convenient elision of the natural heir to the French throne, the Dauphin (Jardine 7, 11). There are also the connections between the opening of Hal's condemnatory speech (*2 Henry IV* 5.5.47–51) and the previous, prophetic speech (*1 Henry IV* 1.2.203) wherein Hal sees that the future holds a transformation for him. The progression from "I know you all" to "I know thee not," is a crucial pronouncement which signals the reformation of Hal into Henry and rings down the curtain on his "former self" and company. The specter of condemnation is all the more evident in the language Shakespeare chose to illustrate Falstaff's fall from grace. The biblical account of the parable of the ten virgins awaiting the bridegroom is significant here, as Christ — the bridegroom — has warned that all the virgins must be ready with full oil lamps when He comes. Five are prepared, and five reason that they can obtain the oil at a moment's notice. When Christ does appear, he rebukes those who are not prepared, who have not followed His counsel: "But he answered and said, Verily I say unto you, *I know you not*" (Matt. 25:12; emphasis added). The five virgins with empty lamps are left without the wedding celebration, condemned for their lack of foresight and ignorance of the bridegroom's warnings. The previously mentioned allusion to Henry as a sort of transformed (or resurrected?) Christ figure (from the mortal Prince Hal to the immortal King Henry) is reinforced as both Christ and Henry transform others into Others, marginalizing those transformed for the eternities on the stage and in the worlds to come. As Other(s), Falstaff is denied admission to the royal abode, and the five virgins lose their eternal inheritance.

The play on words in reference to Henry's imitation of the sun is important, as well, for he is both the brightest in the firmament (or he should be) as the heir apparent and he is also the *son* to his father, the king. The king, however, sees only "riot and dishonor" in his young Henry, and even muses aloud that some magic might have switched Henrys with Lord Northumberland's son, "and called mine Percy, and his Plantagenet!" (1.1.85–89). A theatrical transformation *will* eventually take place, but it will be Hal, and not Hotspur, who will become the "theme of honor's tongue" (1.1.81). Young Henry has to this point imitated without truly representing or ennobling his king's son status; it has been a role for which he has been trained but is ill-suited. Shakespeare's theatrical allusions here are strong, and Henry will only be able to "be himself" when he has assumed the role for which he has been cast, but has yet to perform. It's as if he has been in the tiring house for the early portions of some great play, appearing here and there, out of character and costume, until he finally realizes there lies ahead a cue which he must answer.[3] Henry is the actor capable of donning a new costume and character at will, while, paradoxically, actually becoming himself. This new performance is foreseen, as well, as the young prince promises his premiere will be without parallel:

So when this loose behavior I throw off
And pay the debt I never promised,
By how much better than my word I am,
By so much shall I falsify men's hopes,
And like bright metal on a sullen ground,
My reformation, glitt'ring o'er my fault,
Shall show more goodly and attract more eyes
Than that which hath no foil to set it off.
I'll so offend, to make offense a skill,
Redeeming time when men think least I will [1.2.208–217].

Henry will "throw off" the costume of the scoundrel, exceeding his own estimation of himself ("better than my word I am"), and his transformation ("My reformation") will be presented for all the world to see — including his father, his companions, his enemies, and the groundlings. His prophecies are later fulfilled in *2 Henry IV*, of course, and it is at that time King Henry allows Falstaff a final chance, a chance to see to his own transformation. Falstaff is exiled until such a time as he can "reform" himself, but this re-forming won't be accomplished, and instead he will see "perform'd the tenure" of Henry's sentence: exile and quiet death (5.5.71). He is marginalized, perhaps, as a result of Shakespeare's "hard opinions," his reform made impossible for textual considerations. Richard III also suffers defeat, as will be seen, not because he is evil and must be overthrown, but because he is an actor, and the play must end.

While Hal's blossoming into Henry V is an enriching reformation worthy of a king's son, perhaps the most adept Shakespeare character at this transforming is Richard III, who is not only able to transform himself at will (and into whatever he chooses), but his friends and family into enemies, into Others. Richard manages to transform himself from a wretched, "rudely stamp'd" Other into whatever semblance his connivings require. And, as Anne Barton notes, if it weren't for the "inexorable demand of Fate" nothing — not any character in *Richard III* or even history — should overcome the character Richard (97). These manipulations would not be so effective if Richard weren't able to convince so many others that his machinations were true and correct — he might be a raving lunatic, but not a leader. In *Shakespeare and the Idea of the Play*, Barton further identifies Richard as "impassioned lover, injured friend, plain blunt man" and even "saint" (98). He is the consummate actor, able to take on roles that suit him and his purpose, playing each with equal fervor. But he is also a kind of director who can cast others into whatever roles will most benefit Richard himself; he is given the unusual power by Shakespeare to perform alchemical character transformations—from base metals to gold, or vice versa — often by his mere words. As Henry VI is being taken for burial, Richard tells the corpse bearers to put the king's body down. Anne quickly identifies Richard as the special character that he is: "What black magician conjures up this fiend / To stop devoted charitable deeds?" (*Richard III* 1.2.34–35). Richard answers that the conjured is also the conjurer, and he transforms the bearers to men of evil and from living to dead: "*Villains*, set down the corse, or, by Saint Paul, / I'll *make* a corse of him that disobeys" (emphasis added; 1.2.36–38). The God-like aspects of Richard's character are forwarded by Richard himself and those he manipulates, and, often, other characters reinforce Richard's seeming omnipotence. Anne places him as second only to God — and even co-equal in that only God can truly create — as she condemns him as a "foul devil," one who "hast *made* the happy earth thy hell, / Fill'd it with cursing cries and deep exclaims" (1.2.49, 51–52).[4] Richard is given the power to create and destroy by the very people he so shrewdly manipulates. He seems even beyond reach of mere mortals, and can only destroy himself: "Fouler than heart can think thee, thou canst *make* / No excuse current but to hang thyself" (1.2.83–84). This emphasis on making, on the creation-like or transformational power of Richard the director/maker, pervades *Richard III* and places Richard as perhaps the most complete character/actor ever envisioned by Shakespeare. While Richard counters Anne's vitriol with "rules of charity, / Which renders good for bad, blessings for curses" (1.2.68–69), Anne reaffirms Richard's Alpha and Omega status, calling him both "the cause, and most accurs'd effect" (1.2.120). In this doubling Richard is both friend and Other, and will soon become, for Anne, both murderer and suitor, assailant and husband. Interesting, too, that Stephen Greenblatt attaches this same sort of transformational power back to the author himself:

> [S]o absolute is Shakespeare's achievement that he has himself come to seem like great creating nature: the common bond of humankind, the principle of hope, the symbol of the imagination's power to transcend time-bound beliefs and assumptions, peculiar historical circumstances, and specific artistic conventions [*The Norton Shakespeare* 1].

So Shakespeare is the source for and shares the special abilities with Falstaff and Richard. Richard is able to transform the man he killed, King Henry VI, Anne's (textual) father-in-law, and the man he mortally wounded, Henry's son, Edward, into Others before our eyes and even under the vicious scorning of Anne. Henry and Edward become Others, and Richard is able to gather their treasures—their women, their kingdoms, their reputations, even — as his spoils.

Clarence/George (Richard and Edward's brother) must also be dealt with, and he must also be relegated to Other status to accomplish this feat. Richard vows to set his "brother Clarence [George] and the King / In deadly hate the one against the other" (1.1.34–35), and that Clarence must be seen by Edward as the "G" foretold in prophecy who would destroy Edward and rule in his stead (1.1.39–40). It is clear, as Clarence recounts Edward's encounters with a "wizard" who prophesied the "G" omen, that Richard is actually the wizard in these proceedings, the maker/director able to manipulate his characters into whatever roles he chooses. Clarence is doomed because Richard has succeeded in transforming him into an Other in Edward's eyes. Queen Margaret, Henry's widow — not historically a part of these activities, but included for dramatic purposes nonetheless — must also become an Other, and as Richard rehearses the deeds accomplished in killing the king and Rutland, Margaret finds herself thusly transformed:

> *Glou.* The curse my noble father laid on thee
> When thou didst crown his warlike brows with paper,
> And with thy scorns drew'st rivers from his eyes,
> And then, to dry them, gav'st the Duke a clout
> Steep'd in the faultless blood of pretty Rutland —
> His curses then, from bitterness of soul
> Denounc'd against thee, are all fall'n upon thee;
> And God, not we, hath plagu'd thy bloody deed.
> *Q. Eliz* So just is God, to right the innocent.
> *Hast.* O, 'twas the foulest deed to slay that babe,
> And the most merciless, that e'er was heard of!
> *Riv.* Tyrants themselves wept when it was reported.
> *Dor.* No man but prophesied revenge for it.
> *Buck.* Northumberland, then present, wept to see it.
> *Q. Mar.* What? Were you snarling all before I came,
> Ready to catch each other by the throat,
> And turn you all your hatred now on me? [1.3.173–189].

As the "embodiment of the Lancastrians' blasted hopes" (Evans 718n), Margaret is thrust into hostile territory as representing the failed dynasty, clearly labeled as Other even amongst those who had just moments before been each others' worst enemies. Once again Richard is put on a godlike level, as Margaret warns all who would follow him: "Live each of you the subjects to his hate, / And he to yours, and all of you to God's!" (1.3.301–302). There exists the people, God, and Richard; and Richard here is an Other to everyone, but a success nonetheless. The ailing King Edward is just as skillfully dispatched into Other status as Richard — having facilitated the murder-for-hire of their brother Clarence — lays the onus of responsibility on the king himself, bemoaning the "tardy cripple" who bore the order of leniency, and subtly decrying the original order of death issued by the king (1.4.89–95). Richard also uses this emotional moment to lay blame on the "guilty kindred of the Queen" who "did urge it [Clarence's death] still unto the King" (2.1.136, 138). Here Richard himself even equates his actions to that of deity, which before had only been ascribed to him by others: "God will revenge it" (2.1.139). We know, of course, that since Richard himself masterminded the action, it is Richard who will wreak his vengeance, still the maker/director able to transform others into Others at will. Buckingham's response to Richard's promise of revenge is never more fitting than after this occasion: "We wait upon your *Grace*" (emphasis added; 2.1.141). Richard's assumed kingship, his position and guarantor of royal boons, and even his possible divinity are all now wrapped up in this single word. Still later Richard reasserts his claim to divinity in these earthly matters as he convinces young Prince Edward that his uncles who have been — or will be — arrested are simply purveyors of "sug'red words," men who hide "the poison of their hearts" (3.1.13–14). "God keep you from them, and from such false friends!" Richard says, knowing again that he himself keeps the Prince from his uncles (3.1.15). Richard is transformed, and those who would support Prince Edward are rendered Other, thus ripe for elimination.

As for Hastings, the man who "knew" Richard ("I know he loves me well" [3.4.14]), the transfiguration to Other is as swift as he is blinded by Richard's pleasant "conceit." In fact, a single word, "if," is all Hastings has to utter to give Richard the excuse he needs to cast him as Other and call for his head. As they gather in the Tower, Richard and Buckingham, after conspiring separately (replete with the Catesby's knowledge of Hasting's misgivings about Richard's accession), re-enter with Richard bellowing of "devilish plots" and "damned witchcraft ... that have prevail'd / Upon my body with their hellish charms" (3.4.60–62). Hastings makes the mistake, perhaps, of being the first one to answer:

> *Hast.* If they have done this deed, my noble Lord —
> *Glou.* If? Thou protector of this damned strumpet,
> Talk'st thou to me of "ifs"? Thou art a traitor.
> Off with his head! [3.4.73–76].

Hastings' hasty execution is later defended to the Lord Mayor on the grounds that Hastings was a "subtile traitor" (3.5.37), and when the Lord Mayor balks at the suggestion, Richard invokes the oft-used Other of the Elizabethan stage: "What? think you we are Turks or infidels?" (3.5.41). It is only the most foreign and barbarous of Others who could do such an ignoble thing, and the challenge is thus thrown down to the Lord Mayor to pursue the question further (at his own peril). The Lord Mayor need look no further than the recently-separated head of Hastings for confirmation that Richard and Buckingham "are right noble princes both" (3.5.64), and he concludes that Hastings indeed "deserv'd his death" (3.5.47). Close on the heels of Hastings' demise follows Richard's further estrangement of Edward as he tells Buckingham to spread about "the bastardy of Edward's children," calling into question any claim Edward's heirs might have to the vacant throne. This kind of retroactive Othering (including the suggestion of his own mother's infidelities) exemplifies Richard as what Barton calls "an example of the power wielded by the actor," this power given and commented upon by Shakespeare throughout the play (96). The seductive fiction Richard spins is meant to ensnare both fictional characters on the stage and the viewing audience, and it often seems that the Others Richard creates tend to be accepted by both worlds. Perhaps significant, too, is the fact that Richard is a character developed over three plays, similar to other memorable Shakespeare creations like Falstaff and Hal/Henry. Time and energy is devoted to sculpting a well-rounded character appreciable from many angles, and designed to be appreciated by the audiences of the day who often clamored in the theaters for favorite plays, characters, or even certain portions of plays to be presented to them.[5] As Barton notes, Richard is more than the morality Vice (though he himself notes the similarities in 3.1.82–83), he is "an actor who plays his parts in the real world, rather than on the stage where they would at least be recognized as fabrications" (96). This refers to the Richard known (or assumed to be known) by those within the world of *Richard III* (and, of course, *2 & 3 Henry VI*), but also can hold true for the Elizabethan audience because he is such an "artist in deceit" (96). "Through the power of illusion," Barton concludes, "he blinds honest men and accomplishes their overthrow" (96). It would seem that if there was to be any concern over the content of Elizabethan theater having the ability to affect what Stephen Gosson called a "surfite of the soule," it would not only be the specter of the cross-dressed male or the clown-as-king, but the entirely accessible and insidiously attractive Richard and his ilk (McCollum 41). In *The Anatomie of Abuses* (1583), Phillip Stubbes may have prophesied the list of vices that Richard lays claim to, arguing that there were, indeed things to be learned from the stage:

> Trulie, so there are: if you will learne falsehood, if you will learn cosenage: if you will learn to deceive: if you will learn to play the Hipocrit: to cogge, lye and falsifie: if you will learn to jest, laugh and fleer, to grin, to nodd, and mow: if you will learn to playe the vice, to swear, teare, and blaspheme, both Heaven and Earth: If you

will learne to ... deflour honest wyves: if you will learne to mur-
ther, hate, kill, picke, steal, robbe and rave: If you will learn to
rebel against Princes, to comit treasons, to comsume treasurs ... to
deride, scoffe, mock & flowt, to flatter & smooth ... if you will
learn to become proude, hawtie & arrogant: and finally, if you will
learne to comtemne GOD and al his lawes, to care neither for
heaven nor hel, and to commit al kinde of sinne and mischief you
need to goe to no other schoole, for all these good Examples, may
you see painted before your eyes in enterludes and playes: where-
fore, that man who giveth money for the maintenance of them,
must needs incurre the damage of premunire,[6] that is, eternall
damnation... ["Stage-playes" 8–9].

Richard, of course, is undone in the fifth scene of act five, and Richmond
vows to "unite the White Rose and the Red" (5.5.19), so peace, ultimately,
rules in the end. He is eventually punished, his line removed from the
throne, and Henry VII (Richmond) takes his place on the throne. Perhaps
as important to many of the anti-theatricalists of the period is the fact that
the common actor who would don a king's robes would, at the play's conclusion, have both performed the destruction of a usurper and returned
to his rightful social strata, indistinguishable from any other commoner.
The "revival of medieval sumptuary laws" during the late 1500s may have
contributed, as well, to the anti-theatricalist's charges against the stage, as
the base-born could very easily appear to be royalty with the benefit of a
stage costume (Orgel 15). And if the lower class looked like, then even
acted like nobility, was there not something for the anti-theatricalists to
fear in addition to the effeminized male and the compromised female spectators?

But before peace can truly come, the actor and maker/director
Richard, having ascended the throne in the previous act with the help of
Buckingham and Catesby's mock-theater, must remove the remaining
thorns in his side: the two young princes. Again, Richard the maker/direc-
tor attempts to relegate them to Other status as he tries to persuade Buckingham to kill them in the Tower. Princes Edward and Richard are, after
all, rightful heirs to their father Edward IV, and now–King Richard knows
his claim can never be absolute with them alive. Buckingham, suddenly
somewhat scrupulous and having regained at least a portion of his conscience, refuses to bite when Richard dangles the idea before him, forcing
Richard to be plain: "I want the bastards dead" (4.2.18). In this moment
Richard both transforms the boys into Others as "bastards," thus having
no claim to the crown, and momentarily sheds his actor's garb by revealing his true intentions without falsity or subterfuge. It is then "high-reach-
ing Buckingham" who "grows circumspect," and Richard goes on to

transform both Buckingham and Anne, Richard's new wife, into dispos-
able Others as he plots to marry Elizabeth, Edward's daughter, and unite
the houses of Lancaster and York. The maker/director Richard understands
the possibilities arising from the stopping "of all hopes whose growth may
damage" him (4.2.59). Richard's helpful survey of his accomplishments in
4.3 reads like a nearly-complete list of his "Other" pursuits:

> *K. Rich.* The son of Clarence have I pent up close,
> His daughter meanly have I match'd in marriage,
> The sons of Edward sleep in Abraham's bosom,
> And Anne my wife hath bid this world good night.
> Now for I know the Britain Richmond aims
> At young Elizabeth, my brother's daughter,
> And by that knot looks proudly on the crown,
> To her go I, a jolly thriving wooer [4.3.36–44].

The son and daughter of Clarence have not been killed but marginalized
(as being little threat); Anne and the young Princes have joined the Others in death; and Richmond will be rendered Other (and killed, ideally)
so that Elizabeth can become Richard's wife. Add Henry VI, Edward IV,
Clarence, Margaret, Hastings and Buckingham, and the Other list becomes
more complete. Richard is continually successful as the actor and
maker/director as long as he continually plays the roles he's cast himself
(and others, like Buckingham) into. It isn't until Richard stops being the
player-king and ascends the throne — actually becoming the king and shedding the actor's guise — that his carefully crafted scenario begins to unravel.
Once he is Richard the King — and not Richard the Friend, the Loyalist,
the Wooer, the Avenger, the Pious — once he dons the king's mantle and
puts off the player-king's costume, the fiction he's created collapses under
the weight of not only the stage's demands for a retributive and pleasing
denouement, but also the rigors of historical verisimilitude, which have
been flouted to this point. His attempts to convince Elizabeth that he loves
her daughter and she should be his queen fail, his transforming power at
an ebb:

> *K. Rich.* You mock me, madam, this [is] not the way
> To win your daughter.
> *Q. Eliz.* There is no other way,
> Unless thou couldst put on some other shape
> And not be Richard that hath done all this [4.4.284–288].

Richard cannot "put on some other shape," for he is now the king and has
played his last role — for him, the tiring room holds no other costume, and

the mirror no other visage. Or, truly, he becomes an Other. His attempts to transform his nobles into allies fail, as well, and even his supposed friends will desert him as the battle is ultimately engaged. In the end it is Richard who is the Other, and it is Richard who recognizes his otherness: "My conscience hath a thousand several tongues, / And every tongue brings in a several tale, / And every tale condemns me for a villain" (5.3.193–195). He evolves from consummate actor to consummate Other. Elizabethan theater may be dependent on otherness, as Orgel noted, and Shakespeare's Richard simply could not be without the power Shakespeare gave him to transform himself (as the quintessential actor) and everyone else (as the powerful maker/director) to serve his own ends. The presence of Others on the English stage allowed for the self-definition of Englishmen, just as the later Othering in Python would define and delimit Englishness.

There are at least two fascinating parallels in Python's work wherein Othering is pursued to a deadly end. Both examples occur in *Holy Grail*. The first is early in the film and relies more on the comic, naturally, than Shakespeare's forays into Othering. A plague cart is being pushed through the streets of a filthy hamlet, with a crier leading the way and calling for the dead to be brought out. Bodies are already heaped on the cart, as a man approaches carrying what appears to be yet another corpse over his shoulder. The Large Man (Cleese) asks the Cart Driver (Idle) to take away the obviously living man, even if it's against the rules. The Cart Driver balks, but the Large Man is determined:

> BODY: I think I'll go for a walk.
> LARGE MAN: You're not fooling anyone, you know.
>   (*to* CART DRIVER)
>   Isn't there anything you could do?
> BODY: (*singing unrecognizably*) I feel happy... I feel happy.
> *The* CART DRIVER *looks at the* LARGE MAN *for a moment [...] The* CART DRIVER
>   *swiftly brings up a club and hits the* OLD MAN.
> LARGE MAN: (*handing over the money at last*) Thanks very much [Scene 7].

To satisfy the demands of time and especially efficiency, the old man ("Body") is relegated into Otherness by another, and it doesn't take long for the cart driver to become duplicitous in this effectual — and terminal — Othering. The Large Man insists that his baggage is indeed dead, then not dead but on the way, and finally makes that death wish a reality. He is the director in this scene, and one of his actors — the Cart Driver — becomes a maker for him, a maker of imminent death. The old man might even perdure — in fact we're not even certain he's truly ill, perhaps he's just a nuisance — but the director and maker of the scene transform him into

Other, and from living to dead. For most plague sufferers it was, certainly, only a matter of time, and many plague accounts from the Middle Ages and beyond depict similar desertions when it was thought the victim was infected beyond hope. Hastening the demise, though, in such a banal and offhand way — and for ninepence — adds a level of dark humor reminiscent of Richard's most attractive mischief. This same gleeful malevolence is found again later in *Holy Grail* as Launcelot (Cleese) storms Swamp Castle in search of a damsel in distress. We see that a wedding is in preparation, and that the damsel is actually an effeminate, pasty young man. Launcelot cuts through guards and wedding guests, killing everything in his sight. He is finally stopped by the lord of the castle (Palin), and amidst the bloody carnage the lord makes new plans for his almost-daughter-in-law and "the very brave and deadly" knight. It's clear that the bride-to-be is happy her effeminate fiancé has apparently died, as is his father, and the only remaining business is to make sure her father dies, as well:

> SHOUT FROM BACK: He's not quite dead!
> FATHER: Since the fatal wounding of her father...
> SHOUT FROM BACK: I think he's getting better!
>   *FATHER nods discreetly to a SOLDIER standing to one side. The SOLDIER slips off. FATHER's eyes watch him move round to where the voice came from.*
> FATHER: For ... since her own father ... who ... when he seemed about to recover ... suddenly felt the icy ... hand of death upon him.
>   *A scuffle at the back.*
> SHOUT FROM BACK: Oh, he's died!

So not only is the future daughter-in-law (who, as we've learned previously, has a dowry featuring "huge tracts of land") saved from Otherness in remaining a part of the family, but her father is assisted/directed into Otherness and death. The bride's father goes from tragically dying to being fatally wounded to being actually and permanently dead in just a matter of a few moments, a glance, and a few carefully chosen elegiacal words. The father has already Othered his own son in favor of the more manly Launcelot, but since Herbert hasn't actually died and Launcelot has no interest in the plump princess, the Othering isn't complete as we leave the scene.

Monty Python indulges in similar "otherness" when it comes to foreigners, including creating what has been called "Jabberwocky French" — a farrago of malapropisms delivered with a pronounced French accent — when almost any French character is portrayed (Thompson 33). Germans, Americans, television personalities, establishment figures, aristocrats, and even women (as will be seen) comprise the menagerie of Others that Python identifies and sends up. The Hungarian man (Cleese) in

"The Tobacconist" sketch is forced to read often meaningless but more often sexually and scatalogically charged translations from his Hungarian-English phrase book, and is twice arrested for it (Chapman, et al. 2.25.16–17). The "British" were also sure to be rendered Other, from natives of Scotland, Ireland, and Wales, to members of the far-flung Commonwealth and former Empire. Scotsmen and Scotland often bore the brunt of Python's invectives, a relationship not unlike that which Dr. Samuel Johnson undertook with Scotland during his lifetime. Being at best British and certainly not English, Scotland may have been the nearest and most potentially targetable Other for Monty Python — short of reaching across the Channel to favorite targets such as the French. In fact, even the most common Englishman —"Harold Potter, gardener, and tax official," for instance — was elevated far above the lowly rank of Scotsman. In episode 7, alien saucers arrive and turn Mr. Potter into a Scotsman, a being somewhere below the level of "man":

> Cut to flying saucer sending down ray. Potter freezes ... Shivers and turns into a Scotsman with kilt, and red beard. His hand jerks out in front of him and he spins round and scuttles up road in fast motion, to the accompaniment of bagpipe music. Cut to close-up of newspaper with banner headline: "Man turns into a Scotsman."
> NEWSVENDOR'S VOICE: Read all abaht it! Read all abaht it! Man turns into Scotsman! [1.7.84–85].

A Scotsman in this Python sketch (and elsewhere throughout the Python work) is relegated to Otherness because he is less than a man — he was a(n) (English)man who has become a Scotsman:

> INSPECTOR: Yes. And, er, he never showed any inclination towards being a Scotsman before this happened?
> WIFE: (shocked) No, no, not at all. He was not that sort of person...
> INSPECTOR: He didn't wear a kilt or play the bagpipes?
> WIFE: No, no.
> INSPECTOR: He never got drunk at night or brought home black puddings?
> WIFE: No, no. Not at all.
> INSPECTOR: He didn't have an inadequate brain capacity?
> WIFE: No, no. Not at all [1.7.84–85].

Later in this same episode, Scotsmen are identified as having "no control over [their] own destiny," and are characterized by their country's lack of electricity and indoor plumbing (1.7.86–89). Notice that the vendor above doesn't say an Englishman has turned into a Scotsman, it's even more fundamental than that. A Scotsman isn't even a man, and one can be changed from a man into a Scotsman. Scotsmen also are prone to drinking and suffer from a lesser brain capacity than even the lowliest of Englishmen. This transformation from the purity of Englishness creates an Other, and the "Scotsman as Other" becomes a running gag in *Flying Circus* episodes, with Scotsmen being portrayed as made entirely of wood or tin, or allowing passersby a peek up their kilts.

As Orgel mentioned that the Spanish authorities considered boys dressing as women and girls far more disturbing than actual women on the stage, it may be that Monty Python chose transvestism because it was simply more shocking—thus comedically more effective—than women actors, no matter how talented. More shocking, perhaps, but these men-as-women don't become Other. And as women have been largely excluded from Python's antics, except as "ideal foils"—either played or controlled by the male characters-writers—they must also be considered Other, and their place will be discussed below.

Orgel continues, pointing out that in Elizabethan drama there are multiple *others*, and asserts that, "in fact, Elizabethan drama is often dependent on otherness" (9). Note the otherness of the hypocritical Puritans in Jonson's *The Alchemist*, of the Dolphin and, even, Katherine in *Henry V*, of the "bastard" Don John in *Much Ado*, and, as Orgel mentions, Othello. This otherness creates a need for what Eve Sedgwick and Louis Adrian Montrose call the homosocial, or the necessary male bonding that precedes the facing of the Other (Orgel 9; Sedinger 71). In *Much Ado About Nothing*, it is the conference between Claudio, Don Pedro, and the bastard Don John which precedes the public humiliation of the female character Hero, who has become, by virtue of her supposed lack of virtue, an Other to be despised. She was already, of course, outside of the bonding group because of her gender, but her opportunity to participate even in a symbolic way (via marriage) in the established grouping is temporarily abrogated when another Other, Don John, an Other because of his parentage, accuses her of infidelity. Interesting here that Don John, a sexual Other (being a bastard), is still trusted and kept within the homosocial circle by Claudio and Don Pedro as he accuses Hero of sexual sin. It is Don John who is believed, not the woman, though their separation from the grouping—she because of her sex, he because of his parent's sexual transgression—is similarly libidinal, and is similarly out of their control. As a male, Don John gets the nod for trustworthiness no matter what his background might be, and Hero is painted as the chaste wife-to-be who becomes a whore. Reading *The Winter's Tale*, Orgel notes Leontes' retreat from "women and sex" in his jealousy, and we can see Claudio in *Much Ado* similarly retreating from Hero, marriage, sexual congress (with a woman, at least), and commitment in favor of the homosocial grouping which now more concretely includes Don John, the bastard and false witness. Shakespeare's "Dark Lady" sonnets are mentioned with regard to this chaste wife-to-whore labeling, and "beauty slander'd with a bastard shame" seems appropriately (mis)quoted here in regard to Don John and Hero (127.4). "The better angel is a man right fair, / The worser spirit a woman color'd ill" Shakespeare writes in sonnet 144, which Evans interprets (after warning the reader to avoid literalizing Shakespeare's "deeply metaphorical" language) as the poet assuming a sexual relationship between his Dark Lady and his friend, with "the poet's reaction ... one of concern for the friend rather than ordinary jealousy" (1746). Claudio brings Don John into the homosocial fold as he takes as truth all the bastard's charges, and follows him into the night to witness the supposed betrayal from afar. Claudio had earlier surrendered his own faculties, in a way, by asking Don John to "discover" for him "any impediment" to the marriage, which Don John will of course do without hesitation. Hero, in Don John's words, moves from chastity to outright whoredom in a single, neat phrase: "Even she — Leonato's Hero, your Hero, *every man's Hero*" (emphasis added; 3.2.106–107). Don John's Other status is set aside, for a time, as Hero becomes the "female evil," the ultimate Other.

"There is," Orgel asserts, "a large component of male bonding in Shakespeare," and none should be terribly surprised, as the company Shakespeare wrote for was comprised completely of men. Whether Shakespeare and, by association, other playwrights and companies would have included women in their casts had society not forbidden it is an interesting but moot point. That some of the company regularly dressed as women and acted female parts certainly didn't identify them as Other in this group — this was still an all-boys club. Though not an Other, there is some judgment, at least, in relation to cross-dressing in the course of Shakespeare's plays, specifically *The Merry Wives of Windsor*. Whereas Rosalind was able to don breeches and become Ganymede so that she could make her way to Arden unmolested, and she used her male disguise to her advantage; and whereas Julia in *The Two Gentlemen of Verona* put on a page's costume "to prevent [t]he loose encounters of lascivious men" and, perhaps, to avoid the wagging tongues which might disapprove of a woman making "so unstaid a journey" to Proteus; these are cross-dressings to disguise and for means of escape and safe travel which the texts do not harshly judge with retributive acts or dire consequences (2.7.40–41, 60). It is interesting that Falstaff in *The Merry Wives of Windsor* dons a disguise as well to facilitate an escape, but his disguise leads him to even more mischief. On the verge of being discovered in Mistress Ford's quarters by her husband, Falstaff is forced to search out a disguise, since Master Ford's brothers wait outside the house and Master Ford himself is nearly home. And because he is the "fat knight" there are no hiding places and few believable disguises, so he must become Mrs. Ford's "maid's aunt, the fat woman of Brainford" (4.2.75–76). This woman is hated by Master Ford, as Mrs. Ford relates, but she still allows Falstaff to dress as the old woman. This is a comedy, after all, as Evans reminds the reader, and not a history like the Henriad, so instead of disaster, we are being set up for a comic deflation at Falstaff's expense.

Shakespeare may or may not have "had it in" for his Falstaff character, public and royal popularity notwithstanding, so this chance at humiliation could just as well be in the service of the comedic structure of the play. But there certainly seems to be at least something of a gleeful sadism on the part of the mistresses, as Mrs. Page intones: "Heaven guide him to thy husband's cudgel; and the devil guide his cudgel afterwards!" (4.2.88–89). "We cannot misuse [him] enough," Mistress Page continues, and as the disguised Falstaff is produced, Master Ford sets on old "Mother Prat " (4.2.102–103). Master Ford: "I'll prat her. Out of my door, you witch, you rag, you baggage, you poulcat, you runnion! out, out! I'll conjure you, I'll fortune-tell you!" (4.2.184–186). Master Ford then beats Falstaff/Prat and the cross-dressed knight runs away without a protest. Mistress Page comments on the humiliation of Falstaff, applauding the beating he took and promising to have "the cudgel hallow'd and hung o'er the altar," as it had "done meritorious service" (4.2.204–205). Falstaff in this scene was not only dressed as a woman to disguise and escape, but purposely dressed as a loathed woman who— it was known — would attract only Master Ford's wrath. He is punished not only for being Falstaff, but for being a man and cross-dressing, and he is also being punished as someone else.

The homosocial grouping (Ford, Page, Shallow, Caius and Evans) does not include Falstaff, and he is ostracized and even hunted by these men. He is an Other to this group. Falstaff also does not fit in with nor is he well accepted by the group he chooses to patronize, namely the women of Windsor, and even dressed like these peers he is without the group, thus an Other. Falstaff could echo Viola as the eunuch when she says, "I am not that I play," as Falstaff isn't a brave knight, or an old woman, or even much of a "bully-rook," as the textual abuse he's given (and he takes) indicates. The all-boys club of the King's Men didn't bring Falstaff into the homosocial fold, no matter how he may have (cross-)dressed. And though a necessary staple of the English stage, cross-dressing is also belittled by Beatrice in Much Ado. As her uncles try to convince Beatrice she needs to be more refined and less "shrewd" if she is to secure a husband, she reduces a man without a beard to "less than a man," a man who is only suited for a female's work: "What should I do with him? dress him in my apparel and make him my waiting-gentle-woman?" (2.1.34–36). The cross-dressed man is no more than a feminine servant, and useless as a youth, a man, or a husband. And finally, as we've seen, for a woman (Margaret) to be intentionally confused with another woman (Hero) becomes a sin punishable by the foulest condemnations and ultimate Otherness. This is still cross-dressing, since the boy playing Margaret would also be the boy playing Margaret playing Hero for the audience of Don John, Claudio, and Don Pedro.

In 1969 London nothing comparable to the strictures regarding women on the (sound)stage existed, and Monty Python could have hired any number of women to fill the many female roles written for *Flying Circus* episodes. Or — and this is perhaps more telling — there could have been a female writer/actor brought in as a charter member of Monty Python. Instead, real women become Others as they are treated as objects; useful, apparently, because they have real breasts, an anatomical fact which, paradoxically, also renders them useless as true members of the troupe. Like the King's Men, this was also a boys club. When asked why Python employed men as women rather than bringing women into the troupe, Graham Chapman — the only homosexual cast member, interestingly — answered rather off-handedly: "There were no women actors at Cambridge, and the women we wrote were certainly not to be attractive ... [w]e might as well do them"[7] (Thompson 15). The homosexual as Other (but also as spectacle or object) is also a Python staple, with, as will be discussed later, the homosexual Chapman playing an equal role in the sending up of "pooves," "sods" and "buggers" throughout the *Flying Circus* episodes.

Chapman's short comment above begs many questions, not the least of which involves not only the absence of women but the presence of purposely unattractive cross-dressers. In other words, unlike the Elizabethan stage, Python almost never employed cross-dressing as "in part an attempt to trick others," whether a spectator or another character, as Sedinger claims of the Elizabethan stage (63).[8] The Python cross-dresser is also not an attempt to create heterosexual beauty or attraction, often quite the opposite. And as most critics, including Garber, posit the cross-dresser as visible in a sense, Python must be included, since no effort is made to hide the man in woman's clothing (64). In fact, purposely writing unattractive women's characters foregrounds the constructedness of these images, the Otherness of the images, calling attention to themselves by the sometimes grotesque incongruities of Python's ugly women. The desired effect, then, is not overtly libidinal, but humor via the incongruous. And even as Sedinger has pointed out that much recent scholarship has stepped back from the "boy-actor as mere convention, forgotten by the audience members in their acceptance of the dramatic fiction," the key words in this now challenged phraseology are *dramatic fiction* (64). Python is comedy, the drama being left to whether or not the show would actually air or the weekly battle with the BBC censors would be a win, loss, or draw. We are meant to laugh at the image of a six-foot, five-inch "woman" (John Cleese) with Sandra Dee hair and garish makeup; that, or a plump, slouching, dowdy, slack-faced housewife (Terry Jones) who wears a sweater over her house dress and cooks up rat tarts and jugged rabbit. The image of these grown men dressed as old women in sketches like "Hell's Grannies"— wherein a gang of female senior citizens terrorizes normal folk on the street, young and old like, and even legitimate hoodlums— is funny because it *looks* funny. Python producer Barrie Took calls this sketch "simple reversal ... straight out of the Child's Book of How to Write Comedy. Thugs beating up old ladies? Why not have old ladies ganging up, roaming the streets looking for thugs to bash, young people to bully?" (Hewison 128–29). No homoerotic or homosexual overtones here. This is just one of hundreds of "sight gags" that populate the Python's world, little different from the World War I bunker scene in episode 25 where a Viking, a nun, and an astronaut sit with the doughboys.

In the "Mollusc Live Documentary" sketch both the husband and wife portrayed are wearing large numbers on their backs , as if they are participating in a dance contest; in the "Spanish Inquisition" sketch one of the inquisitors, "Biggles" (Jones), wears the customary red robes but sports a leather aviator's helmet and goggles, as well; in the "Erizabeth L" sketch all the Elizabethan court members are dressed in period attire, but all sit on Vespas; and in the "Our Eamonn" sketch, a young man comes home from a stay in Dublin dressed (and colored) like an African warrior. The fact that the Python *oeuvre* is completely comedic (and slouching toward the absurd) is essential, since tragedy or dramatic fiction often asks that the viewer surrender disbelief at the door. Elizabethan boy-actors, according to Sedinger, have been identified by some critics "as a mere convention, forgotten by the audience members in their acceptance" of the world presented before them. Much current scholarship would have it otherwise, but this possibility actually seems reasonable, especially in regard to cross-dressing and the Monty Python troupe. The real shock may have been the gradual switch to women actors in female parts for Carolean audiences, just as real women in Python's sketches may have become more noticeable than a cross-dressed Pepperpot.

What seems to be consistent with many of these critics (and, to some extent, their Renaissance predecessors) is the notion that cross-dressing is partly done to trick, to deceive other characters. This is true within the confines of plays like *As You Like It*, where Rosalind dresses as Ganymede and "escapes (for a time) being a woman, duke Senior's daughter, the conscious object of Orlando's love" (G. Blakemore Evans 366). It is interesting that Shakespeare allows her to continue this charade long after, according to Evans, the deception is necessary. "Rosalind has only to abandon her disguise as Ganymede — and there is no reason on the level of plot why she should not do this as soon as she is safe in Arden," writes Evans in his introduction to *As You Like It* (365). The cross-dressing is allowed to continue beyond its essential usefulness by the author and the narrative, validating the female-character-as-male ruse.

This deception, according to Sedinger, "both forwards the narrative and produces aesthetic *and erotic* pleasure" (63; emphasis added). But what of the obvious questions? Did not the audience know that the character of Rosalind was being played by a boy, and that even as "she" dressed as a boy, Ganymede, the actor was still male? That Ophelia, Lady Macbeth and Hamlet's mother were all male actors in women's garb? The conventions were such that spectators would hardly be unaware of the stage practices of the time, and that unless the male spectator possessed latent homosexual feelings, there was little chance that the male spectator would be aroused by the sight of a boy in drag. The logical question seems to be: Would the male spectator be necessarily aroused or become overly libidinal if the actor were, in fact, an actress? Contemporary critics like Gosson, Munday, Northbrooke and later Prynne might agree that if a woman in the audience or anywhere near the playhouses was ripe for sordid debasement, then a woman on stage — an insidious, dangerous Other — would certainly be the Siren whose call could not be resisted. Garber's assertion that many recent critics "look *through* rather than *at* the cross-dresser" to avoid a "close encounter" and to "subsume that figure within one of the two traditional genders" seems not only reasonable — since the cross-dresser *is* actually one of the two traditional genders— but seems to fit the expectations of an Elizabethan audience member who views a play for entertainment, rather than libidinal purposes. There seems to be a sort of conflation of the anti-theatricalist's fears in regard to the bawdiness of the play audiences and theater areas with the libidinal capacities of the audience in relation to the staged plays.

This disturbance is defined by Marjorie Garber as the presence of transvestism in culture, leading to a "'category crisis,' disrupting and calling attention to cultural, social, or aesthetic dissonances" (16). Women on the English Renaissance stage in any role would be a disruption, a dissonance in the melody of the time, but boys as women carousing with men reveal "the extraordinary power of transvestism to disrupt, expose, and challenge, putting in question the very notion of the 'original' and of stable identity" (16). Garber defines her "category crisis" as "a failure of definitional distinction," of the crossings between formerly delimited borders between what many would see as binary opposites: black and white, Jew and Christian, master and servant, noble and bourgeois, and even male and female (16). These borders are crossed, often (and without libidinal considerations), in Dekker's *Shoemaker's Holiday*, as simple cobblers cavort with kings and the nobility switch places with the commoner. Henry wanders among his troops in *Henry V*, playing the simple soldier that he might better know the hearts of his men. This category crisis is well exhibited and commented upon in *Hamlet* as Horatio and Hamlet accost the First Clown as he digs Ophelia's grave. Much of the exchange takes the form of a social leveling, or a nonrecognition of Hamlet's authority (or even his person) by the grave digger, resulting in a remarkably witty and guileless exchange. Hamlet and Horatio have listened as the man has sung, and Hamlet determines to speak to this "mad knave" who would toss up skulls and songs with such abandon, asking him whose grave it is he digs:

> *1 Clo.* Mine, sir.
> [Sings.]"[O], a pit of clay for to be made
>   [For such a guest is meet]."
> *Ham.* I think it be thine, indeed, for thou liest in't.
> *1 Clo.* You lie out on't, sir, and therefore 'tis not yours; for my part, I do
>   not lie in't, yet it is mine.
> *Ham.* Thou dost lie in't, to be in't and say it is thine. 'Tis for the dead, not
>   for the quick; therefore thou liest.
> *1 Clo.* "Tis a quick lie, sir, 'twill away again from me to you [5.1.119–129].

It can already be seen that the social classes represented here are appreciated by both men. Hamlet began the conversation by identifying for the grave digger just where each stands in social rank: "Whose grave's this, *sirrah*?" (emphasis added; 5.1.117–118). "Sirrah" is a term one would use to address inferiors, and nowhere else in the exchange does Hamlet use it or any other direct term of address. The Clown uses "sir" as his automatic response of politeness, acknowledging at least their separate social strata. But the "sir" quickly becomes more of a term of forbearance than respect as the Clown answers what to him must seem inane questions. Horatio has already offered the reason for the Clown's seeming nonchalance toward death and even life: "Custom hath made it in him a property of easiness" (5.1.67–68). It won't take long for the "sirs" to disappear and a sort of macabre familiarity to take their stead:

Ham. What man dost thou dig it for?
1 Clo. For no man, sir.
Ham. What woman then?
1 Clo. For none neither.
Ham. Who is to be buried in't?
1 Clo. One that was a woman, sir, but, rest her soul, she's dead.
Ham. How absolute the knave is! We must speak by the card, or equivoca-
    tion will undo us. By the Lord, Horatio, this three years I have took note
    of it: the age is grown so pick'd that the toe of the peasant comes so near
    the heel of the courtier, he galls his kibe [5.1.130–142].

Here Hamlet again reminds all who may care to hear that there is a difference between a "knave" and his peasant's toe and the "we" and his courtier's heel; the "equivocation" of language here highlights the category crisis, the disruption when even verbal jousting tends to favor the rabble rather than the rich. So who is the Other here? The border between Hamlet and the Clown is acknowledged by Hamlet, but not the Clown, who, without intended disrespect or guile, draws the young prince to a level where "in't" and "on't" seem to be very similar.

Beatrice in *Much Ado* is constantly disrupting categories and borders between male and female, the patriarchal and matriarchal orders, and her appointed place (as marriageable): "I had rather hear my dog bark at a crow than a man swear he loves me" (1.1.131–132). She even sees herself as too closely related to men in general to ever be rightfully married: "No, uncle, I'll none. Adam's sons are my brethren, and truly I hold it a sin to match in my kindred" (2.1.63–65). To marry then, for Beatrice, would be a disruption or crossing over of boundaries which God could not ordain: "Not till God make men of some other mettle than earth" (2.1.59–60).

"Crises" such as these may have nothing to do with transvestism — save the fact that any of the female roles would have been played by males — but the crises exist whenever a category is blurred. As Garber later indicates, "category crises can and do mark displacements from the axis of *class* as well as from *race*" (17). And if category crises— especially transvestism — indicate "a borderline that becomes permeable, that permits ... border crossings from one (apparently distinct) category to another," then the Monty Python troupe, donning women's clothing on a regular basis in their comedy, is creating and feeding off of cultural dissonances and the destabilization of identity as they perform.

It didn't take Python long — in fact, during their first and second shows recorded — for the transvestism to emerge, fully formed, in the garb of a "Pepperpot." Since the second *Flying Circus* episode, titled "Sex and Violence," was actually shot first but broadcast second, it is this episode which introduces the "four middle-aged lower-middle-class women (hereinafter referred to as 'Pepperpots') being interviewed" (Chapman, et al. 4). These "women" wear simple dresses and conservative wigs; they often clutch handbags, appear to wear support hose, and speak with lower-middle class accents. None are grossly caricatured with, for example, garish makeup or fright wigs, and all of the Pepperpots seem to exist without the necessary presence of their husbands. The setting is a commercial for Whizzo butter:

> INTERVIEWER (Palin): Yes, you know, we find that nine out of ten British housewives can't tell the difference between Whizzo butter and a dead crab.
> PEPPERPOTS: It's true, we can't. No.
> SECOND PEPPERPOT (Cleese): Here. Here! You're on television, aren't you?
> INTERVIEWER (*modestly*): Yes, yes.
> SECOND PEPPERPOT: He does the thing with one of those silly women who can't tell Whizzo butter from a dead crab.
> THIRD PEPPERPOT (Jones): You try that around here, young man, and we'll slit your face [1.2.4].

Monty Python spent much of their efforts sending up the various television formats and styles, including TV documentaries ("The Commercial Possibilities of Ovine Aviation"), nameless interview shows ("The Man with Three Buttocks"), and TV commercials such as Whizzo butter. Orgel indicates that perhaps "in the largest sense, the Other is theater itself, both a threat and a refuge," and that Elizabethan playwrights had both a safe haven for their socially-challenging sexualities as well as the locus of critical, moral reception (9). Monty Python's penchant for sending up their theater — television — echoes this dichotomy, as one of Python's favorite Other targets is the television format. Television had, until recently, been the safe haven for essential conservatism and the reaffirmation of prescribed Englishness. Frank Kermode notes that as Shakespeare moved through his career his work betrayed a growing understanding of the full ramifications of "theatricality," of the growth of Elizabethan theater and its emerging self-consciousness (Evans 1139). Direct address, by the time of *Hamlet*, no longer was designed to bring the audience in, but actually created a distance between players and audience, the interstices being acknowledged theatricality. Kermode writes:

> This at least gives one a notion of the urgency and complexity of Shakespeare's intentions. *Hamlet* raises issues as to the validity of its own existence as a play — an appearance which dares to comment on reality — and at the same time tells us to attend not so much to the difficulties its hero experiences in the performance of a specific act, as to his difficulties over action in general, to an irreso-

lution which explains itself in terms of the undoubtedly corrupt
society around him. (1139)

Python consistently undercuts its existence as reality, or even as a part of
some continuous unreality, as the artifice of the constructed television performance is refreshed and forwarded. It comments on its own "validity"
as a play, as well, with transvestism being just one way for that validity to
be challenged.

The above Python incidents all appear in the initially recorded episode, and set the tone for much of Python's work over the next few years.
The Pepperpots here are meant to look funny — obvious men in women's
dress, as simple as that — and even sound funny as the male actors pitch
their voices higher and adopt a coarse accent. The Pepperpots initially go
along with the interview, parodying the kind of "housewife-on-the-street"
interview that is so familiar in commercials then and now. The scene is
undercut, however, as one of the women identifies the constructed nature
of the scene ("You're on television, aren't you?"), and another remembers
the somewhat dim light by which these types of commercials display the
ordinary British housewife (she is a "silly" woman "who can't tell whizzo
butter from a dead crab"). Shedding any sense of being duped or of com-
plicity via ignorance, the Third Pepperpot calmly threatens the interviewer
with bodily harm if the standards by which they judge themselves are violated (standards which haven't been forwarded, per se, but will become
apparent in time), and they are made to look stupid.

Far from creating an effeminate man who attracts libidinal attention
from the audience, the Pythons here have created female characters who
don't necessarily act "mannish," but wouldn't get them to a nunnery when
commanded by a man. Sedinger identifies cross-dressers as revealing the
erotic potential of the "failure of representation." In the rupture "between
perception and consciousness" brought on by the transgression of transvestism lies a desire without an object, and this objectlessness is the failure of representation (67). In the epilogue to As You Like It, this failure is
doubly represented, or at least considerably confused. As the play ends Rosalind remains on the stage and announces what many in the audience may
have already been considering, namely that it was "not the fashion to see
the lady the epilogue" (Epilogue 1–2). This is the same character who, during the course of the play, had initially appeared as a woman (Rosalind),
then, in order to effect the wooing of Orlando, became the male Ganymede
and posed as Celia's brother (though Rosalind was actually Celia's cousin).
It was Rosalind as Ganymede who found favor in Phebe's eyes and heart,
and who eventually revealed herself to Duke Senior and Orlando (and

Phebe) in prelude to Hymen's pronouncements. All this, and Rosalind is actually, of course, a boy on the English stage, a boy wooing Orlando and rejecting Phebe.

There is an interesting separation of Rosalind by Rosalind as she gives herself to both her father and Orlando, "To you I give myself, for I am yours," which she says to each in turn (5.4.116–17). It is as if her ability to play both the fettered Rosalind and the equally unfettered (mostly because of "his" gender) Ganymede has given her the ability to serve two masters, her father and her husband-to-be. Perhaps this ability to separate or make distinct one Rosalind (as daughter) from another Rosalind (as wife) arises from the necessary distinction the actor embodies as one gender playing another. The boy-actor will, in a matter of a few years, be obliged to surrender the woman's parts in favor of the male roles to which he's matured, creating yet another separation, a separation wherein he removes his disguise (as female character[s]) and reveals his true gender. Thus the boy-actor wears his infant's dress much longer than boys not of the stage, his "breeches role" waiting for the last vestiges of puberty to resolve. It is here that the "interchangeability of the sexes" seems so appropriate and so vital to the continuance of the English theater that features male-only actors, as well as so threatening to anti-theatricalists (Orgel 13). This fracturing of self creates even more confusion as Rosalind (speaking as daughter, betrothed, and Ganymede) announces "I'll have no father, if you not be he; / I'll have no husband, if you not be he; / Nor ne'er wed woman, if you not be she" (5.4.122–24). In the end she seems unwilling to surrender Ganymede. She will always be her father's daughter, and she will, we know (thanks to Hymen's presence), take Orlando to husband. Thus two of the three lines in this fascinating announcement are essentially given as axiomatic, and the third is at least mildly homoerotic. Rosalind, speaking, we must assume, as at least the vestigial Ganymede, doesn't say she won't marry Phebe, thus refusing to subsume Ganymede back into Rosalind as just the useful, invigorating, and ultimately liberating cloak he had been. This echoes an earlier exchange when everyone was professing their love and Ganymede/Rosalind three times denied that he/she would love a woman, but finally confesses to Phebe, "I would love you if I could" (5.3.111–12). Ganymede/Rosalind then tells Phebe "I will marry you, if ever I marry a woman, and I'll be married tomorrow" (5.3.113–14). She seems to want to have it both ways, which may have proved especially unnerving to anti-theatricalists and reinforced their politics of effeminization.

There also must be considered the rupture created by Rosalind in the epilogue as she, speaking now as the boy-actor, tells the audience: "If I were a woman I would kiss as many of you as had beards that pleas'd me, complexions that lik'd me, and breaths that I defied not" (Epilogue18–20). Not only does she once again straddle the fence as to gender and sexual preference, she also once again refuses to surrender at least a portion of herself—this time the female character played by the boy-actor—as she asserts she will only kiss those men who have pleasing beards, complexions, and breath. (Or, as "he" asserts this, whichever is the case.) This sexually charged offer is completely subject to his/her revocation upon liking, just as the earlier surrender of Ganymede as another self is beset with caveats and conditions. The boy-actor, then, plays the woman who plays the man, all the while playing the audience with gender interchangeability that, seemingly, allows for just about any coupling imaginable to be enacted on the English stage. Any coupling, and, as Orgel indicates, because homosexual behavior goes largely unpunished in the period's stage presentations (Marlowe's *Edward II* excepted), the anti-theatricalists can rage but "there is no indication whatever that Shakespeare is doing something sexually daring" (22).

And where Marlowe accentuates the positive "physical side of homoeroticism" in *Hero and Leander*, creating a source of excitement, and the anti-theatricalists see the interchangeability of gender as instead a "source of ... panic," Monty Python sees this gender malleability and homoeroticism as sources of the comedic. Python's deliberate attempts to create unappealing, unattractive female characters (that is, when the Pythons played the female roles; not so when actual women appeared) in the name of comedy by incongruity and the grotesque, leads away from "failure of representation," since what is being presented or re-presented carries little or no sexuality, instead relying on stereotypical dress and caricature for presentation. The audience isn't to be fooled by these representations, nor are the plots (of the television series) forwarded by the cross-dressing.

More often than not, though, the Pepperpots are offered as bastions of knowledge—knowledge which everyone else in the scene misses completely. In the second appearance of the Pepperpots, a grocery store interviewer asks about local Frenchmen, and the Pepperpots are able to rattle off their favorite French shoppers, including Pascal, Descartes, Voltaire, and Sartre (1.2.16–17). In a sketch where Picasso is attempting to paint while riding a bicycle, an on-the-scene reporter waits for a glimpse of him when he is nudged by a Pepperpot (Michael). The Pepperpot tells the reporter that it's not Picasso but Kandinsky approaching, and just as soon as the reporter admits his error, many cyclists appear, each a modernist painter. The last cyclist to pass is identified by the reporter as "our very own, Kurt Schwitters," and the Pepperpot must correct him again, correctly identifying Schwitters as German (1.1.8–9). Here the Pepperpot can be seen as not only correcting the reporter's misidentification, but as a catalyst, for as soon as she corrects him the one-man event becomes a race of the world's foremost painters. Even though Python's women may be purposely unattractive, they are hardly unattractive characters. They are imbued with both a knowledge that isn't available to others in the texts, especially male characters — who often come across as "gits" — and with an ability to cut through the structured maleness of the situations, whether an interview or mock documentary (or "mockumentary"), and maintain their integrity as viable characters within and across the narrative(s). The above example of the no-nonsense Pepperpot threatening to emasculate the confident interviewer is a case in point. Elsewhere, in the "Mollusc Live Documentary" it is the wife (Graham Chapman) — dressed to the nines and looking very absurd in a blond wig and red sequined evening dress — whose knowledge forwards the narrative:

> MRS JALIN: There's a man at the door with a moustache.
> MR JALIN: Tell him I've already got one. (*Mrs Jalin hits him hard with a newspaper*) All right, all right. What's he want, then?
> MRS JALIN: He says do we want a documentary on molluscs.
> MR JALIN: Molluscs!
> MRS JALIN: Yes.
> MR JALIN: What's he mean, molluscs?
> MRS JALIN: MOLLUSCS! GASTROPODS! LAMELLIBRANCHS! CEPHALOPODS! [2.32. 124].

As the "live documentary" progresses, it is Mr. Jalin who complains of boredom as Mrs. Jalin actually critiques the program, telling the presenter at one point that they "already know that," and tries to switch channels. It isn't until the presenter announces he's about to cover the sex lives of molluscs that they pay more attention. Later in that same episode the Royal Navy is on an expedition to find Lake Pahoe, which, they are certain is located on Runcorn Avenue by Blenheim Crescent. When they reach the address, they find that the houses have been converted to flats, and the husband (Palin) in number 22 has no idea where any lake might be. His wife (Idle), however, first acknowledges the television camera, then tells them: "Oh, you want downstairs, 22A the basement" (2.32.131). Like the Whizzo butter interview cited above, the woman here first notices or acknowledges the situation, then reveals the knowledge she possesses.

One of the longest and most capably sustained satirical scenes involving Python women as narrative catalysts and carriers of knowledge is "Mrs Premise and Mrs Conclusion Visit Jean-Paul Sartre" from episode 27. It can immediately be seen that just the names of the characters themselves —

Premise and Conclusion — serve to acknowledge the structure of not only this particular sketch, which does contain both elements, but also the entire episode, as well as a clever Sartre reference.[9] Far from an attempt to trick the audience, this is almost a Brechtian reminder of the artifice of the performance as performance. Almost.[10] Two women, Mrs Premise (Cleese) and Mrs Conclusion (Chapman) eventually discuss then seek answers to the questions of personal freedom and commitment from Jean-Paul Sartre himself. The two discuss the pros and cons of putting down various pets, with Mrs Premise finally announcing, tangentially: "It's a funny thing freedom. I mean how can any of us be really free when we still have personal possessions" (2.27–54). Here the "stream-of-consciousness" narrative structure emerge, and will be apparent not only throughout the remainder of the scene, but come to characterize the structure of *Flying Circus*. The incongruity of these two women discussing Sartre and personal freedom in a laundromat surrounded by "various shabby folk"— and just after discussing the best do-it-yourself disposal methods for ailing pets— provides a visual element of humor, and the consistent infringing of other narrative ideas/plots into this theme just adds to the scene's rich character. The flow of the scene, as well, will demonstrate that these two women are as in control of the narrative as any character could be in the Python world.

> MRS PREMISE: Sixty new pence for a bottle of Maltese Claret. Well I personally think Jean-Paul Sartre's masterwork is an allegory of man's search for commitment.
> MRS CONCLUSION: No it isn't.
> MRS PREMISE: Yes it is.
> MRS CONCLUSION: Isn't.
> MRS PREMISE: 'Tis.
> MRS CONCLUSION: No it isn't.
> MRS PREMISE: All right. We can soon settle this. We'll ask him.
> MRS CONCLUSION: Do you know him?
> MRS PREMISE: Yes, we met on holiday last year [2.27.54–55].

They reference Genet as well, in this scene, another association that serves to flesh out the scope of knowledge these two Pepperpots possess. Jean Genet, a French novelist and dramatist, is the subject of Sartre's *Saint Genet, comedian et martyr* (Drabble 385–86). And, as Evans mentions of Rosalind in *As You Like It*, who is important enough to be trusted with "the resolution of the plot, such as it is," Mrs Premise and Mrs Conclusion are going to forge ahead, directing the flow of this narrative, such as it is, even when other narratives attempt to sidetrack the flow (a Python staple). They then call Mrs. Sartre, set up a meeting in France, exchange jokes about Jean-Paul's moods, and even converse adroitly in French. Once again, the humor, the insights, and the direction of the plot are within the bailiwick of the women, including Mrs. Sartre on the phone, who is able to make a wry comment regarding her husband's lifelong search for "freedom." There is a jump cut to the ladies sitting on a raft in the ocean, and Mrs. Premise announces that Paris is in sight. The narrative attempts to move off tangentially here, as Mrs Premise and Mrs Conclusion haven't actually reached Paris but are at the North Malden Coast.[11] This is an intrusion from a previous sketch which has made inroads into the narrative on several occasions, and was always able to sidetrack other narrative events during the first two-thirds of the episode. A BBC drama executive (Cleese) takes a phone call and comments on the North Malden's tenacity, then sends us back to the saga. An Icelandic adventure entitled "Njorl's Saga — Part IV," then tries to break in, but with the first shot of the rocky, forbidding Icelandic coast, the Pepperpots enter the scene on the beach. They will not be pushed aside, narratively speaking, and eventually end up in the Sartre flat in Paris. And after all this effort and narrative muscling, Mrs. Premise and Mrs. Conclusion get the answer they've been seeking, and without any of the expected climactic fanfare:

> MRS PREMISE: Coo-ee! Jean-Paul? Jean-Paul! It's only us. Oh pardon. C'est même nous...
>   *They enter. We do not see Jean-Paul although we hear his voice.*
> JEAN-PAUL: Oui.
> MRS PREMISE: Jean-Paul. Your famous trilogy "Rues à Liberté," is it an allegory of man's search for commitment?
> JEAN-PAUL: Oui.
> MRS PREMISE: I told you so.
> MRS CONCLUSION: Oh, coitus [2.27.56–57].

This very abrupt conclusion (voiced by, of course, Mrs. Conclusion) signals the end of the Pepperpots' quest and the end of any mention of this narrative string for the remainder of the show. So while the Pepperpots in this example and others are certainly not sexually attractive, they forcefully propel the narrative to their own ends, and are given the ability to slough off narrative intrusions which might normally supplant the current story line. They are not, then, used as links, or material to lash two sketches together; they are characters critical to the narrative integrity. And just as Wylie Sypher notes the disparate nature of Clarence and his "lyrical sea vision" in *Richard III*, the Pepperpots (transvestism aside) are allowed knowledge and insight beyond their seeming inability and inexperience.

Sypher admits that in Shakespearean drama "some of the most penetrating incursions into human experience are in the mouths of persons ineligible to exhibit these experiences" (47). This knowledge which doesn't quite fit the messenger is also apparent, Kristian Smidt notes, in the character of Claudio in *Measure for Measure* as he discourses on death (x). Smidt continues, furthering Sypher's point, and identifying certain characteristics necessary for such anomalous events— events he terms "unconformities"[12]:

> What Professor Sypher does not say, however, is that "the most intense Shakespearean experience" when associated with characters who would seem incapable of sustaining it, or with events weakly related to it, may serve to raise those characters and events onto a higher level of poetic vision ... [a]nd if it fails to do so it may still remain the most intense Shakespearean experience but it will represent an access of inspiration on a different level from its context and hence exhibit systems of unconformity [x].

In Shakespeare's comedy this undeserving character may be Dogberry, who by means of his bewildering use of the English language can rise to the level of his betters, and even best them as they almost surrender to his perfectly reasonable confusion. In Python's comedy the unconformities are abundant, allowing for "an access of inspiration" on the level of the Pepperpots; peasants who can outline communal rules of order; and a housewife dressed as a ballroom dancer who seems to know a great deal about "molluscs." Smidt continues, identifying the consequences of such unconformities, and noting that as participants

> we must either read the penetrating incursions in isolation from their context and forget for the moment whose mouths they are in, or else recognise one (or several) of three possible effects of the discrepancy: that the speaker, as I said above, is raised (at least momentarily) to the level of the inspired utterance; that the unexpectedness is itself functional in that it startles us into a fuller concentration on the utterance; or that the utterance would have been even more powerful and moving if it had been in conformity with the character of the speaker and the general context [x].

In the case of Falstaff in *2 Henry IV*, the moment when he realizes that Prince Hal has become King Henry elicits this simple but sobering line: "Master Shallow, I owe you a thousand pound" (5.5.72). In this admission of defeat and the Chief Justice's subsequent orders (and Shallow's prophetic speech) Falstaff is raised to an awareness that belies his self-delusion: it is an "inspired utterance" and is most powerful because it does not fit the Falstaff we have come to know and expect. Its unexpectedness is what gives the emotional weight, the pit-of-the-stomach punch to its utterance, and which signals the ultimate demise of Falstaff. This, of course, is reaffirmed just a few lines later by the Chorus, who announces that "(for any thing I know) Falstaff shall die of a sweat, unless already 'a be kill'd with your hard opinions" (Epilogue 29–31). Falstaff is allowed an "inspired utterance," then he is textually marginalized; Python often raises its women characters (albeit, those usually played by males) to higher levels of "vision," then just as often marginalizes the real female actors and "kills" their female (or male, occasionally) characters.

An interesting counterpoint, then, to Python's use of themselves as central female characters is the actual inclusion of women from time to time. Women appeared in the *Flying Circus* episodes almost from the out-set, and more often in the filmed (as opposed to videotaped) segments. Women are also present quite regularly in all three of the Python feature films, as well as the foreign television episodes and filmed performances and compilations. And though we can document the instances of women appearing in Monty Python's productions, their roles and the relative significance of these roles is decidedly limited. Simply put, a real woman is almost never written to be funny. She is also almost exclusively an Other; she is useful and useless because she has breasts. The humorous female characters are always played by men, and the women's roles which actu-ally go to women are written to be supporting (the "straight [wo]man"), often sexually charged, and ultimately perfunctory. In the "Art Gallery" sketch, this marginalization is even commented on in the text, and the female character is told, in essence, that even when she has lines written for her, it might be better to keep her mouth shut. An art critic sits at his desk, choking on a mouthful of Utrillo, when his wife appears:

> WIFE (Katya Wyeth): *(bringing in a water jug and glass on a tray and laying it on his desk)* Watteau, dear?
> CRITIC (Palin): What a terrible joke.
> WIFE: But it's my only line.
> CRITIC: *(rising vehemently)* All right! All right! But you didn't *have* to say it! You could have kept quiet for a change!
> *Wife cries.*
> CRITIC: Oh, that's typical. Talk talk talk. Natter natter natter! [1.4.43].

The very next linking scene brings this same actress back, but into a more typical role as "a sexy girl [who] enters and starts fondling" the Idle char-acter. Episode 6 features a stockbroker who kisses his "attractive wife" goodbye, leaves the house, and "as he does so, she takes off her wrap and two men dressed only in briefs (Chapman and Jones) step out of the kitchen cupboard" (1.6.73). Moments later a "naked young lady gives him a newspaper," and so the scene goes. In fact, there are several occasions which will be highlighted where a woman transgressing-trespassing into the man's prescribed arena is chastened and even "killed," as a character.

Connie Booth, Carol Cleveland and Katya Wyeth appeared semi-regularly in the *Flying Circus* episodes but were never credited as contributing to the shows' writing. There exist, however, two publicity photographs of the entire Python group, and Carol Cleveland appears in both, as if she were considered (at least by the BBC) the seventh Python (Wilmut 132). This inclusion didn't translate into equal creative time, however. Surveying the collected appearances of the actresses, it doesn't take long to categorize their usefulness as "real" females. Referring back to Graham Chapman's comment regarding Python's men-as-women preference — "There were no women actors at Cambridge"— this seems perhaps an inflated estimation of his alma mater's female paucity, "and the women we wrote were certainly not meant to be attractive, *so there was no reason to actually have real breasts*" (emphasis added). With the danger of becoming too reductive, this statement — which John O. Thompson warns "should perhaps be read with caution" as the interview "seems to have been especially ... convivial"— may pinpoint why women were allowed into the Python club (Thompson 15). Dressing up as frumpy housewives or sleazy Parliament groupies is one thing, while trying to get and keep a wide audience without a female actor in sight may have been quite another. Connie Booth, Carol Cleveland, and Katya Wyeth had breasts, as did the hundreds of naked or semi-naked animations created as linking material by Terry Gilliam, as did the various other young women who appeared from time to time.

Carol Cleveland is introduced in the second episode (shot first, aired second) and described in the telescript as "a beautiful blond buxom wench, in full bloom of her young womanhood," and is offered as a sexual object (1.2.19). The sketch involves a marriage counselor making advances on the wife of a witless man, with the counselor and the wife eventually asking the husband to leave so they can couple privately. Carol appears again in the same episode, this time as an appropriately dressed showgirl who hands cards to a linkman (Michael) in "The Amazing Kargol and Janet" show. She appears, offers the cards, the linkman picks one, and Kargol "reads" the card without looking. The linkman thanks Janet, she "postures and exits" (1.2.26).

Just a few episodes later Donna Reading, yet another buxom blond, is playing what at first appears to be a somewhat straight-up part — a woman in a sci-fi film whose father has been turned into a Scotsman — but she is quickly shown to be both a sexual object and somewhat hapless.

She is introduced in a passionate kiss with Chapman, and described as "none too intelligent" in the stage directions. The camera pulls out to reveal that she is wearing "something absurdly sexy" and he is dressed as a scientist. He asks her questions, and she gives incorrect answers, and finally she is exposed as the "none too intelligent" character earlier described. This short scene offers the woman as sexual object, as capable of holding little or no significant knowledge that can further the plot, and unable to comprehend either the language conventions (i.e., rhetorical speaking, metaphors), or even the conventions of the sci-fi genre in regards to incidental music, which she thinks is a doorbell chiming. Charles and she reappear later in the same episode, with her dimness continuing, and she is eventually dealt with in a very final way. She is first seen "sitting suggestively on a stool" in the laboratory. After a series of inane answers to easy questions, Charles asks her to look into the microscope, then hits her with a sand-filled sock, and "she collapses out of sight under the desk" (1.7.92–93). Toward the end of the episode "She" wakes momentarily, only to be clubbed again by the scientist. Occurring in episode 7 during the first year of the series' run, this violent means of ending a female character's contributions to a sketch sets the trend for many episodes to follow, and becomes an accepted way to deal with a female character who has outlived her usefulness. It is important to note that many male characters are dealt with in a similar fashion, and that many characters are similarly offered as dense, "none too intelligent" types (e.g., The Gumbies). Python seemed able to offend or poke fun at just about everyone, but the upside for these other characters, like The Gumbies or one of Terry Jones' frumpy housewife roles or even Ken Shabby (Palin), is that they are purposely written to be both interesting and amusing — something the female actors and their characters rarely are allowed. Finally, "she" isn't even given a name in the script or in the performed version — she is "She" throughout — as if she represents all women in her "none too intelligent" state. Her only appellation beyond "she" is the highly objectified "darling" as voiced by Charles during their passionate kiss. Thus she is reduced to her gender and her libidinal economy.

Other instances abound where female actors are silenced by means of a violent act. In "The Lost World of Roiurama," four explorers wander through the jungle, including "Brian" (Carol Cleveland), who wears a false moustache. Brian's lines are banal, at best, including "Terrific idea" when describing the jungle diner they've found; "Er quiche lorraine, please" when ordering at the jungle diner (she's the only one to order quiche); and "God knows" and "You don't think that's where they're taking us?" after they've been captured (2.29.81–85).[13] Brian gets just two more short lines before she speaks her final line — "Baboon of the Yard?" — to the interloping Scotland Yard inspector. The inspector is making an arrest in their sketch, when Baboon tells Brian to shut up and shoots her dead. Without comment the sketch continues on around her. In "Full Frontal Nudity" (episode 8) we revisit the Art Critic (Palin) and his wife (Katya). After the wife makes another terrible pun, a voice-over is heard: "But there let us leave the art critic to strangle his wife and move on to pastures new" (1.8.99).[14] The camera pans across on idyllic countryside, catching the art critic strangling his wife; he tries to look innocent as the camera moves on, then continues strangling as they move out of camera range.

But just as the door may seem to be shut against Python as patriarchal woman-haters, we have to acknowledge moments — and they are just moments — when a female actor does do something substantive, and is allowed to be more fully realized as a character. In "The Spanish Inquisition" sketch, Carol Cleveland plays Lady Mountback, the mill owner's wife, and she is allowed to participate in the setup for the jarring entrance of the Inquisitors. She is nearly given equal status in regards to dialogue and narrative importance throughout the sketch. In fact, she remains in the sketch as an active participant even after Chapman, whose character instigated the initial action, has left for another sketch (1.15.192–94). It is in this same episode that the Spanish Inquisition characters reappear two more times, the first as a "Dear Old Lady" (Marjorie Wilde) — an actual old lady — is showing snapshots to a young woman (Cleveland). The Dear Old Lady shows photos to her young friend, and the young friend tears up each one. This continues until the Dear Old Lady finds a photo depicting "the Spanish Inquisition hiding behind the coal shed," and the young woman, predictably, is suddenly interested: "Oh! I didn't expect the Spanish Inquisition" (1.15.197). At that moment Cardinal Ximenez (Palin), Biggles (Jones), and Fang (Gilliam) appear, and the Dear Old Lady is taken to a dungeon to be tortured with soft pillows and a comfy chair. What is anomalous here is the very natural, very real old woman character played by Wilde. She is appealing in her innocence, professing not to understand the accusations against her, and reacting with a warm smile as the Inquisitors "torture" her in the comfy chair. She is not a cross-dressed Pepperpot-type, so the humor isn't entirely visual or incongruous due to gross caricature, though these elements must be considered. It may be that this scene works *because* she is an old woman; she is the sweet grandmum who good-naturedly puts up with the boys' shenanigans, and the brutality and horror which should accompany such an evocation ("the Spanish Inquisition") is undercut by her mere presence. By this time (episode 15) *Flying Circus* had launched into its second run,[15] the audience having been exposed to Python's cross-dressing tactics for what amounted to an entire television season, and certainly at least somewhat inured to the "shock" (or disruption) of seeing a man in women's clothing (Chapman, et al. 320). What this means is that the audience can now view the specter of a real old woman — not Terry Jones as a dowdy Pepperpot — as a sort of disruption that transvestism might have perpetrated, but which through time and repetition has become the norm. It is thus incongruous to see a "Dear Old Lady" being tortured by the Inquisitors, and the humor is generated from this reversal.

The "Dear Old Lady" is allowed to act and react to the silliness going on around her, as is Carol Cleveland in this and the very next scene, "The Semaphore Version of Wuthering Heights." As Catherine, Cleveland is the star of this adaptation, and actually gets more screen time than any other character, including Heathcliffe (Jones). Using semaphore flags, Catherine first is intimate with Heathcliffe, then admits to her husband she has been seeing her lover again:

> Cut to front door again. Exterior. Husband is waiting. Catherine comes up the path towards him. As she approaches he flags.
> SUBTITLE: YES! YES! I'VE BEEN SEEING HEATHCLIFFE, AND WHY NOT? HE'S THE ONLY MAN I EVER LOVED. HE'S FINE. HE'S STRONG. HE'S ALL THE THINGS YOU'LL NEVER BE, AND WHAT'S MORE... [1.15.199].

Here Cleveland commands the scene, looks no more silly than anyone else as she waves her flags, and manages to carry off the scene very effectively. This is one of the rare occasions when the male writers/actors don't undercut or marginalize their female actor or character. (Though, the fact that she is unable to speak a word and can only signal her utterances is worth mentioning as perhaps another example of the female being muted in the Python world.)

With characters like the Pepperpots and various Pythons dressed as Victoria or Elizabeth or the female members of "The Most Awful Family in Britain, 1974," there is the essential notion that the end result is humor by visual incongruity. Philip Thompson identifies the caricature and the grotesque as separated by degrees, the former able to become the latter with just a tweak of exaggeration. A caricature may be a "recognizable or typical person or characteristic distorted (or stylized) in a ridiculous and amusing way" (Thompson 17). The Pepperpots might fit this category. The grotesque is broached as the characteristics are distorted beyond "the norm for caricaturistic exaggeration — a norm of abnormality," and the caricature can become disgusting or fearsome, approaching the "realm of the monstrous" (17–18). Characters in this category may include those which are not only disgusting visually, such as Valerie Garibaldi (Chapman) from

"The Most Awful Family in Britain" with her mini skirt, beehive hair and absolutely garish makeup, but perhaps morally or emotionally or sexually, such as those male-as-female performances with homoerotic undertones, including Mother (Jones) in *Life of Brian* who, it is suggested, regularly performs fellatio on a centurion. In *The Meaning of Life* we are presented with the Protestant couple (Chapman and Idle) who discuss condom use, with the wife (Idle), eventually becoming aroused enough to ask "Have you got one?" In the same film there is a quick visual of an older American couple (Palin and Idle) in an elevator, and the wife (Idle again) is kneeling before her husband, blowing on his camera's lens cap. This libidinal factor gets raised to the monstrous in *The Meaning of Life*'s "Live Organ Donors" sketch (discussed in chapter 4), wherein the wife of a live organ donor is wooed by one of the men harvesting her husband's liver. When she finally agrees to donate her own liver, the bloody carnage that will necessarily follow changes the caricature from homoerotic to monstrous. And this monstrosity is clearly useful to Python in the quest for visual humor based on sexual underpinnings elevated to the grotesque by the specter of cross-dressed men.

On the Shakespearean stage, cross-dressed men and boys—albeit "pretty" boys to play pretty girls—confused at least some theater-goers as contradictory emotional and physical responses were generated. The attraction and revulsion can exist simultaneously, as noted by Thompson:

> It should be clear that ... the classic reaction to the grotesque — the experience of amusement and disgust, laughter and horror, mirth and revulsion, simultaneously, is partly at least a reaction to the highly *abnormal*. For the abnormal may be funny (this is accurately reflected in the everyday usage of "funny" to mean both "amusing" and "strange") and on the other hand it may be fearsome or disgusting [18].

Interestingly, when it came down to it, a real woman played the birthing mother and a real woman disrobed and played the wife in the sex education scene with Cleese in *The Meaning of Life*, and a real woman stood naked before Brian's mother in *Life of Brian*. Near the end of *The Meaning of Life* a man (Chapman) is allowed to choose his method of execution, and opts to be chased over a cliff by a group of topless women. Python seems to want to draw the line between caricature and the grotesque when it suits them. The visual incongruity of a man dressing as an ugly woman can undercut the homoerotic or even heteroerotic subtext by its grotesque nature; it becomes funny, and not sexual. Or it can become funny and sexually disturbing when the gender lines are blurred and a disruptive crisis occurs, which sounds a lot like an echo of the Elizabethan anti-theatri-calist argument. An ideal example of this can be seen in the opening seg-ment of a *Flying Circus* episode where the camera tracks slowly along a line of bikini-clad beauties, each in a seductive stance. Each posing beauty is meant to be sexually attractive, and the music and languorous camera movement reinforce this sexuality. Four and five women are passed and appraised, until the camera comes to rest on Cleese, who is lounging across the top of the familiar desk he inhabits for the beginning of each episode. Cleese wear panties and bra, and nothing else. He delivers his "And now for something completely different" line with a seductive look, and the show begins. (But not before there is a cut to the "'It's' Man" (Palin), who is just as hirsute as he ever is but also wearing panties and a bra.) The sex-uality then, is undercut by the "grotesque" visions of Cleese and Palin in drag underclothes. The sexuality is even further genericized (or sanitized) by the following segment called "How to recognize different parts of the body" (1.22.294). Superimposed arrows point to (clad) body parts as a narrator is overheard. The arrows point out a foot, Venus de Milo's shoul-der, another foot, a bridge of a nose, and "the naughty bits," with the arrow pointed at a man's polka dot shorts (1.22.294). The body is dis-membered in these segments (which appear throughout the episode), effectively desexualizing the images in favor of discrete anatomical units. Later the motif reappears and we are shown "more naughty bits," includ-ing the (clothed, again) naughty bits of a lady, a horse, an ant, and Regi-nald Maudling (1.22.297). Also, these grotesqueries became more and more prevalent *after* the *Flying Circus* episodes, in the feature films, though "Poet Problems" (*Flying Circus* episode 17) offers a bored housewife (Jones) attempting to seduce her poet reader (Palin). She comments on the size of his torch, the volts of his batteries, gets positively enraptured when he unscrews his flashlight, and pulls him onto the couch asking that he take her to "the place where eternity knows no bounds, where the garden of love encloses us round" (1.17.230). There is perhaps far more homoerot-ica in the *Flying Circus* episodes without any subconscious cross-dressing elements or the outright gay lifestyle accoutrements (Karl Marx and Che Guevara first making out, then relaxing in bed; or the interviewers in the "Two Sheds" sketch).[16]

The homosexual as Other in Monty Python appears regularly, often including or instigated by the troupe's only homosexual member, Graham Chapman. The presence of a homosexual cast member would seem to pre-sent two possibilities for the troupe: avoid the subject out of respect for the feelings of Chapman, or treat same-sex attraction like any other human endeavor and send it up. They obviously chose the latter, becoming equal opportunity offenders. The homosexual character and homosexual tendencies (male to male, not female to female) are, however, given Other status in the bulk of Python's work, and are often used as definitives or ways to classify one as an Other. Being Other, however, doesn't necessarily mean that the homosexual will be marginalized or textually destroyed. The homosexual, after all, is still a man, and still can partake of the homosocial bonding. Like Don John, who is an Other because he is a bastard (a sexual classification, in a sense), he is still a male and trusted more than the female. In fact, often it is more likely that the homosexual Other will be treated kindl,, though comically, and allowed to exist as at least some kind of significant part of the Monty Python world. But the homosexual as Other must be addressed, as well.

The faculty of the Philosophy Department at the University of Woolamaloo is welcoming its newest faculty member, and they are singularly concerned with the new hire's sexual orientation:

> FOURTH BRUCE (Cleese): No right, well gentlemen, I'll just remind you of the faculty rules. Rule one — no pooftahs. Rule two — no member of the faculty is to maltreat the Abbos in any way whatsoever, if there's anyone watching. Rule three — no pooftahs. Rule four — I don't want to catch anyone not drinking in their room after lights out. Rule five — no pooftahs. Rule six — there is *no* rule six. Rule seven — no pooftahs [1.22.296].

Four of the six rules, as can be seen, forbid the admission of homosexuals into the faculty — an Australian faculty, but a faculty nonetheless. Like the previous treatment of Scotsmen, the Australians are lampooned here in a broad manner and treated distinctly as Other. They are not only not English, they are also either homophobic (by checking sexuality credentials) or latently homosexual (for the same reason), both ascriptions meriting Other status. But Michael, the newest hire, is already something of an Other by virtue of his name, which isn't Bruce:

> FOURTH BRUCE: Michael Baldwin — this is Bruce. Michael Baldwin — this is Bruce. Michael Baldwin — this is Bruce.
> FIRST BRUCE: Is your name not Bruce, then?
> MICHAEL: No, it's Michael.
> SECOND BRUCE: That's going to cause a little confusion.
> THIRD BRUCE: Yeah. Mind if we call you Bruce, just to keep it clear? [1.2.295].

Before he can become one of the dominant grouping, he must not only change his name to match everyone else, but must also renounce any "alternative" sexuality than what the homosocial grouping allows. This preference is signaled as the sketch ends with a prayer and one of the Bruces says,

"Right, let's get some Sheilas" (1.2.296). Just as foreigners are often portrayed as Other on the Elizabethan stage, the Australians here are given
Other status by virtue of their outrageously pronounced accents, their uni-
formity (each dresses and is named exactly the same), their homophobic
and homosocial tendencies, and even their dietary and religious habits.
Perhaps most importantly they are not English. They are an Other, though
certainly a part of the Commonwealth. They all admire the Queen as "a
good Sheila ... and not at all stuck up" (1.2.295). They are British, then,
in the largest sense of the empire, as opposed to English, and are therefore Others.

The references to homosexuality in Shakespeare and even on the Elizabethan stage were fewer and often well-obscured in the play texts. Some
of the most remarkable examples are Antonio and Sebastian in *Twelfth
Night*; the homoeroticism of Marlowe's *Edward II*, and the opening scene
of *Dido, Queen of Carthage*; and mentions of homosexual behavior or characteristics in Jonson's *Epicoene* and *Poetaster*, as well as Middleton's *Father
Hubbard's Tales* (Porter 128; Orgel 19–20). Stephen Orgel identifies the
"selective blindness" employed by the English when confronted with
sodomitical acts, and the ability which allowed them to "associate [homo-
sexuality] on the whole only with foreigners, not with themselves" (20).
The stage, then, became a place for "the easy life of a London playboy"—
a life which included an "ingle" or catamite (a boy kept by a pederast)—
to be played out in a relatively tame and socially ignorable manner (20–21).
The term "homosexuality," even, is problematic. As Alan Bray notes in
Homosexuality in Renaissance England, the word wasn't used in English
until the 1890s, and "sodomite," a word having more particular connota-
tions today, was during Elizabethan times a dumping ground for myriad
nonreproductive sexual acts, and was often not logically applied as a legal
category (Bray 14; Sedinger 75–76; Coke 58–59). Sodomy was also almost
always publicly connected to "other kinds of subversion," as Orgel mentions. Orgel continues, writing that sodomy "becomes visible in Elizabethan society only when it intersects with some other behavior that is
recognized as dangerous and antisocial ... an aspect of atheism, papistry,
sedition, witchcraft" (20–21). Sodomy (including homosexuality, though
not separable at the time) therefore became the avenue through which
these subversions were both accomplished and then made public.

It was through these combinations of political and religious subversions with sexual perversions that Christopher Marlowe was posthumously
accused; among others Richard Baines accused Marlowe of partaking
explicitly in all three areas (Porter 128). Marlowe's proclivities— he is
described as "intermittently misogynistic, aggressively sensual, and

flagrantly homoerotic"[17]— are well-known, however, and his treatment of the relationship between young King Edward II and his favorite Gaveston (and then Spenser), as well as his description of Edward's grotesquely ironic death trumpet the homosexual or at the least basely effeminized characters and practices with the trappings of the Other. In *Edward II*, Lancaster calls Gaveston "base and obscure," while Mortimer (junior) describes Edward and his preferences as "brain-sick" (1.1.101, 125). Orgel identifies this relationship as "the only dramatic instance of a homosexual relationship presented in the terms in which the culture formally conceived it — as antisocial, seditious, [and] ultimately disastrous" (25). Though still often railed against, homosexuality was, according to Orgel, treated as more acceptable or tolerable at the time than destructive heterosexuality, perhaps at least partly attributable to the fact that homosexuality rarely ran afoul of the patriarchal order (like heterosexual affairs could and did) or threatened bloodlines or inheritances (25–27). Plus, of course, many of the practitioners would have been the very men who ruled the society, made and enforced the laws, and saw to the continuation of the patriarchy and status quo hierarchy. But as Bray points out, the overwhelming abundance of textual evidence (evidence somehow ignored by early homosexual apologists like Havelock Ellis and, to a certain extent, later ones like Orgel) betrays the "deep horror with which homosexuality was widely regarded" (7). No matter who was practicing it, high or low, aristocrat or commoner, the homosexual and homosexuality was a person and a category firmly labeled "Other." The difficulty with which historians approach the syncretism of more recent terms and age-old practices demonstrates the complete Otherness surrounding homosexuality. Bray writes: "To talk of an individual in this period as being or not being 'a homosexual' is an anachronism and ruinously misleading" (16). The more fruitful approach is to realize a broader description, Bray concludes: "The temptation to debauchery, from which homosexuality was not clearly distinguished, *was accepted as part of the common lot, be it never so abhorred*" (emphasis added; 16–17). A bit later and off the stage (but on another, far more visible stage) King James I may have just been following the fashion of so-called "tolerated indiscretions" and commonly accepted debauchery as he wooed Buckingham, for instance, calling him "wife," and himself "widower" if they were ever parted (Akrigg 431).

The treatment of outright homosexual behavior in Monty Python is, of course, comedic, and can be as derisive and mocking as any other taboo subject being sent up. Episode 22 mentioned above in reference to "pooftahs" is a veritable dumping ground of sodomitical humor, and the targets are establishment figures. Like *Corona Regia* (1615), an attack on James

I and his homosexual tendencies (probably written by the German Caspar Schoppe), this Python episode posits the faculty of a commonwealth university, an eminent and knighted plastic surgeon specialist, and a squad of soldiers as partaking in some way in the homosexual arena of culture. The specialist (Cleese) agrees to do an unnecessary nose job if the patient (Chapman) will "come on a holiday camping" with him (1.22.299). The patient, Mr. Luxury Yacht, immediately turns to the camera and says excitedly: "He asked me! He asked me!" What follows is a filmed section featuring Mr. Luxury Yacht and the Specialist holding hands and skipping through the woods, in slow motion, their tent in the background. The gag is both continued and a segue accomplished as an Interviewer (Palin) appears: "Next week we'll be showing you how to pick up an architect, how to pull a prime minister, and how to have fun with a wholesale poulterer" (1.22.299). But included amongst the more obvious same-sex attraction jokes in this sketch are more subtle references to homosexuality. Mr. Luxury Yacht has come to the specialist for plastic surgery, and he's obviously wearing an enormous false nose, but the specialist doesn't seem to notice the nose. Moreover, Mr. Luxury Yacht isn't able to say exactly why he's there, or even who he is:

> MR LUXURY YACHT: Ah, no, no. My name is *spelt* "Luxury Yacht" but it's pronounced Throatwobbler Mangrove.
> SPECIALIST: Well, do sit down then Mr Throatwobbler Mangrove.
> MR LUXURY YACHT: Thank you.
> SPECIALIST: Now, what seems to be the trouble?
> MR LUXURY YACHT: Um, I'd like you to perform some plastic surgery on me.
> SPECIALIST: I see. And what particular feature of your anatomy is causing you distress? [1.2.298].

From the very start the obvious must be discounted. The patient's name is spelled one way and pronounced in a completely different way, the patient's enormous nose (fake or otherwise) isn't noticed by the specialist, and the patient can't seem to bring himself to mention just what part of his body he wants the specialist to examine. When the specialist finally notices and mentions the oversized proboscis, the patient at first denies that he's come about his "enormous hooter," then admits he wants the specialist to "hack a bit off" (1.2.299). Another bit of misdirection awaits as the interview progresses, leading us further away from a simple plastic surgery visit and closer to a same-sex flirtation:

> SPECIALIST: Fine. It is a startler, isn't it. Er, do you mind if I ... er.
> MR LUXURY YACHT: What?
> SPECIALIST: Oh, no nothing, then, well, I'll just examine your nose [1.2.299].

Just what the specialist wanted to do before examining the nose isn't voiced, but certainly implied, and especially so as the sketch progresses. The nose is found to be fake, but the patient still wants "an" operation — it's no longer clear that it's a nose operation at all he wants. The scene is brought to a close as the specialist agrees to do an operation if the patient will come on holiday with him, and we see them frolicking through the woods. And if the audience hasn't picked up on the homosexuality theme of this episode, the sketch following the Interviewer's interjection is described as "a precision display of bad temper" from "the men of the Derbyshire Light Infantry" (1.2.299). In two separate shots the light infantry men prance about in unison, "mincing" and camping it up as they drill (1.2.299). Still later in the show it is announced that the winner of the "Where to put Edward Heath's statue" Competition — won by a Mr. Ivy North — will receive a cash prize and "a visit to the Sailors Quarters" (1.2.301). It becomes apparent that much of Monty Python's world is ruled and supported by the homosocial bond that stems from the all-male cast and is translated into same-sex couplings on the stage. Women are often cast as Other then marginalized or textually destroyed in favor of the homosocial, while the same-sex couplings are often celebrated — this even as Python ridicules and "camps up" homosexuality. Authority figures are often cast as homosexuals, perhaps because they are traditional and therefore easy targets for comic deflation, or perhaps because, like the Elizabethan practitioners of sodomy, it is the authority figures who can most easily get away with such practices. In episode 13 a man (Palin) approaches a police inspector (Cleese) to report that his wallet's been stolen. The aimlessness of this link becomes obvious as both participants seem to be "acting," as if they're just going through the motions, and the result brings into question the veracity of the entire episode:

> MAN: I'm terribly sorry but I was sitting on a park bench over there, took my coat off for a minute and then I found my wallet had been stolen and £15 taken from it.
> INSPECTOR: Well did you er, did you see anyone take it, anyone hanging around or...
> MAN: No no, there was no one there at all.
> INSPECTOR: Well there's not very much we can do about that, sir.
> MAN: Do you want to come back to my place?
> INSPECTOR: ...Yeah all right [1.13.168].

The Inspector's lack of real interest ("Uh huh"), the apology from the man who has been wronged, and just the terseness of the summary judgment delivered by the Inspector lend an odd air to the link. With the payoff becoming evident — and certainly by virtue of its libidinal nature — it seems as if the entire dialogue has been nothing more than an elaborate code sequence to precipitate the coupling. This also hearkens back to the encounter between the Specialist and Mr. Luxury Yacht, where the patient was only in the office, as it turns out, to secure a "date" with the object of his affection. Later in this same episode (episode 13) the "policeman-as-fairy" scenario ("fairy" here carrying the double meaning of homosexual *and* supernatural being) is revisited, with officers wearing tutus and carrying magic wands (1.13.170).

The lip-locked Karl Marx and Che Guevara, the happy male couple who go on a camping holiday, and even men at the highest levels of society, as will be seen, partake of these homosexual relationships, often either before or after they distance themselves from a heterosexual coupling. In the feature film *Monty Python and the Holy Grail*, the virtuous Sir Galahad (Palin) is surrounded by a bevy of beautiful and scantily-clad women, but is "saved from almost certain temptation" by Lancelot (Cleese), who threatens the women with his sword ("Back foul temptress!") as they escape. Galahad protests, "Bet you're gay," to which Lancelot answers that he is not. Female sexuality is a trap, a temptation which will, if succumbed to, compromise the homosocial grouping and the quest. In episode 3 of *Flying Circus*, a milkman delivers to a suburban house where he is greeted by a "seductively dressed young lady" (1.3.38). The woman gestures for him to come inside; he does, following her upstairs. She leads him into a room, and as she locks him in, he sees several other milkmen, all elderly, "who have obviously been there for a very long time" (1.3.38). She is the femme fatale, her sexuality a trap. Men going home or going out with other men are not dealt with retributively, their couplings are camped up, certainly, but in an attractive, humorous way. Not unlike the "natural revulsion at the imperfection of women" Stephen Orgel discusses *vis à vis* Renaissance society and especially the male of the period, the successful couplings in the Python's world are almost exclusively either same-sex (male-male) or cross-dressed (13). Karl Marx and Che Guevara are first seen kissing, then later they are seen "lying post-coitally" in bed (Chapman, et al. ? 25.19–25). "Lust effeminates," Orgel continues, citing Renaissance medical and scholastic opinion, "[and] makes men incapable of manly pursuits" (14). This is heterosexual lust, certainly, and not the affection shared by the same-sex couples discussed above. And not only are the heterosexual couplings kept at a distance, but are also simply replaced with men playing the women's part within the reality of the story. One or more members may cross-dress and play women when unattractive women are called for, but in the case of the "Dad's Pooves" skit, a man dresses as a woman to become the sexual partner of another man:

CONTINUITY VOICE (Eric): ...Week two sees the return of the wacky exploits of the oddest couple you've ever seen — yes, "Dad's Pooves"!
A kitchen set. A man (Terry G) in sexy female underwear. Another man (Terry J) dressed as a judge, runs in with flowers.
SUPERIMPOSED CAPTION: "DAD'S POOVES"
CONTINUITY VOICE: ...the kooky oddball laugh-a-minute fun-a-plenty world of unnatural sexual practices *(the first man spanks the judge with a string of sausages)* [2.38.227].

This is something of a departure for Python. In a very short scene we are presented with a cross-dressed man who is cross-dressed for the purpose of sexual excitement within the fictional world, and not just to play a role. Though, of course, in the sexual exchange depicted he is playing a role — that of the feminine. His partner the judge carries on the Python penchant for depicting sexual perversities at the highest levels of government and society. This is a true disruption (to use Garber's term), since it is so multivalent. Is the man depicted actually a judge, or is he simply playing a role, not unlike the man wearing women's underwear?

There is another example of a noteworthy disruption, this based on Python's accepted practice of having men play women without any textual acknowledgment that the woman is actually a man. Jones as a frumpy housewife or Cleese as a female interviewee on a talk show play their female roles straight, as it were, never winking to the audience or even other characters that cross-dressing is being performed. In one instance (in episode 14) a gangster documentary is being exhibited focusing on the infamous Dinsdale brothers. Once again the disruption is evident in relation to a same-sex innuendo, but mingled with (and possibly confused by) the cross-dressing acknowledgment. Gloria (Cleese) sits at a bar and responds to an off-screen interviewer's questions:

GLORIA: I walked out with Dinsdale on many occasions and found him a most charming and erudite companion. He was wont to introduce one to many eminent persons, celebrated American singers, members of the aristocracy and other gangleaders.
INTERVIEWER (Idle): *(off-screen)* How had he met them?
GLORIA: Through his work for charity. He took a warm interest in Boys' Clubs, Sailors' Homes, Choristers' Associations, Scouting Jamborees and of course the Household Cavalry [1.14.188–189].

The pederastic inferences cast Dinsdale in the same-sex attraction role, and the fact that he is dating a man dressed as a woman named Gloria becomes especially interesting when Gloria acknowledges his true identity: "And what's more he knew how to treat a female impersonator" (1.14.189). To my knowledge this is only one of two instances in the Monty Python works where transvestism is forwarded as an identity, a category which serves to disrupt the already codified category of men dressing as women without the reflexive moment.[18] And like the Renaissance practices noted by Orgel, Porter, and Bray, among others, this "perversion" is attached to an inferred category of same-sex attraction. In the Renaissance the charge of sodomy was a rider or companion charge to political or religious corruption; in Monty Python homosexuality is a companion to acknowledged cross-dressing, and is also very frequently attached to political and religious authority figures like Edward Heath, members of parliament, judges, and well-connected criminals like the Dinsdales. These category crises exist at multiple levels and truly call into question the identity of these characters, and are perhaps a modern enactment of the universal effeminization and the blurring of genders which anti-theatricalists so feared and railed against. Many times the heterosexual couplings aren't even allowed. In episode 5, a man and woman (Jones and Cleveland) are kissing passionately:

> SHE: Oh, oh, oh Bevis, should we?
> HE: Oh Dora. Why not?
> SHE: Be gentle with me [1.5.63].

What follows is a filmed montage of metaphorically sexual images — a smokestack rising, waves crashing, a volcano erupting — ending with several of the suggestive images reversing themselves (smokestack falling, tree crashing). The girl sits alone on the bed:

> SHE: Oh Bevis, are you going to *do* anything or are you just going to show me films all evening?
> *We see Bevis, with small projector.*
> BEVIS: Just one more, dear.
> SHE: Oh [1.5.63].

The answer to the man's "Why not?" is becoming more obvious, as this coupling between a man and a woman is interrupted before consummation. In episode 43 the newlyweds (Jones and Cleveland again) are reduced to sitting nude in their wedding bed with her father (Chapman), whom she has invited to stay with them. And without the interference of female sexuality, there even seems to be a conspicuous absence of jealousy between homosexual characters. In episode 21, two judges (Idle and Palin) in the Old Bailey enter an "oak-panelled robing chamber" wearing their wigs and red robes:

SECOND JUDGE: I could see that foreman eyeing me.
FIRST JUDGE: Really?
SECOND: Yes, cheeky devil.
FIRST JUDGE: Was he that tall man with that very big...?
SECOND JUDGE: No, just a minute — I must finish you know. Anyway, I finished up with "the actions of these vicious men is a violent stain on the community and the full penalty of the law is scarcely sufficient to deal with their ghastly crimes," and I waggled my wig! Just ever so slightly, but it was a stunning effect [1.21.287–288].

These are well-known homosexual stereotypes, to be sure, but delivered without the threat of violence or judgment often found in the heterosexual couplings. And like the Renaissance notion that men must be left to men's pursuits, only entangling themselves with women when absolutely necessary (i.e., for procreation), this homosocial bonding (without the explicit mention of homosexual intercourse) rings fairly harmless and ultimately funny. As Alan Bray and Orgel note, the crime of heterosexual fornication during the Renaissance "was much more energetically prosecuted" than homosexual behaviors (Orgel 19). This toleration (as, again, no bastard children or corrupted inheritances arose from homosexuality) is echoed in Python's work, as the homosexual is often portrayed in a humorous and not derisive light. Indeed, as we have seen, it is the heterosexual coupling which is often interrupted, as in the "Housewives of Britain" sketch, wherein a group of ladies rids the country of Others (foreign literature, strikers), including pulling Othello from Desdemona's bed during a performance of *Othello* (2.32.121). Here the Other is both foreign and heterosexual — perhaps the ultimate Other. In episode 9 a man (Chapman) and a woman (Cleveland) are sitting on a sofa, "beginning to make passes at each other" (1.9.117). As they woo, they move closer and closer and are just about to kiss when the doorbell rings. The man promises to get rid of the intruder, but instead, of course, another man (Idle) enters who will interrupt for the duration their attempts at successful cuddling. Into the formerly quiet room comes a procession of ghastly people, including a flatulent and vulgar married couple (Cleese and Jones), an outrageously dressed "poof" and his "gorgeous little man" (Gilliam and Palin), a goat and a group of Welsh coal miners (1.9.118–120). The woman (Cleveland) is sexually harassed and runs screaming from the room, and the man (Chapman) is eventually shot and killed. The heterosexual coupling here is not only textually averted, but the Otherness of this situation is signaled early on. Just before the sketch began (and in the last moments of the episode) the catch-phrase "And now for something completely different" is heard. The heterosexual coupling is what ranks as difference here, not the cross-dressed couple or even the homosexual couple introduced later in the sketch. Heterosexuality, then, becomes Other.

Again, admittedly, it's difficult to pronounce judgment on Monty Python as being misogynistic in their abuse of female characters and actors, since the abuse is fairly widespread amongst both genders, all races, classes, prejudices, and is most often self-deprecating. Their consistent marginalization of the female actor may just be attributable to a writing style and skill that doesn't allow for interesting female roles that don't have to be camped up. Shakespeare was able to write females who were fascinating even though they had to be played by men; Python wrote females who were funny because they were played (and informed) by men. The goal finally was entertainment, as contemporary newspaper critic Alan Brien pointed out: "The Python humour ... is notorious for being infantile hysterics inflated often to the level of genius ... [and] much of it is intended to be nothing more than loony outrageousness ... but everything means something" (Thompson 6). Dressing up as unattractive women who then are often knowledgeable beyond any other character in the sketch; or, embodying the "Tory Housewives" who set about to clean up British labor (or, perhaps, "Labour") standards, and, "talking of windmills, aren't afraid to tilt at the permissive society" as they clean up modern art, Shakespearean stage practices, and even the BBC — these are strong characters that often go beyond caricature (2.32.121). These women characters, finally, their often outrageous attire and habits, and the other people, ideals and organizations which Python regularly targets allow for a mixture of the grotesque, satire, and general lampooning in the quest for entertainment. As William Davis wrote in the *Telegraph*, Monty Python "is very funny, but it is more than routine comedy performed by professionals prepared to behave foolishly for the sake of entertaining the public. It is pure satire, and it is all the more effective because of its underlying contempt" (Thompson 9). The contempt, however, isn't always (or even usually) present, as the familiar and often warm depictions of female characters (by males) and homosexual characters betray a tenderness bred, perhaps, by familiarity.

The Others in the works of both Shakespeare and Monty Python are myriad and, finally, essential. Just as Elizabethan drama was dependent upon otherness for a complete self-definition of what it was to be English, Monty Python relies on the sending up of foreigners, the British, authority figures, homosexuality and, paradoxically, heterosexuality and the rigidity of a multitude social, sexual, political, and economic roles and categories to define Englishness and further the reading of the National Poet Shakespeare and his "others." There is a tolerance in both Shakespeare and Python, a tolerance which allows for necessary condemnations and fondly-realized approbations (often in near-simultaneity) of characters like Falstaff and Hero, Richard and Reginald Maudling, swishy judges and the Pepperpots. These binary tensions reflect works which resonate on many levels and across multiple categories, blurring distinctions without homogenizing, becoming "at once a containment of subversiveness and a creation of subtle new subversiveness" (Porter 132). This subversiveness has been visible before, in Shakespeare's undercutting of the conventions of the stage, of the unities, and his acknowledgment of the artifice of the stage; and it has been visible in Python's reflexiveness, anachronistic tendencies, and general disavowal of the boundaries between fantasy and reality, between the stage and life.

Notes

1. Shakespeare's absence from this list is intentional, since it has yet to be proven that he attended any university. Even the certainty of his grammar school education is unclear (since there are no surviving records indicating his matriculation anywhere), but his educational history been anecdotally reconstructed by many scholars from extant sources. See Matus, 32, 35.

2. For a brief discussion of this phenomenon see Braunmuller's and Hattaway's *English Renaissance Drama* (Cambridge: Cambridge UP, 1994). The play referred to is *The Concealed Fancies*, and was acted by the Cavendish girls. Orgel seems to be right, as well, when he notes that most scholars brush right over the "male only" convention of the English stage.

3. Shakespeare through Henry even seems to push the theatrical allusion further, remarking on the occasional nature of theater, its spectacle and allure:

> If all the year were playing holidays,
> To sport would be as tedious as to work;
> But when they seldom come, they wish'd for come,
> And nothing pleaseth but rare accidents. (1.2.204–207)

"Playing" in the afternoons at the Globe or the Swan, either before or after a day's work, is an opportunity for the citizenry to both see a play and have their own play time away from the labors of the day. Has young Henry grown tired of or accustomed to the dissolute life he's experienced regularly since he was a child? Is it simply time to put down the playthings in favor of adult life, and only pick up those childish baubles as if they were "playing holidays" that come but a few times a year?

4. Cf. *Genesis* 1, 2 for the creation motif. See *Revelations* 20:1, 3 for a reference to the devil as arising from, confined within, and cast back into the pit, as well as his millennial probationary reign on earth before the final judgment. Richard is given qualities seemingly reserved for the Prince of Darkness during the apex of his prophesied power. He is both Creator and Destroyer, perhaps an allusion also to the dual nature of man, and thus a more fully realized character because of his duality, his shortcomings, his darker side.

5. See Gurr, 103–113 and 212–230 *passim* for some of the proclivities of the Elizabethan audience.

6. This was the act with which Henry VIII sought to humble the clergy in his dispute with Rome. "Premunire" refers to the act of obeying a foreign power or monarch at the expense of one's own fealty to king and country, in this particular case, Henry VIII and his causes. Stubbes does refer to the stage flaunting the disobedience to "Princes" and the committing of "treasons" in his charges against performance and players.

7. This assertion is, of course, without base. There were female actors and writers at both Cambridge and Oxford, but none happened to be later chosen for the Python troupe. See Wilmut, 1–27 *passim*. Author Marina Warner attended Oxford at about the time Terry Jones and Michael Palin were there, and Graham Chapman and John Cleese were at Cambridge. In a recent interview with *The Guardian*, she mentions Oxford as being less than receptive to intelligent females:

> They weren't used to undergraduates who were modern women, and the sense of decorum was oppressive. It was assumed that any woman who was interested in clothes must be a silly goose. Now one is used to meeting a woman with a first in philosophy wearing the latest nose ring, or whatever. In those days if you went to a tutorial in a mini skirt it meant you weren't serious about study. (22 January 2000)

8. The case of cross-dressing as a means to deceive other (albeit dim) characters and forward the plot is utilized quite effectively in *Life of Brian* and virtually nowhere else in the Python *œuvre*. In Jerusalem in Christ's time, the film depicts a "men-only" stoning policy. Women were not allowed to participate in the actual execution process. When Brian's mother (Jones) wants to go to a stoning, Brian (Chapman) agrees, but they must make a stop on the way at a roadside vendor who sells stones and packets of gravel. Brian's mother purchases stones but also buys a beard, which she must wear if she is to participate in the men-only stoning. At the stoning, we don't see Brian and his mother participate, but hear the charge of heresy leveled against the stonee for using the word "Jehovah." We quickly hear that most of those who are ready to stone the man are women wearing false beards. Actually, several are Pythons dressed as women wearing men's beards, and the rest are women just wearing beards. The man heading up the stoning (Cleese) even asks at one point if there are any women in the crowd, with the "no" answers starting off high-pitched but quickly pitched lower. When someone throws a stone too soon, the moderator asks who did it, and many high-pitched voices answer "She did! She did!" They again quickly change to lower pitched voices and shout "He did!" and point at the offender, who is sent to the back of the crowd. Not only are the male characters in charge of the stoning duped, but the female as Other is forwarded within the historical context of the film. And as the women who don beards to participate in the stoning show a good deal of initiative as they transgress defined boundaries, they are also portrayed as vicious and sadistic in their pursuit of this death sentence. They are then Other because they cannot participate, and Other because they do participate in this male-only ritual.

9. Jeffrey Miller in *Something Completely Different* identifies the "snob merit" aspects of Python's comedy, a style of comedy which the educated — like the Pythons themselves — will "get" and the rude and unwashed will not. Miller con-

tinues: "The names of the two old women — Premise and Conclusion — also set up the final joke of the sketch: when Sartre confirms Mrs. Premise's premise that '*Rues a Liberte* is an allegory of man's search for commitment,' Mrs. Conclusion concludes the sketch..." (135–36). Miller looks at the entire episode in some detail. See 134–137.

10. Brechtian to a point, perhaps, but Kristin Thompson points out in "Sawing Through the Bough: *Tout va Bien* as a Brechtian Film" (*Wide Angle* 1:3, 1976), that Brecht separated himself from the Dadaists and surrealists and their interpretations of alienation. Ben Brewster's article "From Shklovsky to Brecht: A Reply" (*Screen* 15:2), quotes Brecht: "Their objects do not return from alienation" (Thompson 30). Brecht saw those practitioners essentially paralyzing the function of their art, so that "as far as its effect is concerned, it ends in an amusement" (30). Much of Python's work (especially the *Flying Circus* episodes) is explicitly created to undercut any return, to deny any progress other than that which leads to a comedic, shocking and often open-ended end. In other words, to end in an amusement.

11. Just another purposeful anachronism? Malden has no coast, and is perhaps given one to better serve the premise of leaving England for France. The show did, after all, shoot all the exterior location shots in a single trip, so being at the seaside and calling it North Malden might just have been easier. See Kim Johnson, Roger Wilmut.

12. "Unconformity" is a useful term borrowed from geology, though appropriated somewhat haphazardly. In geologic terms, "unconformity" is actually a relationship which most pointedly establishes a break in *time*, i.e., evidence in sedimentary deposition where/when sediments are *not* being deposited. There are also various kinds of unconformities (angular, etc.). "Nonconformities" are relationships which represent, again, a break in time, and which feature units that have nothing in common, i.e., an intrusive igneous dike in a sedimentary deposition. A "disconformity" is characterized by (in sediment) layers of differing sedimentary deposition sharing a similar dip, often due to erosion and new deposition. In short, Smidt and his sources, A.P. Rossiter and M.R. Ridley, have taken a geologic term and invested it with a broader range of meaning than the term originally allowed. As can be seen, all three terms can (and perhaps should) be used when referring to Smidt's definition of "unconformity":

> Unconformities are recognized chiefly by breaks in narrative continuity, contradictions as to cause and effect, impossible or incredible sequences of events, or unexplained and surprising changes in the characters portrayed. They also have to do with proportion and distribution of parts and functions and with the stability of thematic concerns. Sometimes they will be signaled by formal irregularities, such as meaningless repetitions or shifts in styles of speech and the patterns of verse and prose. (ix)

See Smidt's *Unconformities in Shakespeare's History Plays* and *Unconformities in Shakespeare's Early Comedies* (London: Macmillan, 1982 and 1986); see also Ridley's *Shakespeare's Plays: A Commentary* (Dent, 1937) and Rossiter's "The Structure of Richard the Third" in *Durham University Journal* 31 (1938): 44–75.

13. The other characters in this scene, all male, are given the lines which forward the narrative and link the disparate elements together. This is a standard practice and can be researched thanks to the complete printed telescripts, *The Complete Monty Python's Flying Circus: All the Words* (Pantheon: New York, 1989).

14. "Pastures new" is of course a reference from Milton's *Lycidas*, line 193. See Merritt Y. Hughes edition, *John Milton: Complete Poems and Major Prose* (New York and Indianapolis: Odyssey, 1957): 125. See also Virgil's *Eclogues X*, lines 70–77.

15. The first series aired from October 5, 1969 to January 11, 1970, and comprised episodes 1–13. The second series began its televised run on September 15, 1970 (episode 14) and finished with episode 23 on December 1, 1970. Episode 15 was aired on September 22, 1970, and was the second episode broadcast that season. For more complete transmission details, see Chapman, et al. *All the Words*, Appendix.

16. Karl Marx (Jones) and Che Guevara appear in "World Forum" (2.25.19); "Dad's Pooves" is found in episode 38 (2.38.227); and the "Arthur 'Two Sheds' Jackson" sketch is located in episode 1 (1.1.9).

17. See Joseph A. Porter's "Marlowe, Shakespeare, and the Canonization of Heterosexuality" in *The South Atlantic Quarterly* 88.1 (Winter 1989): 128.

18. The reflexive moment would occur when the character who is dressed as a woman admits such, and this rarely happens in Monty Python's work. The two exceptions to this rule are the female impersonator mentioned above, and the lumberjack in episode 9. The "I'm a Lumberjack" song and scene (1.9.114–115) offers transvestism in relation to the manly, male-centered Canadian lumberjack profession. The chorus and the girl become horrified, and she runs off as he is pelted with rotten fruit. Certainly an Other here, and certainly disrupting a category and blurring roles, perhaps the Britishness of the participants (they are Canadian, not English) reduces their ability to tolerate the admitted cross-dresser, much as was seen in the Australian-dominated Philosophy Dept. faculty sketch.

Conclusion

I mentioned above that Jean Marsden in 1991 looked at the state of Shakespeare scholarship and saw a lack, a missing field of study rendered conspicuous by its absence. She asked why there weren't more studies which set out to "demonstrate the widespread presence of Shakespeare," not only in adaptations, but in the structures and nuances of literature (especially the novel), the theater, and literary criticism. One stated goal of my study — now more than ten years on from Marsden's — was to take a giant step toward addressing that absence. Shakespeare has become a cultural symbol, an accretion of the man, the myth, the works, and the appropriations attempted over a four-hundred-year span. The Monty Python troupe read "Shakespeare," England's National Poet, as well as his fellow English dramatists of the time, then responded to, appropriated, and sent them up. Ultimately, though, this reexamination of England's shared cultural past becomes not simple mockery but valorization — the English Renaissance dramatists are valued anew. It is just such a revitalizing and refreshing of the legacy of The Bard that keeps Shakespeare fresh in the minds of artists, viewers, academicians and critics alike.

Monty Python didn't, of course, arise out of nowhere, or spring fully-formed from nothingness. There are too many instance of comparison, of similarity, of obvious appropriation of Shakespeare, Jonson and Dekker, et al. to dismiss the troupe's debt to the English Renaissance. Comparisons could have been made elsewhere, for there is obviously a significant appreciation of and influence from others as disparate as Swift, Brecht, and Joyce, or just the consistent inspiration of daily British television. *Monty Python* is, after all, an omnium-gatherum of influences, a seemingly indiscriminate mill accepting grist from anywhere, even everywhere, and only a close reading reveals the methods behind the madness. The point here is that Python's connections to Shakespeare are very real, the comedic troupe's work adding to the cultural myth that is Shakespeare.

We have examined Shakespeare and Monty Python as versions of the English National Poet, both speaking a language that comes to be known as "Englishness." They have provided generations of English (and British) men and women with shared cultural icons and a common heritage, which is both quotable and eminently worth appropriating. Monty Python read the National Poet Shakespeare and, like many had done before, appropriated The Bard to their own comedic ends. We looked at the "theatricality" of Shakespeare, Jonson and Python, their utilizations of actors, characters, caricatures, troupe configurations, and writing styles. Their uses of incongruities, anachronisms, elements of satire, and their respective knowledges of the literary and historical world all figured into their ultimate *mise en scène*. We have approached their uses and abuses of history, acknowledging the living organism-like nature that both Python and Shakespeare attributed to history. History became useful to Shakespeare as a loose framework upon and around which was draped the fabric of plot and story; and for Python as a grab bag of characters and antique notions in the construction of their anarchic comedy. Elements of satire, the grotesque, carnival and ribald wordplay characterize much of the humor of Shakespeare, Jonson and Python, where a humble shoemaker or filthy peasant or even a puppet (in *BF*) can carry the (narrative) day. Finally, the lengthy prospect of treating the specter of "Other" on the English Renaissance stage and in Python's works begs further study. There are so many Others in Python alone, to paraphrase Orgel, that I feel the surface has just been scratched, and continued study can and will yield good fruit. Foreigners? Women? Homosexuals? Stuffy establishment types? British (as opposed to English)? Royalty? There are many Others. Even the so-called commoner — the solid middle-class or the poor — can be treated as Other, and, as we saw in the case of Richard III, friends can be "othered" into marginality and death. These seem areas of rich possibilities for future work.

And much work remains to be done. *Flying Circus* as Jonsonian (or Middletonian) London city or citizen comedy? A particular vogue of the early seventeenth century, the city comedy genre is revisited by Python as, often, the city meets the country (or the south meets the north) in myriad *Flying Circus* episodes. Admittedly shot and written within just minutes of the city's center (due primarily to budgetary constraints), *Flying Circus* often takes as its ammunition the peoples and mores that might be particular to London. In-jokes, recognizable localized settings and subjects, topical humor of current political and cultural figures and trends, working class subjects—city comedy and *Flying Circus* weren't seriously discussed here, as the subject should prove to be enormous. In episode 2 a City Gent and a Rustic — the first on holiday, the latter chewing grass and thickly-accented — discuss the possible implications of flying sheep (1.2.15–16). This same visual incongruity resurfaces in episode 25 in an art gallery, as two smartly-dressed and well-spoken art critics are juxtaposed against another rustic (called a "bumpkin" in the script) who identifies himself as being the man from "The Hay Wain" painting by Constable (2.25.22). Looking more closely at just one example in *Flying Circus*, Python explores the friction between father and son, between the working class and the cultural sophisticate, between the city and the country, all in a single scene. In typical Python fashion, though, nothing is quite as one might expect in such a setting:

> DAD (Chapman): Aye, 'ampstead wasn't good enough for you, was it? ... you had to go poncing off to Barnsley, you and yer coal-mining friends. *(spits)*
> KEN (Idle): Coal-mining is a wonderful thing father, but it's something you'll never understand. Just look at you!
> MUM (Jones): Oh Ken! Be careful! You know what he's like after a few novels.
> DAD: Oh come on lad! Come on, out wi' it! What's wrong wi' me? ... yer *tit!*
> KEN: I'll tell you what's wrong with you. Your head's addled with novels and poems, you come home every evening reeling of Château La Tour... [1.2.22–23].

The reversals in this section put a new spin on relations between classes and between London and the north, and offer a tantalizing example of the possibilities that could be realized by study of Python's workings of the city/citizen comedy.[1] Another fruitful area of study might be the troupe's feature film work. Less attention was paid herein to the feature films than the *Flying Circus* episodes, for two reasons. First, the television shows were given priority because of the distance separating the film format from the television stage and the latter's discussed affinities with the Elizabethan stage and conventions; second, because approaching the films in their entirety could have protracted the analyses almost indefinitely. But perhaps most tantalizing is the prospect of studying *Monty Python* as a true cultural phenomenon. *Flying Circus*, after all, was a television show with a relatively short lifespan. How do we really account for its continued popularity? Especially in an age where viewing choice has expanded exponentially, the Pythonesque and Pythonisms still reverberate on both sides of the Atlantic. It might be beneficial to look at another popular television show with roughly the same broadcast duration and which was even being produced at nearly the same time as *Flying Circus*: *Star Trek* (1966–1969).

Both shows fared well in their initial runs, but weren't runaway hits; both lasted only a few years before disappearing from live production; both have provided words and phrases to our cultural lexicon; and, both have endured in syndication and fan memorialization to become acknowledged television cult classics.

Significantly helpful to future scholars and aficionados of Python's Englishness would be an annotated version of *Flying Circus*. I came to appreciate the necessity of a thoroughly annotated text as I studied Edmund Spenser's expansive *Faerie Queene*. The editor, A.C. Hamilton, admitted that even though each page featured many lines of annotation — notes which defined archaic terms and diction, identified classical and contemporary sources and inspirations, and just illuminated what could be a mystifyingly allegorical text — there were many references lost to the modern reader thanks to the passage of time and changes in writing and learning and literary representation (vii). As we move further away from Shakespeare's English usage and his cultural-historical sensibilities, reading Shakespeare without the help of copious notes grows more and more difficult. Colloquial English being what it is — protean and transformative — it is reasonable to assume that careful annotations become more rather than less important with the passage of time. These notes help keep the spirit of the original text alive. The same holds true for Python's work. There already exists a certain level of accessibility built in to the *Flying Circus* texts — the topical political and social references, the various film and video clips of people and places, the animated cut-outs — all these become eye or ear candy for the viewer/reader who couldn't distinguish Edward Heath from Alan Whicker on a dare, nor would most know who either man was to begin with.[2] As shown in Chapter 4, the political and socio-historical implications of a simple photo — in this instance, of Ian Smith — would be completely lost on the viewer or reader without benefit of a careful gloss which ultimately fleshes out the apparently one-dimensional comedy. The synchronic (as opposed to diachronic) study of Monty Python and Shakespeare (and Spenser) blossoms when accurate and plentiful cultural, historical, and social information can be studied in context with the text. And just as Spenser or Shakespeare are still moving or poignant or just accessible without annotation, the depth of experience and the broader range of association becomes apparent in Python with improved referential/allusory understanding. A better understanding of what audiences of the time found funny, as well — and why — will help us better appreciate the art form.

Finally, I have to return to Hans Robert Jauss's comment in Chapter 1 regarding the importance of even mentioning Shakespeare and the dramatic titans of the English Renaissance *vis à vis* Monty Python: "A literary event can continue to have an effect only if those who come after it still or once again respond to it — if there are readers who again appropriate the past work or authors who want to imitate, outdo or refute it" (22). No matter what the literary event, if there are none who come after and reassess, reevaluate, challenge, confront, or appropriate that event, it will die a certain death in obscurity. Shakespeare is the National Poet because he is still appropriated and pored over, both Shakespeare the man and Shakespeare the constructed, mythological thing. Shakespeare endures because he is constantly compared and contrasted with and against the later Stuart playwrights and poets, the Restoration, eighteenth-century, Victorian, and Romantic playwrights and poets, and so on. He is even mentioned in the same breath as the Beatles and Monty Python, and the wheel of fortune swings 'round again. This book is the very kind of study that — by association, by historical connection, and by comparison — aims to invigorate Shakespeare studies, especially where his continued influence across the arts is concerned. I come not to bury Shakespeare in a grave dug by Monty Python, but to praise him. This isn't wild-eyed Bardolatry or even Pythonolatry, but informed appreciation and sincere study. We are, ultimately, "ciphers to this great accompt" as well, as we look again at Shakespeare in the light of the English cultural icon Monty Python, and reckon the increased worth of both.

Notes

1. This is also a terrific send-up of the British film and literary movements of the 1950s and 1960s, the so-called "Angry Young Men" and "kitchen sink" dramas based, often, in working-class neighborhoods, mill towns, and the lower end of the middle management world. Texts such as *Look Back in Anger* and *This Sporting Life* examined the lack of real choices and freedoms faced by the first postwar youth generation, and the stultifying effects of the British class system.

2. Edward Heath became Tory PM in 1970 when Harold Wilson unexpectedly lost the election which he had himself called, ushering in the Conservatives and civil unrest (specifically labor strikes). Wilson and Labour would return to office four years later. See "This Sceptred Isle" website. Available www.bbc.co.uk/radio4/sceptred_isle/page/233.shtml?question=233. Alan Whicker was the host of *Tonight* and *Whicker's World,* and his interview styles are lampooned in various advertising films made by several of the Pythons and in *Flying Circus* during the third season. Scenes in episode 27 feature a host of Whickers on a desert island desperately looking for someone to interview. Credits to the episode also give the last or middle name "Whicker" to the entire cast and crew. See Chapman, et al. 2.27; Wilmut 215.

Bibliography

Abrams, M. H. *A Glossary of Literary Terms*. 4th ed. New York: Holt, Rhinehart and Winston, 1981.

Akrigg, G. P. V., ed. *Letters of King James VI & I*. Berkeley: U of California P, 1984.

Axton, Marie. *The Queen's Two Bodies: Drama and the Elizabethan Succession*. London: Royal Historical Society, 1977.

Bakhtin, Mikhail. *Rabelais and His World*. Trans. Helene Iswolsky. Bloomington: Indiana UP, 1984.

Baldwin, T. W. *Organisation and Personnel of the Shakespearean Company*. Princeton: Princeton UP, 1927.

Barish, Jonas A. *The Antitheatrical Prejudice*. Berkeley: U of California P, 1980.

Barkan, Leonard, ed. *Renaissance Drama*. New Ser. 14. Evanston, IL: Northwestern UP, 1983.

Barker, Francis. "Which Dead?: *Hamlet* and the Ends of History." Barker, Hilme, and Iversen 47–75.

_____, Peter Hulme, and Margaret Iversen, eds. *Uses of History: Marxism, Postmodernism and the Renaissance*. Manchester, England, and New York: Manchester UP, 1991.

Barroll, J. Leeds, III, ed. *Medieval and Renaissance Drama in England*. Vol. 2. New York: AMS P, 1985.

_____. *Politics, Plague, and Shakespeare's Theater: The Stuart Years*. Ithaca and London: Cornell UP, 1991.

Bartlett, John, and Justin Kaplan, eds. *Bartlett's Familiar Quotations*. 16th ed. Boston, Toronto and London: Little, Brown and Co., 1992.

Barton, Anne. "The King Disguised: Shakespeare's *Henry V* and the Comical History." Price 92–117.

_____. *Shakespeare and the Idea of the Play*. Westport, CT: Greenwood, 1977.

Bate, Jonathan. *The Genius of Shakespeare*. London: Picador, 1997.

Baugh, Albert C. *A Literary History of England*. 2nd ed. Englewood Cliffs, NJ: Prentice-Hall, 1948.

Beckerman, Bernard. "Shakespeare's Dramatic Methods." *William Shakespeare: His Work*. Ed. John F. Andrews. New York: Charles Scribner's Sons, 1985. 397–416.

Belsey, Catherine. "Making Histories Then and Now: Shakespeare from *Richard II* to *Henry V*." Barker, Hilme, and Iversen 24–46.

Bennett, Robert B. "Four Stages of Time: The Shape of History in Shakespeare's Second Tetralogy." *Shakespeare Studies* 19. Ed. J. Leeds Barroll. New York: Burt Franklin, 1987.

Bentley, Gerald. "The Swan of Avon and the Bricklayer of Westminster." College of English. Princeton University, 15 Mar. 1946.

Berger, Harry, Jr. "The Pepys Show: Ghost-writing and Documentary Desire in *The Diary*." *ELH* 65.3 (1998): 557–591.

Bergeron, David M. *Shakespeare: A Study and Research Guide*. London: Macmillan, 1975.

_____. "Shakespeare Makes History: *2 Henry IV*." *Studies in English Literature* 31.2 (1991): 231–245.

Berube, Gerald, and Michael Graff. "Dubious and Wasteful Academic Habits." *The Chronicle of Higher Education* 41.23 (17 February 1995): B2.

Bishop, Ellen. "Bakhtin, Carnival and Comedy: The New Grotesque in *Monty Python and the Holy Grail*." *Film Criticism* 15.1 (Fall 1990): 49–64.

Blanchard, W. Scott. *Scholar's Bedlam: Menippean Satire in the Renaissance*. Lewisburg, PA: Bucknell UP, 1995.

Bliss, Lee. "Three Plays in One: Shakespeare and *Pilaster*." *Medieval and Renaissance Drama in England*. Vol. 2. Ed. Bloom, Harold. *Falstaff*. New York and Philadelphia: Chelsea House P, 1992.

Bluestone, Max, and Norman Rabkin, eds. *Shakespeare's Contemporaries*. 2nd ed. Englewood Cliffs, NJ: Prentice-Hall, 1970.

Braunmuller, A. R., and Michael Hattaway, eds. *The Cambridge Companion to English Renaissance Drama*. Cambridge, England: Cambridge UP, 1990.

Bray, Alan. "Homosexuality and the Signs of Male Friendship in Elizabethan England." Goldberg 16–17.

_____. *Homosexuality in Renaissance England*. London: Gay Men's Press, 1982.

Bretzius, Stephen. *Shakespeare in Theory: The Postmodern Academy and the Early Modern Theater*. Ann Arbor: U of Michigan P, 1997.

Brock, D. Heyward. *A Ben Jonson Companion*. Bloomington: Indiana UP, 1983.

Bryant, J. A. *The Compassionate Satirist: Ben Jonson and His Imperfect World*. Athens: U of Georgia P, 1972.

Bullough, Geoffrey. "Theobald on Shakespeare's Sources." *Mirror Up to Shakespeare: Essays in Honor of G. R. Hibbard*. Ed. J. C. Gray. Toronto: U of Toronto P, 1984. 13–21.

Burden, Dennis H. "Shakespeare's History Plays: 1952–1983." *Shakespeare Survey* 38. Ed. Stanley Wells. Cambridge, England: Cambridge UP, 1985. 1–11.

Butt, John, ed. *The Poems of Alexander Pope*. New Haven: Yale UP, 1963.

Calderwood, James L. *To Be and Not to Be: Negation and Metadrama in Hamlet*. New York: Columbia UP, 1983.

Callaghan, Dympna. *Shakespeare Without Women: Representing Gender and Race on the Renaissance Stage*. London and New York: Routledge, 2000.

Callans, Johan. *From Middleton and Rowley's Changeling to Sam Shepard's Bodyguard: A Contemporary Appropriation of a Renaissance Drama*. New York and Wales: Mellen Press, 1997.

Campbell, Oscar James. *Shakespeare's Satire*. London, New York, Toronto: Oxford UP, 1943.

Cartelli, Thomas. "*Bartholomew Fair* as Urban Arcadia: Jonson Responds to Shakespeare." *Renaissance Drama*. New Ser. 14. Evanston, IL: Northwestern UP, 1983. 151–72.

Certeau, Michel de. *The Writing of History*. Trans. Tom Conley. New York: Columbia UP, 1988.

Chapman, Graham, John Cleese, Terry Gilliam, Eric Idle, Terry Jones, and Michael Palin. *The Complete Monty Python's Flying Circus: All the Words*, 2 vols. New York: Pantheon, 1989.

____, ____, ____, ____, ____, and ____. *The Monty Python Song Book*. New York: Harper Trade, 1995.

____, ____, ____, ____, ____, and ____. *Monty Python's Big Red Book*. New York: Contemporary Books, 1980.

Coke, Edward. *The Third Part of the Institutes of the Laws of England*. London, 1644.

Cook, Ann Jennalie. "'Bargaines of Incontinencie': Bawdy Behavior in the Playhouses." *Shakespeare Survey* 10 (1977): 271–286.

Corner, John, ed. *Popular Television in Britain: Studies in Cultural History*. London: BFI, 1991.

Coward, Mat. "Clinch That Cliche." *New Statesman & Society* (26 May 1995): xxvi–xxviii.

Cox, John D., and David Scott Kastan, eds. *A New History of Early English Drama*. New York: Columbia UP, 1997.

Crisell, Andrew. "Filth, Sedition and Blasphemy: The Rise and Fall of Television Satire." Corner 145–158.

Day, David. "Monty Python and the Medieval Other." Harty, *Cinema Arthuriana* 83–92.

Dekker, Thomas. *The Shoemakers Holiday*. *Drama of the English Renaissance: The Tudor Period*. Eds. Russell A. Fraser and Norman Rabkin. New York: Macmillan, 1976.

Diamond, John. "Once I Was British." *The Times* (Jan 14, 1995): 1.

DiGangi, Mario. *The Homoerotics of Early Modern Drama*. Cambridge, England: Cambridge UP, 1997.

Dobson, Michael. "Accents Yet Unknown: Canonisation and the Claiming of *Julius Caesar*." Marsden 11–28.

____. *The Making of a National Poet: Shakespeare, Adaptation and Authorship, 1660–1769*. Oxford, England: Clarendon P, 1992.

Dollimore, Jonathan, and Alan Sinfield. "History and Ideology: The Instance of *Henry V*." Drakakis 206–227.

____ and ____, eds. *Political Shakespeare: Essays in Cultural Materialism*. 2nd ed. Manchester, England: Manchester UP, 1994.

Drabble, Margaret. *The Oxford Companion to English Literature*. 5th ed. Oxford, England: Oxford UP, 1985.

Drakakis, John, ed. *Alternative Shakespeares*. London and New York: Routledge, 1990.

Ellison, Paul A. *Oldcastle: The Man and the Legend*. Online. Exeter Revels. Internet. 11 Dec. 1998. http://www.ex.ac.uk/~Pellison/revels/oldc/contents.html

Elmer-Dewitt, Phillip. "I've Been Spammed!" *Time Magazine* 147.12 (18 March 1996): 44.

Evans, G. Blakemore, ed. "Richard II." *The Riverside Shakespeare*. Boston: Houghton Mifflin, 1974. 803–804.

Evans, Robert C. "Shakespeare, Sutton, and Theatrical Satire: An Unreported Allusion to Falstaff." *Shakespeare Quarterly* 40 (1989): 493–94.

Evelyn, John. *The Diary of John Evelyn, Vol. III, Kalendarium 1650–1672.* Ed. E. S. de Beer. Oxford, England: Clarendon P, 1955.

Faber, J. A. "Thomas Dekker's Gentle Craft: An Essay on *The Shoemakers Holiday.*" *Iowa State Journal of Research* 61.3 (Feb. 1987): 359–71.

Fairlie, Henry. "Maggie's Flying Circus." *The New Republic* 202.1 (Jan. 1, 1990): 22–25.

Farrell, Kirby. "Prophetic Behavior in Shakespeare's Histories." *Shakespeare Studies* 19 (1987): 17–40.

Felperin, Howard. "'Cultural Poetics' Versus 'Cultural Materialism': The Two New Historicisms in Renaissance Studies." Barker, Hilme, and Iversen 76–100.

Finegan, Jack. "Nineveh." *Collier's Encyclopedia.* Ed. William D. Halsey. 1966 ed.

Foakes, R. A. "The Descent of Iago: Satire, Ben Jonson, and Shakespeare's *Othello.*" Honigmann 16–30.

_____. "Playhouses and Players." Braunmuller and Hattaway, *The Cambridge Companion to English Renaissance Drama* 1–52.

Fox-Genovese, Elizabeth. "Literary Criticism and the Politics of the New Historicism." *The New Historicism.* Ed. H. Aram Veeser. New York and London: Routledge, 1989. 216–223.

Fraser, Russell A., and Norman Rabkin, eds. *Drama of the English Renaissance I: The Tudor Period.* New York: Macmillan, 1976.

_____ and _____. *Drama of the English Renaissance II: The Stuart Period.* New York: Macmillan, 1976.

Fries, Maureen. "How to Handle a Woman, or Morgan at the Movies." Harty, *King Arthur* 67–80.

Geng, Veronica. "It's…: *The Complete Monty Python's Flying Circus: All the Words.*" *The New Republic* 202.17 (Apr. 23, 1990): 32–35.

Godzich, Wlad. "The Holy Grail: The End of the Quest." *North Dakota Quarterly* 51.1 (Winter 1983): 74–81).

Goldberg, Jonathan, ed. *Queering the Renaissance.* Durham, NC, and London: Duke UP, 1994.

_____. "Sodomy and Society: The Case of Christopher Marlowe." *Southwest Review* 69 (1984): 371–378.

Goldie, Grace Wyndham. *Facing the Nation: Television and Politics 1936–1976.* London: The Bodley Head, 1977.

Gosson, Stephen. *The Schoole of Abuse.* Ed. Edward Arber. London, 1869.

Grancsay, Stephen V. "Armor." *Collier's Encyclopedia.* Ed. William D. Halsey. 1966 ed.

Greenblatt, Stephen, ed. *The Norton Shakespeare.* New York: W. W. Norton, 1997.

Griffin, Dustin. *Satire: A Critical Reintroduction.* Lexington: UP of Kentucky, 1994.

Gurr, Andrew. *The Shakespearean Stage 1574–1642.* Cambridge, England: Cambridge UP, 1992.

_____, J. R. Mulryne, Ronnie Mulryne, and Margaret Shewring, eds. *Shakespeare's Globe Rebuilt.* Cambridge, England: Cambridge UP, 1997.

Gutwirth, Marcel. *Laughing Matter: An Essay on the Comic.* Ithaca, and London: Cornell UP, 1993.

_____. *Shakespeare's Impact on His Contemporaries.* Ottawa: Barnes & Noble, 1982.

Harbage, Alfred. "Introduction." Bluestone and Rabkin xi–xvi.

Harlow, John. "'Ello 'ello, it's a German Python." *The Sunday Times* (4 October 1998): 10.

Hart, Jonathan. *Theater and World: The Problematics of Shakespeare's History.* Boston: Northeastern UP, 1992.

Harty, Kevin J. *Cinema Arthuriana: Essays on Arthurian Film.* New York, and London: Garland, 1991.

_____. *King Arthur on Film: New Essays on Arthurian Cinema.* Jefferson, NC, and London: McFarland, 1999.

_____. "Lights! Camelot! Action!" Harty, *King Arthur* 5–37.

Hattaway, Michael, Derek Roper, and Boika Sokolova, eds. *Shakespeare in the New Europe.* Sheffield, U.K.: Sheffield Academic P, 1994.

Hertzberg, Hendrik. "Onward and Upward with the Arts: Naughty Bits." *New Yorker* (29 March 1976): 69–70.

Hewison, Robert. *Monty Python: The Case Against.* London: Eyre Methuen, 1981.

Holderness, Graham. "Illogical, Captain!" *Oxford Quarterly* (Spring-Summer 1997): 43–46.

_____. *Shakespeare Recycled: The Making of Historical Drama.* Hertfordshire, England: Harvester Wheatsheaf, 1992.

_____. *Shakespeare's History.* New York: St. Martin's P, 1985.

_____ and Andrew Murphy. "Shakespeare's England: Britain's Shakespeare." Joughin 19–41.

Honigmann, E. A. J., ed. *Shakespeare and His Contemporaries.* Manchester: Manchester UP, 1986.

_____. *Shakespeare's Impact on His Contemporaries.* London: Macmillan, 1982.

Hubert, Judd D. *Metatheater: The Example of Shakespeare.* Lincoln: U of Nebraska P, 1991.

Jardine, Lisa. "'No offence i' the' world': *Hamlet* and Unlawful Marriage." Barker, Hilme, and Iversen 123–139.

_____. *Reading Shakespeare Historically.* London and New York: Routledge: 1996.

Jauss, Hans Robert. "Literary History as a Challenge to Literary Theory." *Towards an Aesthetic of Reception.* Trans. Timothy Bahti. Minneapolis: U of Minnesota P, 1982.

Johnson, Kim. *And Now for Something Completely Trivial: The Monty Python Trivia and Quiz Book.* New York: St. Martin's P, 1991.

_____. *The First 20 Years of Monty Python.* New York: St. Martin's P, 1989.

_____. *The First 28 Years of Monty Python.* New York: St. Martin's P, 1998.

_____. *Life (Before and) After Monty Python: The Solo Flights of the Flying Circus.* New York: St. Martin's P, 1993.

Johnson, Samuel. *London: A Poem in Imitation of the Third Satire of Juvenal.* 1738 first folio edition. Ed. Jack Lynch. Online. London: R. Doddesley, 1738. Samuel Johnson Archive. Rutgers U Library. 6 March 2000. http://www.andromeda. rutgers.edu/~jlynch/Texts/london.html

Jones, Tom B. "Babylonia and Assyria." *Collier's Encyclopedia.* Ed. William D. Halsey. 1966 ed.

Jonson, Ben. *The Alchemist. Drama of the English Renaissance II: The Stuart Period.* Eds. Russell Fraser and Norman Rabkin. New York: Macmillan, 1976.

_____. *Bartholomew Fair. Drama of the English Renaissance II: The Stuart Period.* Eds. Russell Fraser and Norman Rabkin. New York: Macmillan, 1976.

_____. "Conversations with Drummond." *Ben Jonson*. Eds. Ch. H. Herford and Percy Simpson. Vol. 1. Oxford, England: Clarendon, 1925. 138.

_____. *Volpone. Drama of the English Renaissance II: The Stuart Period*. Eds. Russell Fraser and Norman Rabkin. New York: Macmillan, 1976.

Joughin, John J., ed. *Shakespeare and National Culture*. Manchester, and New York: Manchester UP, 1997.

Kastan, David Scott, ed. *A Companion to Shakespeare*. Oxford, England: Blackwell, 1999.

Kavenik, Frances M. *British Drama, 1660–1779: A Critical History*. New York: Twayne, 1995.

Keen, Maurice. *The Outlaws of Medieval Legend*. London: Routledge and Kegan Paul, 1961.

Kelley, Henry A. *Divine Providence and the England of Shakespeare's Histories*. Cambridge, MA: Harvard UP, 1970.

Kerins, Frank. "The Crafty Enchaunter: Ironic Satires and Jonson's *Every Man Out of His Humour*." *Renaissance Drama*. New Ser. 14. Ed. Leonard Barkan. Evanston, IL: Northwestern UP, 1983. 125–50.

Knights, L. C. *Shakespeare: The Histories*. London: Longmans, Green & Co., 1962.

Lanier, Douglas M. "The Prison-House of the Canon: Allegorical Form and Posterity in Ben Jonson's *The Staple of News*." *Medieval and Renaissance Drama in England*. Vol. 2. Ed. J. Leeds Barroll, III. New York: AMS P, 1985. 253–68.

Latham, Robert. *The Shorter Pepys*. Los Angeles: U of California P, 1985.

Levenson, Jill. "Dramatists at (Meta) Play: Shakespeare's *Hamlet* and Pirandello's *Henry IV*. *Modern Drama* 24.3 (Sept. 1981): 330–337.

Levine, Laura. *Men in Women's Clothing: Anti-Theatricality and Effeminization 1579–1642*. Cambridge, England: Cambridge UP, 1994.

Life of Brian. Dir. Terry Jones. With Graham Chapman, John Cleese, Terry Gilliam, Eric Idle, Terry Jones, and Michael Palin. Handmade Films, 1979.

Lim, Walter S. H. "Representing the Other: *Othello*, Colonialism, Discourse." *The Upstart Crow* 13 (1993): 57–78.

Londre, Felicia. "Elizabethan Views of the "Other": French, Spanish, and Russians in *Love's Labor's Lost*." *The Elizabethan Review* 3.1 (Spring/Summer 1995): 3–20.

MacCabe, Colin. *The Eloquence of the Vulgar*. London: BFI, 1999.

MacDonald, Ronald R. "Uneasy Lies: Language and History in Shakespeare's Tetralogy." *Shakespeare Quarterly* 35.1 (Spring 1984): 22–39.

Maconie, Stuart. "Don't Run Your Flag Up My Flagpole." Online. *The Times* (25 February 2000). http://www.the-times.co.uk/news/pages/resources/times_search page.html.

Madigan, Timothy J. "Opus Dei and Secret Societies: The Open Society and the Open Mind." *Free Inquiry* 15.1 (Winter 1995): 12–14.

Maley, Willy. "'This sceptred isle': Shakespeare and the British Problem." Joughin 83–108.

Manheim, Michael. "The English History Play on the Screen." *Shakespeare and the Moving Image*. Eds. Anthony Davies and Stanley Wells. Cambridge, England: Cambridge UP, 1994. 121–145.

Mano, D. Keith. "Why Americans Feel Inferior to the British ... and Why We Shouldn't." *Forbes* (13 March 1995): 123–126.

Marsden, Jean I, ed. *The Appropriation of Shakespeare: Post-Renaissance Reconstructions of the Works and the Myth.* New York: St. Martin's P, 1991.

_____. *The Re-Imagined Text: Shakespeare, Adaptation and Eighteenth-Century Literary Theory.* Lexington, KY: UP of Kentucky, 1995.

Marston, John. *The Dutch Courtesan. Drama of the English Renaissance II: The Stuart Period.* Eds. Russell Fraser and Norman Rabkin. New York: Macmillan, 1976.

Matus, Irvin. *Shakespeare, In Fact.* New York: Continuum, 1994.

McCollum, John I., ed. *The Age of Elizabeth.* "Stephen Gosson. *The Schoole of Abuse* (1579)." Edited by Edward Arber, London, 1869." Boston: Houghton Mifflin, 1960.

McPherson, David. "Three Charges Against Sixteenth- and Seventeenth-Century Playwrights: Libel, Bawdy, and Blasphemy." *Medieval and Renaissance Drama in England.* Vol.2. Ed J. Leeds Barroll, III. New York; AMS P, 1985. 269–82.

Meagher, John C. *Shakespeare's Shakespeare: How the Plays Were Made.* New York: Continuum, 1997.

Miles, Rosalind. *Ben Jonson: His Life and Work.* London and New York: Routledge and Kegan Paul, 1986.

_____. "Will Power." *Toronto* 110.3 (April 1995): 32–37.

Miller, Jeffrey S. *Something Completely Different: British Television and American Culture.* Minneapolis: U of Minnesota P, 2000.

Miller, Paul Allen. "Sidney, Petrarch, and Ovid, or Imitation as Subversion." *ELH* 58.3 (Autumn 1991): 499–522.

Mink, Louis O. "Narrative Form as a Cognitive Instrument." *Historical Understanding.* Eds. Brian Fay, Eugene O. Golob, and Richard T. Vann. Ithaca, NY: Cornell UP, 1987.

Monty Python and the Holy Grail. Dir. Terry Jones and Terry Gilliam. With Graham Chapman, John Cleese, Terry Gilliam, Eric Idle, Terry Jones, and Michael Palin. National Film Trustee Co., Ltd., 1974. (90 min., color.)

Monty Python Live at the Hollywood Bowl. Dir. Terry Hughes. With Graham Chapman, John Cleese, Terry Gilliam, Eric Idle, Terry Jones, and Michael Palin. Handmade Films, 1982. (73 min., color.)

Monty Python's Flying Circus. Vol. 1–24. Dir Ian McNaughton. With Graham Chapman, John Cleese, Terry Gilliam, Eric Idle, Terry Jones, and Michael Palin. London: BBC. Duvalier Ent., 1969–74.

Monty Python's Meaning of Life. Dir. Terry Jones. With Graham Chapman, John Cleese, Terry Gilliam, Eric Idle, Terry Jones, and Michael Palin. Handmade Films, 1983. (103 min., color)

Morgan, David. "Monty Is 30." *The Observer* 3 October 1999.

_____. *Monty Python Speaks.* New York: Avon, 1999.

Morreall, John. "A New Theory of Laughter." *The Philosophy of Laughter and Humor.* Ed. John Morreall. Albany: State U of New York P, 1987. 128–38.

Musgrove, S. *Shakespeare and Jonson: The Macmillan Brown Lectures.* Auckland: Auckland UP, 1957.

Neale, Steve, and Frank Krutnik. *Popular Film & Television Comedy.* New York: Routledge, 1990.

Nickel, Helmut, ed. "Armor." Section IV. Online. *Microsoft Encarta Online Encyclopedia 2000.* 23 Mar. 2000. http://encarta.msn.com.

_____. "Arms and Armor in Arthurian Films." Harty, *Cinema Arthuriana* 181–201.

Noble, Adrian. "How Will Invented History." *The Daily Telegraph* (1 April 2000): 7.

Northbrooke, John. *A Treatise Wherein Dicing, Dauncing, Vaine Playes, or Enterluds ... Are Reproued.* Ed. John P. Collier. London: Shakespeare Society, 1843.

O'Connor, Evangeline M. *Who's Who and What's What in Shakespeare.* New York: Gramercy, 1996.

Orgel, Stephen. "Nobody's Perfect: Or Why Did the English Stage Take Boys for Women?" *The South Atlantic Quarterly* 88.1 (1989): 7–29.

Osberg, Richard H. and Michael E. Crow. "Language Then and Language Now in Arthurian Film." Harty, *King Arthur* 39–66.

Oxford English Dictionary. 2nd ed. Oxford, England: Clarendon P, 1989.

Palmer, Jerry. *Taking Humour Seriously.* London and New York: Routledge, 1994.

Paxman, Jeremy. "The English." *The Sunday-Times* 27 September 1998: 1–8.

_____. "The Joy of Thuggery." *The Sunday-Times* 11 October 1998: 1–5.

_____. "The Land of Lost Content." *The Sunday-Times* 4 October 1998: 1–6.

Pepys, Samuel. *Diary.* Eds. Robert Latham and William Matthews. Vols. III and IV. London: G. Bell and Sons, 1970.

Perry, George. *Life of Python.* London: Pavilion Books Ltd., 1983.

Phillips, Andrew. "Europe In Crisis." *Maclean's* 105.40 (5 Oct. 1992): 34–37.

Pope, Alexander. "The Dunciad Variorum." Butt 317–460.

Porter, Joseph A. "Marlowe, Shakespeare, and the Canonization of Heterosexuality." *The South Atlantic Quarterly* 88.1 (Winter 1989): 127–147.

Price, Joseph G. *The Triple Bond: Plays, Mainly Shakespearean, in Performance.* University Park, and London: Pennsylvania State UP, 1975.

Pugliatti, Paola. "'*Res fictae in fabula vera*': Towards a Study of Invention in Shakespeare's History Plays." *Strumenti Critici* 8.1 (1993): 19–35.

"Quidnunc." *The Times* (Jun 18, 1995): 1.

Rackin, Phyllis. "Anti-Historians: Women's Roles in Shakespeare's Histories." *Theatre Journal* 37.3 (1985): 329–345.

_____. "Temporality, Anachronism, and Presence in Shakespeare's Histories." *Renaissance Drama.* New Ser. 17. Evanston, IL: Northwestern UP, 1986. 101–23.

Radel, Nicholas F. "Fletcherian Tragicomedy, Cross-dressing, and the Construction of Homoerotic Desire in Early Modern England." *Renaissance Drama.* Ed. Mary Beth Rose. Evanston, IL: Northwestern UP and Newberry Library Center for Renaissance Studies, 1995. 53–82.

Randall, Dale. *Winter Fruit: English Drama, 1642–1660.* Lexington: UP of Kentucky, 1995: 1–2.

Reeves, Bill. "Mad Max, Larry, and the Bard: *Hamlet* Then, and Now." *Popular Culture Review* 6:1 (Feb. 1995): 21–27.

Reschke, Mark. "Historicizing Homophobia: *Hamlet* and the Anti-Theatrical Tracts." *Hamlet Studies* 19.1–2 (Summer and Winter 1997): 47–63.

Rhodes, Neil. *Elizabethan Grotesque.* London: Routledge & Kegan Paul, 1980.

_____. *The Power of Eloquence and English Renaissance Literature.* New York: St. Martin's P, 1992.

Ribner, Irving. *The English History Play in the Age of Shakespeare.* Princeton: Princeton UP, 1957.

Rollins, Hyder E., and Herschel Baker, eds. *The Renaissance in England: Non-Dramatic Prose and Verse of the Sixteenth Century.* Prospect Heights, IL: Waveland, 1992.

Rose, Margaret. *Parody: Ancient, Modern, and Post-Modern.* Cambridge, England: Cambric̓ ʒe UP, 1993.

Ross, Charles. *The Wars of the Roses: A Concise History.* London: Thames and Hudson, 1992.

Ross, Robert. *The Monty Python Encyclopedia.* New York: TV Books, 1999.

Rubenstein, Lenny. "Monty Python Strikes Again." *Cineaste* 14.2 (1985): 6–9.

Schuler, Robert M. "Jonson's Alchemists, Epicures, and Puritans." Barroll, *Drama* 171–208.

Scoufos, Alice⸱ Lyle. *Shakespeare's Typological Satire: A Study of the Falstaff-Oldcastle Problem.* Athens: Ohio UP, 1979.

Seary, Peter. *Lewis Theobald and the Editing of Shakespeare.* Oxford, England: Clarendon P, 1990.

Sedgwick, Eve Kosofsky. *Between Men: English Literature and Male Homosocial Desire.* New York: Columbia UP, 1985.

Sedinger, Tracey. "'If sight and shape be true': The Epistemology of Crossdressing on the London Stage." *Shakespeare Quarterly* 48.1 (Spring 1997): 63–79.

Shakespeare, William. *As You Like It. The Riverside Shakespeare.* Ed. G. Blakemore Evans. Boston: Houghton Mifflin, 1974.

_____. *Coriolanus. The Riverside Shakespeare.* Ed G. Blakemore Evans. Boston: Houghton Mifflin, 1974.

_____. *Hamlet. The Riverside Shakespeare.* Ed. G. Blakemore Evans. Boston: Houghton Mifflin, 1974.

_____. *Henry V. The Complete Oxford Shakespeare: Vol. 1— Histories.* Eds. Stanley Wells and Gary Taylor. Oxford, England: Oxford UP, 1994.

_____. *Henry V. The Riverside Shakespeare.* Ed. G. Blakemore Evans. Boston: Houghton Mifflin, 1974.

_____. *1 Henry IV. The Complete Oxford Shakespeare: Vol. 1— Histories.* Eds. Stanley Wells and Gary Taylor. Oxford, England: Oxford UP, 1994.

_____. *2 Henry IV. The Complete Oxford Shakespeare: Vol. 1— Histories.* Eds. Stanley Wells and Gary Taylor. Oxford, England: Oxford UP, 1994.

_____. *1 Henry VI. The Riverside Shakespeare.* Ed. G. Blakemore Evans. Boston: Houghton Mifflin, 1974.

_____. *Julius Caesar. The Riverside Shakespeare.* Ed. G. Blakemore Evans. Boston: Houghton Mifflin, 1974.

_____. *King John. The Riverside Shakespeare.* Ed. G. Blakemore Evans. Boston: Houghton Mifflin, 1974.

_____. *King Lear. The Riverside Shakespeare.* Ed. G. Blakemore Evans. Boston: Houghton Mifflin, 1974.

_____. *The Merry Wives of Windsor. The Riverside Shakespeare.* Ed. G. Blakemore Evans. Boston: Houghton Mifflin, 1974.

_____. *Much Ado About Nothing. The Riverside Shakespeare.* Ed. G. Blakemore Evans. Boston: Houghton Mifflin, 1974.

_____. *Richard II. The Riverside Shakespeare.* Ed. G. Blakemore Evans. Boston: Houghton Mifflin, 1974.

_____. *Richard III. The Norton Shakespeare.* Ed. Stephen Greenblatt. New York: W. W. Norton, 1997.

_____. *Richard III. The Riverside Shakespeare.* Ed. G. Blakemore Evans. Boston: Houghton Mifflin, 1974.

_____. *Troilus and Cressida*. *The Riverside Shakespeare*. Ed. G. Blakemore Evans. Boston: Houghton Mifflin, 1974.

_____. *The Winter's Tale*. *The Riverside Shakespeare*. Ed. G. Blakemore Evans. Boston: Houghton Mifflin, 1974.

Sinfield, Alan. *Cultural Politics — Queer Reading*. Philadelphia: U of Pennsylvania P, 1994.

Smidt, Kristian. *Unconformities in Shakespeare's Early Comedies*. London: Macmillan, 1986.

_____. *Unconformities in Shakespeare's History Plays*. London: Macmillan, 1982.

Shooter, Anne. "Parrots Beware, Monty Python's Circus Looks to Fly Again." *Daily Mail* (30 August 1997): 9.

Smith, Hallett. "Shakespeare's Path from History to Tragedy." *Huntington Library Quarterly* 50.3 (1987): 179–198.

Spencer, Hazelton. *Shakespeare Improved*. Cambridge: Harvard UP, 1927.

Spenser, Edmund. *The Faerie Queene*. Ed. A. C. Hamilton. London and New York: Longman, 1998.

Stam, Robert. *Subversive Pleasures: Bakhtin, Cultural Criticism, and Film*. Baltimore: Johns Hopkins UP, 1989.

Stewart, Susan. *Nonsense: Aspects of Intertextuality in Folklore and Literature*. Baltimore and London: Johns Hopkins UP, 1979.

Stubbes, Phillip. *The Anatomie of Abuses, 1583*. New York: Da Capo P, 1972.

The Sunday Times. "Letters to the Editor." 4 October 1998: 18.

Sypher, Wylie. *The Ethic of Time; Structures of Experience in Shakespeare*. New York: Seabury P, 1976.

Thompson, Raymond H. "The Ironic Tradition in Arthurian Films." Harty, *Cinema Arthuriana* 93–104.

Tillotson, Geoffrey, Paul Fussell, and Marshall Waingrow, eds. *Eighteenth-Century English Literature*. New York: Harcourt Brace Jovanovich, 1969.

Tillyard, E. M. W. *Shakespeare's History Plays*. London: Chatto and Windus, 1944.

Topping, Richard. *Monty Python: A Celebration*. London: Virgin P, 1999.

Van Lennep, W., ed. *The London stage, 1660–1800; a calendar of plays, entertainments & afterpieces, together with casts, box-receipts and contemporary comment. Compiled from the playbills, newspapers and theatrical diaries of the period*. Carbondale: Southern Illinois UP, 1960–68.

Waugh, W. T. "Sir John Oldcastle." *English Historical Review* 20 (1905): 434–456, 637–658.

Webster, John. *The White Devil*. Fraser and Rabkin, II: 432–474.

Wells, Robin Headlam. "The Fortunes of Tillyard: Twentieth-Century Critical Debate on Shakespeare's History Plays." *English Studies: A Journal of English Language and Literature* 66.5 (1985): 391–403.

Wells, Stanley, and Gary Taylor. *The Complete Oxford Shakespeare: Vol. 1— Histories*. Oxford, England: Oxford UP, 1994.

White, Roland. "No Laughing Matter." *The Times* (Jul 2, 1995): 1.

Wickham, Glynne W. G. *Early English Stages, 1300 to 1660*. London: Routledge & Kegan Paul, 1980.

Williams, Precious, and Jason Nisse. "Gates Summons Help from Python Spam." *The Independent* 23 January 2000, foreign ed.: 12.

Willson, Robert F., Jr., *Shakespeare's Reflexive Endings*. Lewiston, Queenston, Lampeter, England: Edwin Mellen P, 1990.

Wilmut, Roger. *From Fringe to Flying Circus: Celebrating a Unique Generation of Comedy*. London: Methuen, 1980.

Worden, Blair. "Shakespeare and Politics." *Shakespeare Survey* 44 (1992): 1–15.

Yoakum, Jim. *The Monty Python (Non-Inflatable) TV Companion*. New York: Dowling P, 1999.

Index